WARSHIPS
& SEA BATTLES
OF WORLD WAR 1

BEEKMAN HOUSE, NEW YORK

WARSHIPS
& SEA BATTLES
OF WORLD WAR I

BEEKMAN HOUSE, NEW YORK

Introduction

When the German Fleet surrendered in 1918, it was without a fight. The naval race between Britain and Germany in the years leading up to the First World War had left Britain with a fleet so superior in numbers that it was never seriously challenged by the Germans. Apart from the abortive confrontation at Jutland, no full scale engagement between the two fleets had taken place.

Yet the war at sea was to prove decisive in a way few had anticipated. The German U-boat campaign against merchant shipping came within a hair's breadth of crippling Britain's ability to wage war, and it was Britain's policy of distant blockade, rather than any military breakthrough, which ultimately brought Germany to her knees.

In this book we present a comprehensive account of the First World War at sea, and of the ships that fought that war. Those sea battles that did take place are discussed in depth, as well as the gallant exploits of individual ships. Far more significant for the future, however, were the technological developments inspired by the war. Mines, torpedoes, submarines, and the various devices employed to combat them, are described and illustrated in full. The illustration throughout—action photographs and detailed full colour drawings—is magnificent, and combines with the authoritative text to make this one of the most readable and informative accounts of the warships and sea battles of the First World War ever published.

Edited by Bernard Fitzsimons

Phoebus, London.

This edition © BPC Publishing Ltd. 1973

Published by Beekman House, New York, a division of Crown Publishers, Inc.

First published in Purnell's History of the First World War

First published in this form 1973

ISBN 0-517-130912

Printed in Belgium - H. Proost & Cie p.v.b.a. Turnhout - Belgium

Contents

Britannia rules the waves

H.M.S. MARLBOROUGH.
Battleship, 25,000 tons.

H.M.S. THUNDERER,
Super Dreadnought, 22,500 tons.

H.M.S. LORD NELSON.
Battleship, 16,500 tons.

H.M.S. Swiftsure.

H.M.S. DREADNOUGHT.
Battleship, 17,900 tons.

H.M.S. Africa, Battleship.

H.M.S. Southampton.

H.M.S. COLLINGWOOD.
Super Dreadnought, 19,250 tons.

The British public felt the same loyalty and affection toward their navy
as the Germans did toward their army. These postcards reflect the public
interest in the names and types of ships

BALANCE OF NAVAL POWER AUGUST 1914

The British, with very few exceptions, believed they had the best navy in the world in 1914. Their superiority over Germany in numbers and tradition was obvious, but their inferiority in certain technical fields, especially mines and torpedoes, was not generally realised. *Below: Tegetthof,* one of Austria-Hungary's four dreadnought-class ships

Lieutenant-Commander P. Kemp

Britain, in August 1914, had retained her immense lead in battleships and battle-cruisers over all other European nations. In spite of the periodical scares over the rate of German building during the immediate pre-war years, her own building rate had been just more than enough to maintain the declared 60% numerical superiority over Germany. These were her own ships, built for her own navy, but an immediate bonus was available on the outbreak of war in the shape of three dreadnought battleships being built (and virtually completed) in Britain for foreign navies. The *Almirante Latorre*, ordered by Chile, was taken over in September 1914 and commissioned as HMS *Canada*, and two battleships built for Turkey, the *Osman I* and *Rashadieh*, were requisitioned in August and added to the Grand Fleet as HMS *Agincourt* and HMS *Erin*. The two Turkish ships raised the British total of dreadnoughts at the outbreak of war to 24, to which Germany could reply with only 13. And looking ahead, the comparison was brighter still, with 13 British dreadnoughts on the stocks in various stages of construction (with two due to join the fleet later in 1914) and only ten laid down by Germany (of which two were also due later in 1914). Among the 13 British ships were five of the new *Queen Elizabeth* class, faster and more powerfully armed than any others in the world.

The battle-cruiser comparison was almost equally favourable in numbers. Counting HMS *Tiger*, to which only the finishing touches in the dockyard were required, there were ten British battle-cruisers, although one of these, HMS *Australia*, was in the service of the Australian government. And on the German side, counting SMS *Derfflinger* which was in the same state of completion as the *Tiger*, there were six such ships in commission. But they included the *Blücher*, a 15,800-ton armoured cruiser which carried only 8.2-inch guns compared with the 11-inch and 12-inch of the later German battle-cruisers and the 12-inch and 13.5-inch of the British battle-cruisers.

Of the other nations concerned, France and Russia were slightly ahead of Austria-Hungary and Italy. France had four battleships of the *Courbet* class, all launched in 1913 and 1914, of 23,500 tons and armed with twelve 12-inch guns,

whilst almost complete at the outbreak of war were three larger battleships of the *Bretagne* class, carrying ten 13.4-inch guns. And in addition she had six *Danton* class battleships, technically pre-dreadnoughts because of their mixed armament of 12-inch and 9.4-inch guns but, like the two British *Lord Nelsons*, being counted as dreadnoughts because of their recent construction and ability to maintain the speed of the dreadnought fleet.

The Russian fleet was divided into two, one part in the Baltic and the other in the Black Sea. There were four dreadnought battleships of the *Gangoot* class in the Baltic—each carrying twelve 12-inch guns in four triple turrets—and four more on the stocks, big ships of the *Borodino* class, 28,000 tons with nine 14-inch guns in triple turrets and a designed speed of 26½ knots. Also in the Baltic was the armoured

A huge disparity in overall strength . . .

cruiser *Rurik,* which compared roughly with the German *Blücher*.

There were no dreadnoughts in the Black Sea though there were three in process of completion which were just about equal in displacement and gunpower to those owned by Austria-Hungary. But as far as the Entente Powers were concerned, the Russian Black Sea fleet could count for little unless Turkey could be brought into the war on the side of Britain, France and Russia, and any prospect of this, remote at the best of times, was made even more unlikely in August 1914 by the British requisitioning of two Turkish battleships which had just been completed in Britain.

Austria-Hungary, whose only access to the sea was in the northern Adriatic, had three new dreadnoughts launched in 1914, with a fourth due to be launched in 1915. These were the *Viribus Unitis* class, ships of 22,000 tons with twelve 12-inch guns. She also had three *Franz Ferdinands*, small pre-dreadnoughts of 14,500 tons with a mixed armament of 12-inch and 9.4-inch guns, and thus ships of little value in terms of naval warfare in 1914. Like Russia in the Black Sea, the fleet's only

exit into the Mediterranean was through the Straits of Otranto, a comparatively narrow stretch of sea which the navies of Britain and France would have little difficulty in blocking.

An uneasy partner
The third member of the Triple Alliance was Italy, and it was no secret in London or Paris that she was an uneasy partner in the arms of Germany and Austria-Hungary. It was not expected that she would follow them into a European war, but in terms of the European political grouping her navy had to be counted. She had one dreadnought, the *Alighieri*, completed in 1912, and three more on the verge of completion. These, on paper, were powerful ships, carrying thirteen 12-inch guns in three triple and two twin turrets, but their displacement of 22,000 tons argued that they were either over-gunned or under-armoured.

A crude addition of dreadnought-type ships on both sides gave a superiority to the Entente Powers over those of the Alliance of 49 to 33. Such a comparison was virtually meaningless, if only because Britain's naval commitments were world-wide while those of Germany, apart from a tiny sprinkling of colonial possessions which were indefensible in war, were confined only to the North Sea and the Baltic. There were many other considerations which went a long way further to reduce the apparent disparity in overall dreadnought strength, but these will be discussed later in this article.

In smaller ships, the overall ratios were much the same as with the capital ships. Neither Britain nor Germany had built heavy cruisers after the step-up to battle-cruisers, but in what were known as light cruisers, Britain had 18, with eight being built, and Germany eight, and eight more projected. Only France, and to a lesser extent Russia, had continued to build heavy cruisers. France had four, headed by the *Quinet* and *Rousseau* of 14,000 tons and carrying fourteen 7.6-inch guns, while the Russian Baltic fleet had two *Bayan* class cruisers of 7,750 tons with a mixed armament of 8-inch and 6-inch guns.

In Britain's Royal Navy were 225 destroyers, of which 127 were fast, modern boats and the remainder, though mostly more than ten years old, still valuable in

A German naval squadron steaming in line ahead off Heligoland in ships designed primarily for operations in the North Sea terms of the many naval duties which fell to the lot of destroyers in war. The comparable German figures were 152 overall, 108 fast and modern, and 44 more elderly though still useful. British submarines outnumbered German U-boats by 75 to 30, but most of the British boats were small and of use only in coastal operations. Germany, at the outbreak of war, had more submarines capable of overseas operations than Britain, and also more being built and projected.

Of the other nations concerned in the European line-up in 1914, France could muster 81 destroyers and 67 submarines, Russia, in the Baltic and Black Sea combined, 106 destroyers and 36 submarines, Austria-Hungary, 18 destroyers and 11 submarines, while Italy had 33 destroyers and 14 submarines.

Outside Europe there was one other navy to be taken into account, that of Japan. Under the Anglo-Japanese alliance of 1902 there was no obligation for Japan to enter the war, since the actual declaration on August 4, was a British initiative, but it was very obvious that, in her expansionist mood, she would do so. Her acquisitive eyes had long been focused on the well-equipped German base at Tsingtao in China, and there were German colonial islands in the Pacific which might come her way at the final peace discussions were she involved in a successful war. From the British point of view, the Japanese fleet had a potential value in war to cover and track down the powerful German East Asiatic Squadron and thereby release British ships for other operations nearer home. Japan had a useful fleet of four dreadnought-type capital ships, of which her two *Kongo* class battle-cruisers were as large, as powerfully armed (eight 14-inch, sixteen 6-inch), and as fast (27 knots) as any others in the world. The battleship *Asi* was a mixed armament ship which, however, ranked as a dreadnought, and her capital ship fleet was supported by two first-class *Nisshin* type cruisers and three second-class *Hirato* type, together with the older *Tone*. Of her 54 destroyers, all were of British design and most of them built in Britain.

Counting up their ships, the three Entente powers appeared overwhelmingly strong. Moreover, with Britain lying across the German exits from the North Sea into the world's oceans, the High Seas Fleet

was pinned into its home waters and unable to intervene in operations in other parts of the world. This geographical advantage had been rammed home in the naval staff talks between Britain and France in 1912 in which the French had agreed to withdraw their Atlantic and Channel squadrons, together with their Far East and Pacific squadrons, and concentrate them all in the Mediterranean, accepting naval responsibility for the whole of that sea. This decision, it is true, owed something to the effect of the Balkan War of 1912/13, as well as to the naval staff talks in London and Paris, but it effectively released the battleships of the British Mediterranean Fleet to swell the number of those in home waters.

Numbers, however, counted for little. It was quality which mattered more than quantity when it came to the actual test

... but quality not quantity when it came to the test

of battle. In pure design, there was little to choose between the British and German dreadnoughts, and although there were some naval experts, even in 1914 and before the results in action had pointed to deficiencies in the British ships, who thought the German design superior. They were eventually proved wrong when the battleship *Bayern* was raised after the holocaust in Scapa Flow at the end of the war. A minute examination of her construction proved that British naval architects in 1914 had nothing to learn from their German counterparts.

One of the considerable disabilities from which the British capital ships suffered in comparison with the German was their lack of beam. Successive Liberal governments in Britain, voted into power on promises of social benefits to all, had refused to spend money on new docks so that all British ships had to be built to fit the existing docks instead of the other way round. This meant that no British dreadnought could be built with a beam of more than 90 feet. At Wilhelmshaven there were two docks to take ships up to a beam of 102 feet; at Kiel there was a floating

dock with an available beam of 131 feet: while between the two new locks on the Kiel Canal at Holtenau was a huge space large enough to accommodate anything. In this respect Germany had a great advantage.

Ship for ship, all the German battleships and battle-cruisers had about 10 feet more on the beam than the British. This gave them an immediate advantage in that they were less susceptible to damage by mine or torpedo. It also enabled them to carry thicker armour on sides and gun turrets, a possibility which was enhanced by a considerable saving in weight which arose from the different functions of British and German ships. British ships were designed for a world-wide rôle. Their crews lived permanently on board, and they carried enough coal to give them a steaming radius of 4,000-5,000 miles. German capital ships were designed purely for North Sea or Baltic operations. Their crews lived ashore in barracks when the ships were in harbour, and the fuel they carried gave them a steaming radius of under 2,000 miles. Their great beam, allied to the saving in weight in fuel alone, and combined with the fact that crew habitability was not of primary importance in view of their short endurance and the living accommodation ashore, enabled a much more complete watertight subdivision below decks to be built into their hulls. As a result, the German capital ships were more nearly unsinkable than any of the British.

It all came down to the size of the available docks. When Admiral Jellicoe visited Kiel in 1910, the Kaiser told him that in Germany they built docks to take the ships, and not ships to fit the docks. Writing after the war, Sir Eustace Tennyson-d'Eyncourt, the Director of Naval Construction, had this to say: 'Had wider docks been available, and had it been possible to go to a greater beam, the designs on the same length and draught could have embodied more fighting qualities, such as armour, armament, greater stability in case of damage, and improved underwater protection.' With their greater beam, and therefore greater displacement, the German ships could have a considerably thicker armour belt built into them. In the first dreadnoughts, the British armour belt was 10 to 11 inches up to the main deck only, while the comparable German dreadnoughts carried 12 inches. In the *Orion* to *Iron Duke* classes, British armour was 12 inches thick, but in the comparable *Kaiser* and *König* class, German side armour was 13¾ inches thick.

There was something of the same story in a comparison of the big guns of the two fleets. A considerable amount of capital had been invested by the main British gun manufacturers in wire-wound guns, and therefore all British big naval guns were wire-wound. The German navy had gone for the built-up gun, which had proved itself not only more robust but with a longer life. There was a tendency for the muzzles of big wire-wound guns to droop fractionally after firing a few rounds, with consequent inaccuracy in range keeping, while their life was estimated (by the Germans, it is true) as 80-100 rounds. The life of the built-up gun was estimated (again by the Germans) at 220 rounds. They fired their shells with a considerably

endorsed by Admiral Jellicoe, also a gunnery expert, ran into opposition from the Navy's Inspector of Target Practice, who argued strongly for the retention of individual gunlaying. This battle of opinions continued until the end of 1912 when a test between HMS *Thunderer,* fitted with Scott's director system, and her sister ship HMS *Orion,* using individual gunlayers, clinched the argument. In three minutes of firing at a range of 9,000 yards, with the ships steaming at 12 knots, the *Thunderer* scored six times as many hits as the *Orion.* But by now time was running short, and with opposition still being expressed by the diehards, only eight battleships in the Grand Fleet had been fitted with director firing by August 1914.

The Germans had a system of director firing, known as *Richtungsweiser,* which had much in common with Scott's director except that it was mounted in the ship's conningtower and not in the foretop. If

indeed throughout all British naval history up to that year, the gun was always the dominant weapon. Officers who had specialised in gunnery had always enjoyed a better record for promotion to the higher ranks than officers of other specialities, and in this veneration of the gun as the queen of the naval battlefield, other weapons had had less drive put behind them in the race towards perfection. British torpedoes were unreliable in their running, and not infrequently ran deep or sank to the bottom after being fired; a somewhat strange state of affairs when it is remembered that the Royal Navy had pioneered the torpedo from its very birth. By 1914 the 21-inch torpedo had largely replaced the earlier 18-inch, and all the dreadnought battleships and all modern destroyers carried the larger version. The German navy had also two sizes of torpedo, 450-mm (17.7-inch) and 500-mm (19.7-inch), with a larger 600-mm (23.6-inch) torpedo under develop-

Although in 1914 Italy had only one dreadnought, her commanding position in the Mediterranean made her navy a factor to be reckoned with

greater muzzle velocity, and the muzzles did not droop.

Gun for gun, the German was smaller than the British. Taking ships comparable in size and date of completion, where the British fitted 12-inch guns, the Germans fitted 11-inch; when the British went up to 13.5 inches, the Germans replied with 12-inch. Allowing for the higher muzzle velocity of the German guns, there was nothing in the disparity of size so far as range was concerned, though the British ships held a substantial advantage in weight of broadside. Given equal accuracy in ranging and in shell and fuse design, this advantage could have been considerable since heavier shells are more accurate at long ranges than lighter ones.

In the ten years ending in 1914, the Royal Navy had made a striking advance in the range and accuracy of its gunnery. Whereas in 1904, battle practice ranges had been 3,000-4,000 yards and often with a stationary target, by 1914 the range had grown to 16,000 yards at towed targets. Accuracy was very good, but the individual gunlayers in the turrets were always handicapped by the smoke of burnt cordite, funnel smoke, shell splashes, and the difficulty of identification of the target. In 1911 Admiral Sir Percy Scott, who had been recognised as the greatest expert in gunnery in the Royal Navy, brought out his director system, by which all guns were trained, laid, and fired by a master sight in the foretop, well above the smoke. In addition to obtaining a clear view, the director sight made certain that all turrets were trained onto the same enemy ship, for the individual gunlayers in the turrets had merely to follow the electrically repeated elevation and bearing of the master sight.

Scott's director system, enthusiastically

there were any diehards in the German navy they were never permitted to interfere with technological development, and the *Richtungsweiser* system had been introduced throughout the High Seas Fleet by 1914. German gunnery was always excellent, their salvoes compact with very little spread, and always remarkably accurate for range.

This accuracy was based on the stereoscopic rangefinder, which had a telling advantage over the British type in that it absorbed very little light. This was particularly valuable in the North Sea, where in the frequent mist and bad light, little could be seen through the British type because of the high absorption of light through the lenses and prisms.

It was a similar story in shells, mines and torpedoes. When Jellicoe had been Third Sea Lord and Controller in 1910 he had sent a memorandum to the Ordnance Board asking them to produce an armour-piercing shell that would penetrate armour at oblique impact and burst inside. At the end of the year Jellicoe went to sea, and the responsibility to see this development through to its conclusion fell to his successor, Admiral Sir John Briggs, who was anything but energetic. Nothing had been done by 1914 on this requirement, and this sorry tale of incompetence had its result in the war when the British armour-piercing shell broke up on oblique impact against the German armour instead of penetrating and bursting inside.

German superiority

The German superiority in torpedoes and mines lay as much in better and more sophisticated workmanship as in a fatal British tendency to regard these as the weapons of a weaker power. In 1914, and

ment. The four earliest German dreadnoughts (*Nassau* class) had the 450-mm, as also did the *Blücher* and *Von der Tann* among the battle-cruisers. All other dreadnoughts and all destroyers and U-boats from *G.174* and *U.19* onwards had the 500-mm torpedo. Any older boats which were still operational had the old 17.7-inch torpedo. But although slightly smaller, size for size, the German torpedo was a more reliable weapon in range, running, and depth-keeping than the British.

Negligence and inefficiency

If the performance of British torpedoes left much to be desired, that of British mines was shocking. No one at the Admiralty had been given responsibility to think out the use or value of mines in terms of naval strategy or tactics; no one had been charged with the technical development of mines. Those with which Britain went to war in 1914 were thoroughly inefficient, either breaking away from their moorings when laid or else frequently failing to explode when hit by an enemy ship. In the German navy as much attention was paid to the development of the mine as to every other weapon, and the sinking of the new dreadnought battleship *Audacious* by a single mine within a very few weeks of the declaration of war told the story.

In smaller ships of war, the Germans were in every way as good as the British. All their destroyers, to which they still gave the older name of torpedoboats, were excellent seaboats and very strongly constructed. Unlike British practice, they were in every case tested by running their acceptance trials in really bad weather to guarantee against leaking and straining. Their U-boats, too, were as well constructed as British submarines throughout, not even excluding the new British E-class boats which were one of the most successful classes of submarines ever built in Britain at least up to 1925, and they had turned their attention to the long endurance submarine for ocean warfare some years before Britain had faced this challenge.

One reason for this German superiority in *materiel* was that in Germany, technology in the metallurgy, engineering, shipbuilding, and chemical industries was in a very advanced state. This stemmed, at least in part, from the different educational backgrounds of the two countries. In England, most higher education was devoted to training for the professions, but in Germany its main emphasis was on training for trade purposes. All through the naval *materiel* picture in Germany was an emphasis on attention to detail which extended right through from top to bottom. It was not only in shells and fuses, rangefinders, mines, and torpedoes that they were far ahead. Their attention to detail even reached down as far as saving life after ships had been sunk in action. While the British navy still relied on the boats carried on board to save life after action, the German ships were · issued with sufficient special lifejackets for the whole crew designed to hold men upright while floating in the water.

This was a product of the basic German mentality and planning, meticulous in every detail and allied to an urge to be prepared for any and every emergency. The British mentality was not geared in that age to so deep a regard for perfection in

The crucial ratio – the balance of dreadnoughts

Below: **SMS Rheinland**, of the *Westfalen* class, the first German dreadnoughts. *Displacement:* 18,900 tons. *Length:* 472 feet. *Beam:* 89 feet. *Armament:* Twelve 11-inch, twelve 5·9-inch and sixteen 3·4-inch plus six 17·7-inch torpedo tubes. *Power/speed:* 26,100 hp/20 knots. *Armour:* Belt 11½ inches, turrets 11 inches. *Crew:* 963

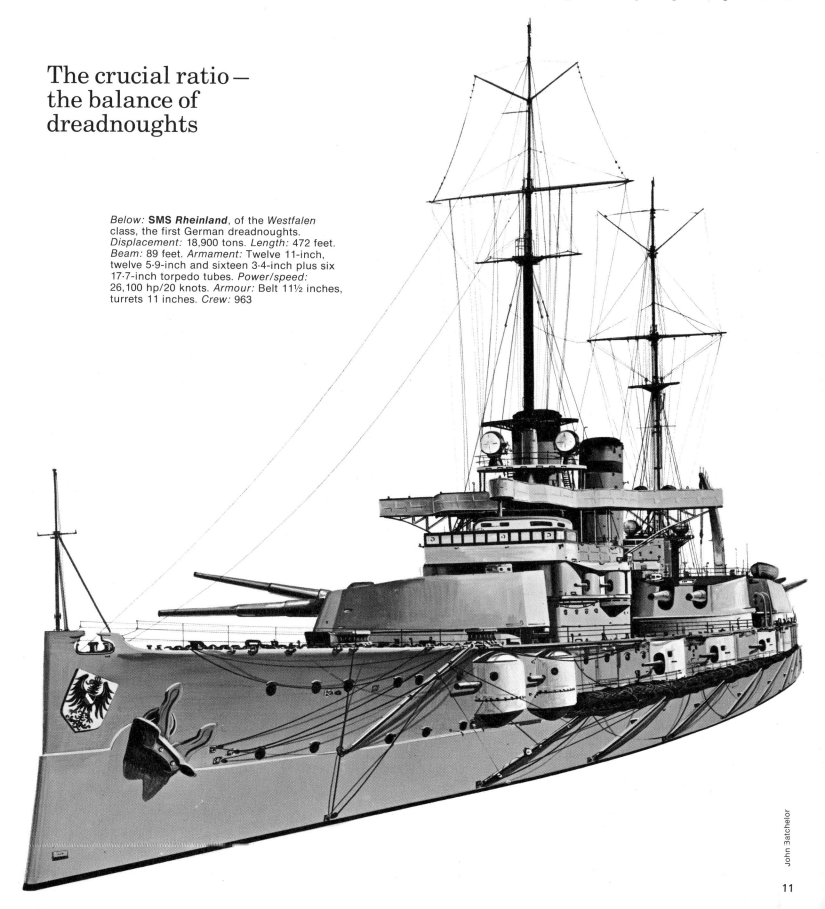

John Batchelor

such detail. Britain had its engineers and shipbuilders who were in every way as brilliant as any in Germany, but their attitude was more that of the gentlemanly amateur than that of the dedicated technologist. There was a complacency in Britain, founded upon its broad industrial base which could guarantee a faster rate of naval building than Germany could ever achieve, which perhaps militated against such a perfectionist doctrine. Every argument which was produced to sustain the naval race against Germany in the decade leading up to 1914 was based entirely on quantitative rather than qualitative superiority. What was perhaps perplexing was the sincere belief in Britain, and particularly in the British Admiralty, that ship for ship, those built in Britain were undoubtedly superior to those built in Germany. There had been no lack of reports from the British Naval Attaché in Berlin stressing the excellence of German ships, as well as of their guns, their gunnery results, their shells and fuses and their torpedoes. Yet the belief in British superiority was quite genuinely held and believed. One man only seemed to have doubts, but this one man was Admiral Jellicoe, the Commander-in-Chief designate of the Grand Fleet in the event of a war against Germany. Three weeks before the outbreak of the war, in a memorandum addressed to Churchill, the First Lord of the Admiralty, he drew attention to the 'very striking inferiority' of the armour

and underwater protection of British battleships and battle-cruisers as compared with German. He concluded with a statement that it was 'highly dangerous to consider that our ships as a whole are superior or even equal fighting machines'.

This memorandum by Jellicoe followed a speech a few days earlier by Churchill in which he spoke of 'the undoubted superiority of our ships unit for unit'. Churchill was quite sincere when he said that, and was in fact only echoing the genuine beliefs of the Admiralty as a whole.

This German thoroughness and attention to detail extended to dockyards as well as to ships. Theirs were not only magnificently organised for the building, equipping, and repairing of warships but were also tied into the German system of mobilisation, the whole operation being brought together under a single directing staff. The German dockyards had benefitted, of course, not only from the fact that they were relatively new and had thus been initially planned and laid out to cope with modern methods of warship design and construction, but also from ungrudging investment of public money in the needs and growth of the new navy. Britain's dockyards, on the other hand, had been developed through the centuries, originally planned and laid out for a sailing navy, and adapted time after time to try to keep pace with the technological changes of

'Undoubted superiority' or 'Striking inferiority'?

The dreadnought battleship — Queen of the seas. Before the war it had been assumed that the British and German fleets would immediately fight it out to a finish in a fleet action similar to Trafalgar. But until 1916 at Jutland, no such confrontation took place. For the greater period of the war, the Grand Fleet waited at Scapa Flow and exerted a tacit authority over the Germans. HMS *Dreadnought. Displacement:* 17,900/20,700 tons. *Length:* 526 feet. *Beam:* 82 feet. *Power/speed:* 22,000 hp/22 knots. *Armament:* Ten 12-inch and 24 12-pounder guns. *Armour:* Belt 11 inches, turrets 8 inches. *Crew:* 862 men

naval warfare. Not that they were inefficient—the *Dreadnought* had been built in Portsmouth Dockyard in the incredibly short space of 11 months—but many of their facilities suffered from a lack of modern layout and from the legacy of the more unhurried days of sail.

Obsolete dockyards

Of more immediate importance in the context of a war against Germany was the actual situation of the three major British dockyards at Chatham, Portsmouth and Devonport. Their position had largely been dictated by the wars of the 16th, 17th and 18th Centuries when the traditional enemies of Britain had been Spain, Holland, and France. The western approaches to Britain, the English Channel, and the southern North Sea had been the naval battlegrounds of those years, and the English dockyards had been developed on the strategic realities of war against the traditional foes. But with the emergence of Germany as the only obvious enemy, the focus of naval warfare had shifted from the Channel to the northern half of the North Sea, and Chatham, the only major dockyard on the east coast of Britain, was too far south to provide immediate support to a Grand Fleet which would necessarily have to be stationed in the north of Britain.

The need for a fully equipped base in the north had been recognised by the British Admiralty as far back as 1903 when it was decided to develop Rosyth, on the northern side of the Firth of Forth, as a first-class naval base. When Sir John Fisher came to the Admiralty in 1904 as First Sea Lord he did his best to hold back the work at Rosyth partly because he had doubts about the safety of Rosyth as a fleet anchorage and partly because he preferred the Cromarty Firth on the grounds that it was farther north than Rosyth and thus a better base from which to command the northern exit from the North Sea into the Atlantic.

Farther north still, in the Orkney Islands,

was the immense anchorage of Scapa Flow. Having decided on the development of Rosyth as a first-class dockyard against Fisher's opposition—first-class being defined as a port where the dockyard was capable of building, equipping, and repairing warships of any size in every respect, where permanent depots of men and stores of all descriptions were maintained, and where the scale of defence was heavy enough to deter attacks by battleships, the Admiralty next considered the possibility of developing a second-class base in the north to back up Rosyth—second-class being defined as a base where smaller repairs could be undertaken and only stocks of the more immediate stores were maintained. The choice lay between Cromarty and Scapa Flow, and after much discussion Cromarty was chosen. Scapa Flow was designated as a fleet anchorage in war, but the Committee of Imperial Defence, to whom the whole question of east coast bases was referred, recommended that no defences should be erected there. The Admiralty protested, but when it was discovered that the cost of setting up fixed defences would come to £379,000 and that the annual cost of upkeep would amount to £55,000, even the Admiralty agreed that it was time the financial horns were pulled in.

When war came in August 1914, the plight of the Grand Fleet in respect of bases was frightening. The strategic requirements of the policy of distant blockade dictated the stationing of the Grand Fleet as far to the northward as possible in order to command the northern North Sea between the Orkneys and the Norwegian coast, and Scapa Flow was the only answer. It was completely undefended, with no nets or booms to prevent entry by U-boat, and no searchlights to detect enemy marauders by night. Both Cromarty and Rosyth had by 1914 been given a sketchy coastal artillery defence designed to keep surface ships at bay, but both were wide open to U-boat attack and their approaches were easy to mine. The dockyard at Rosyth, which had been subject to interminable delays on the grounds of economy, had only just been begun to be constructed and would not be operational for some years later. Only Chatham still remained as a first-class east coast base, but was much too far away adequately to nourish a Grand Fleet with Scapa Flow as its main operational base. There was, it is true, a second-class base at Harwich, but that again was too far south for the Grand Fleet and was in any case earmarked as a base for light craft.

The situation in Germany was exactly the opposite. On the German North Sea coast, protected by the island of Heligoland, were two of the three main fleet bases, Cuxhaven and Wilhelmshaven. In the Baltic, but readily accessible to those in the North Sea through the Kiel Canal which had been widened and dredged to take dreadnoughts, was the third great naval base at Kiel. Subsidiary bases at Hamburg, Bremen, and Emden were interconnected through the rivers Elbe and Weser, and the Ems-Jade Canal. The islands of Heligoland, which protected the mouths of the Elbe and Weser rivers, and Borkum, which provided the same service for the Ems, were both heavily fortified, and at strategic points along the coast, powerful forts and gun emplacements gave

additional security. Nature, too, had been kind to Germany by providing shoals and sandbanks off the coast which restricted approach by heavy ships to narrow channels which were easily defensible.

One final area of comparison on the *materiel* side lay in the air. Both Britain and Germany had recognised the possible importance of aircraft in sea warfare at roughly the same time, mainly for use as advanced scouts. Whereas Germany had fixed her eyes firmly on the rigid airship as the most desirable means of long-distance scouting, Britain had vacillated between airships and aeroplanes. Her airship policy had been a sorry tale of indecision throughout. Money for a rigid airship had been voted in the 1909 Naval Estimates, but the resultant *Mayfly* had had her back broken during her trials when a gust of wind caught her when she was halfway out of her hanger. This was in 1911, the same year in which Jellicoe, during a visit to Germany, had been taken for a flight in a Zeppelin, and returned to London with glowing accounts of their value to a fleet at sea. However Jellicoe's enthusiasm carried less weight with the Board of Admiralty than the disaster to the *Mayfly,* and in 1912 the Committee of Imperial Defence agreed with the Admiralty that airships were useless. This odd decision, which went in the face of all German experience, was largely influenced by Admiral of the Fleet Sir Arthur K. Wilson, First Sea Lord until December 1911, who argued that airships presented as large a target as battleships and could be brought down by naval guns. He did not explain, and nobody seems to have asked him, how the guns were to be sufficiently elevated to engage a Zeppelin and how the fall of shot was to be spotted. Nevertheless, in 1914 the Royal Navy ordered eight rigid airships, none of which were ready by the outbreak of war. There were already seven small non-rigid airships, of which four were too unreliable for operations at sea and one was used for training.

The first aircraft-carrier

Such enthusiasm as the Admiralty could muster for naval flying was directed mainly into heavier-than-air machines. In 1912 an aircraft had been successfully launched from the deck of HMS *Africa* while the ship was at anchor. In 1912, during the course of the naval review at Weymouth, an aircraft was successfully flown off from the forecastle of HMS *Hibernia* while she was under way. In 1913 the old cruiser HMS *Hermes* was commissioned as the first aircraft-carrier in any of the world's navies, accommodating three seaplanes. When war came in 1914, the Royal Naval Air Service could boast a strength of 52 seaplanes (though only 26 of them were airworthy) and 39 land-based aeroplanes.

In Germany there had been no deviation from the Zeppelin programme. They were based mainly at Cuxhaven and, while their primary rôle was for scouting purposes over the North Sea, they had a subsidiary rôle as potential bombers against land targets. In 1914 there were some 28 available for fleet work, though some of these could be withdrawn temporarily for other purposes. In addition, seaplanes and land-based aircraft for naval purposes were stationed at air bases around the German North Sea coast.

Above: 'Kaiser-class' dreadnought SMS *Kaiserin. Left:* Admiral Reinhard Scheer, Commander-in-Chief of the High Seas Fleet. *Below:* SMS *Prinzregent Luitpold,* a 'Kaiser-class' dreadnought. The five 'Kaiser-class' dreadnoughts — SMS *Kaiser, Friedrich der Grösse, Kaiserin, Prinzregent Luitpold, König Albert* — were completed between October 1912 and August 1913. In 1914 *Friedrich der Grösse* became the flagship of the C-in-C, the others formed the *3rd Battle Squadron.* All except *König Albert* were at Jutland. *Displacement:* 24,380 tons. *Length:* 564 feet. *Beam:* 95¼ feet. *Power/speed:* 30–35,000 hp/21–23 knots. *Armament:* Ten 12-inch, 14 5.9-inch, eight 3.4-inch, four 3.4-inch anti-aircraft guns and five 19.7-inch torpedo tubes. *Armour:* Belt 13¾ inches, turrets 11¾ inches. *Crew:* 1,088–1,178 men

The evolution of strategic thought in the two major naval powers, Britain and Germany, during the years leading to the outbreak of war is interesting. Both navies had been obsessed more by the development in material than by its relation to strategy and tactics, and little thought was given to the best way in which these magnificent new fighting ships should be used. It was not the day of the naval thinker but the day of the naval specialist. Almost the whole of naval education in both countries was directed towards the technical aspects of a naval life, and virtually none to its more philosophical aspects of the strategical and tactical uses of a fleet. In Britain, with her long heritage and expertise in the use of sea power on a world scale, this was inexcusable. In Germany it was, if not wise, at least understandable for her experience of sea power extended back less than 20 years.

A second Trafalgar?
Most British naval officers were at least aware of the fact that in most of the wars of the past the principle of close blockade of an enemy in his ports had led to satisfactory conclusions in the end. When, in about 1904, it became apparent that the next enemy upon the seas would be Germany, it was accepted that the general war strategy would consist of a close blockade of the German North Sea coast. Its total length was no more than 150 miles in the form roughly of a right angle, so that a blockade would lie roughly along the hypotenuse. A corollary of this close blockade was the capture of one or more of the German islands—Sylt and Heligoland were those most frequently mentioned—for development as a forward British base for light craft charged with the blockade. Behind the advanced light forces would lie the main fleet of Britain, ready to engage the High Seas Fleet as it came out and inflict upon it a second battle of Trafalgar.

It took a long time for the realities of modern naval warfare to impinge upon this strongly held British belief. It was, of course, unrealistic even in 1904, for the mine and the torpedo, the submarine and the torpedo-boat, and the long-range coastal gun were all realities before that date. At least as late as 1907, in a series of war plans drawn up in that year, and later still in the minds of many senior admirals whose task it was to decide British naval strategy, the doctrine of close blockade held sway. Even when at last the facts did percolate through naval thinking, the plan was modified to a close blockade in daylight hours by light craft with fleet support and a withdrawal of the supporting fleet at night to a distance beyond which German light forces could not reach if they sailed at sunset and were back in their harbours by sunrise the next morning. This distance was worked out as 170 miles, and the scheme incorporated in the war plans.

By as late as August 1911 close blockade was still in fashion. In a memorandum issued during that month by the Commander-in-Chief Home Fleet, the agreed strategy was indicated in some detail: *The present War Plans provide for a blockade of the Heligoland Bight by the 1st and 2nd Destroyer Flotillas, supported by the 1st, 2nd and 3rd Cruiser Squadrons, with the principal objects of*
● *preventing raiding expeditions leaving German ports in the earlier stages of hostilites;*
● *preventing the German Fleet putting to sea without the British Commander-in-Chief knowing it and, when it is known to be at sea, conveying him such information as to its movements as will enable it to be brought to action by the British Main Fleet.* Here we were, back to the days of Hawke, Cornwallis and Nelson!

By 1912, at long last, even the naval diehards had come to the conclusion that close blockade was too risky an operation to consider. The German islands, on the capture of which the original scheme had depended, were now heavily fortified. German submarines and torpedo boats, it was at last agreed, could carry out a war of attrition against British advanced forces that could, in a reasonably short time, whittle away the numerical advantage on which the ultimate safety of the nation depended. Some other scheme was needed.

It took the form of a proposed 'observational blockade', to consist of a line of cruisers and destroyers stretching from the south-westerly tip of Norway to a point in the centre of the North Sea, and then southward to the coast of Holland. The main battle fleets would be at sea to the westward of this line. As the 1912 War Plans stated: 'The general idea of these plans is to exercise pressure upon Germany by shutting off German shipping from oceanic trade through the action of patrolling cruisers on lines drawn across the approaches to the North Sea, and supporting these cruisers and covering the British coasts by two battle fleets stationed so as to be in a position to bring the enemy's fleet to action should it proceed to sea with the object of driving the cruisers off or undertaking other offensive action.'

'Observational blockade'
For the next two years, almost to the brink of war, the 'observational blockade' remained the official strategy of the Royal Navy, in spite of the obvious impossibility of maintaining a blockade line of 300 miles in length with its invitation to the enemy to attack the blockading ships one by one in a series of concentrated raids. But right at the end, in the war plans issued to the fleet in July 1914, the overall strategy was changed finally to that which in the final reckoning would bring victory to Britain. The observational blockade was abandoned and the policy of distant blockade adopted, closing the two exits from the North Sea, first, by the Channel Fleet in the Dover Straits, and second, by the Grand Fleet stationed in the north of Scotland to guard a line from the Orkney Islands to the Norwegian coast. *The maritime domination of the North Sea,* ran the new War Plan, *upon which our whole policy must be based, will be established as far as practicable by occasional driving or sweeping movements carried out by the Grand Fleet traversing in superior force the area between the 54th and 58th parallels [roughly the latitudes of Heligoland and the southern tip of Norway]. The movements should be sufficiently frequent and sufficiently advanced to impress upon the enemy that he cannot at any time venture far from his home ports without such serious risk of encountering an overwhelming force that no enterprise is likely to reach its destination.*

German basic strategy had gone through changes almost as radical as those in Britain. It had begun with the *Riskflotte* theory, with the building of a fleet strong enough to dissuade a British encounter with it because of the resultant British inferiority with the navies of France and Russia. After 1904, with the entente with France, and especially after 1907, when Russia, too, joined hands with Britain, a new strategy had to be worked out, and a satisfactory one was found based on the known British policy of a close blockade of the German North Sea coast. During such a blockade, the German Admiralty expected, there would be countless opportunities for bringing to action detached squadrons of the British fleet whose duty it would be to support the blockade. This attritional warfare, in which by reason of the proximity of their bases the German fleet could ensure local superiority, would in the end produce the situation where the numerical superiority of the Royal Navy had been whittled away, and in which the High Seas Fleet could risk the full-scale battle.

The British change from close blockade to observational blockade, and from that to distant blockade, was unknown in Germany. It was realised in naval circles in Berlin that close blockade was no longer a feasible operation of war in the face of modern weapons, and that Britain was bound to modify her plans to a distant blockade. They confidently expected the Royal Navy to use both forms of blockade, which would 'alternate frequently or merge into one another as the situation changes. It is very probable that during the first days of the war, when attacks on our part may be expected, our waters will be closely blockaded, also when it is intended to transport the Expeditionary Force to France'. These were the occasions, it was thought, when a sudden *sortie* of the High Seas Fleet could make a killing of a detached squadron of British ships.

From the very start, the High Seas Fleet had no intention of coming out into the North Sea to try conclusions with the Grand Fleet. That was never a part of their basic strategy. It remained, even after it became clear that there was to be no close British blockade, based on the hope of meeting, in superior force, detached British squadrons and destroying them until parity with the Grand Fleet had been reached. Britain, on the other hand, so misread the German strategy that she was convinced that the High Seas Fleet would steam out into the North Sea within a few days of the declaration of war to do battle with the Grand Fleet. It would have suited her book admirably, but the Germans were much too wise to risk everything on one such desperate fling.

If Britain had somehow stumbled, so far as the Navy was concerned, into a correct strategical posture for a war against Germany, the evolution of the tactical art had taken a long step backwards.

The line of battle
The line of battle, hallowed for centuries in the *Fighting Instructions* of the sailing navy, had always been a producer of sterile battles at sea, and it had only been when admirals like Hawke or Boscawen in the Seven Years' War, or Rodney in the War of American Independence, or Nelson in the Napoleonic War, had risked their reputations and disregarded the rules of the *Fighting Instructions* that decisive actions had resulted. Now, in the age of steam

when the wind no longer dictated the course a ship could steer, there was a fine chance to break clear from the straight-jacket of the rigid line of battle. All it needed was men of vision, admirals who were prepared to trust their subordinate commanders of squadrons and divisions to do the right thing in the stress of battle. But in the Royal Navy, and very largely in the German navy too, there were few such admirals. Command at sea was centralised in the Commander-in-Chief, and for a junior admiral to act on his own initiative was to court relegation to an operational backwater. All tactical training in the past 50 years had consisted of intricate manoeuvres executed by signal from the flagship, not unlike an old-fashioned courtly dance by mastodons on the surface of the sea. Even when the manoeuvres ordered involved ships in danger of collision, there was no questioning an admiral's instructions, and in 1893 the battleship *Victoria* had been rammed and sunk by the battleship *Camperdown* because the Commander-in-Chief had ordered a particular manoeuvre with too little sea room in which to perform it. No one questioned him. The manoeuvre was carried out and the *Victoria* was sunk.

In battle, with smoke from funnels and guns reducing visibility and with a line of ships which might stretch as far as five miles, tactical manoeuvring by signal from the flagship was fraught with hazard. It took time to pass the signal by visual means up and down the line (Jellicoe, for example, distrusted wireless), and often the flagship was obscured from the view of cruiser squadrons and destroyer flotillas in attendance on the fleet, when signals never got through at all. Although in the various fleet battle orders there was a certain amount of lip service paid to decentralisation and individual initiative, it never worked out in practice. The fleet battle orders were themselves too rigid and too mandatory to allow any individual leeway.

It was not very different in the High Seas Fleet, though admirals commanding squadrons were allowed some discretion in the tactical handling of their ships. But in general, like the British, once the line of battle had been formed it was subject to centralised control. The only real difference between the two fleets lay in their night-fighting capabilities. One or two British attempts to introduce night encounters in the pre-war fleet manoeuvres had ended in uncertainty and muddle, and Jellicoe in particular would have none of it. 'The difficulty of distinguishing friend from foe,' he wrote, 'and the exceeding uncertainty of the result, confirmed the opinion I had long held that a night action between fleets was a pure lottery.' The German fleet, on the other hand, had practised night action in a big way, and had made itself very proficient in the art.

For all the German advantages, and they were many in such things as broad-beamed ships, better guns and shells, better rangefinders and searchlights, and a more meticulous attention to every detail of naval warfare, there was one sphere in which the Royal Navy excelled. It was a long-service fleet, manned by officers and men who were volunteers and who were making service in the Royal Navy their career. German sailors were enrolled on a short-service basis, and their training was

neither as long nor as thorough as that of the British seamen. There were other weaknesses as well, and one over-riding handicap was the incredibly chaotic arrangement whereby naval policy was placed under the control of the General Staff of the army. But it was the short-service basis of German enrolment which was the telling factor. Three years was the service spell of the German seaman, compared with 12 years, and a chance of re-enlistment for a further ten to qualify for a pension, which was the British system. Compared with the German, British ships spent far more time exercising at sea, and the innate sense of seamanship which this developed amongst officers and men stood them in good stead in the war which was coming.

Of the qualities of leadership, there was not much to choose between British and German. If Jellicoe's weakness was an excess of caution allied to an inability to decentralise in the control of an immense fleet, his opposite numbers in the High Seas Fleet, first Ingenohl and later his successor, Pohl, were no better, if in fact as good. Lower down the scale, in the vice- and rear-admirals and captains, there was about an equal proportion of good and bad on both sides, if one counts ship handling, tactical skill, and professional knowledge as the criteria of judgment.

One priceless intangible
Above this, however, there remained for the Royal Navy one priceless intangible. The officers and the men they led had no knowledge of the *materiel* advantages of the German fleet, of more robust ships and more efficient weapons, nor would they have believed it if they had. They had complete confidence in the ships and weapons they manned, complete confidence in their leaders, and complete confidence that in their own skills and training they held the key to invincibility. This supreme confidence, as clearly recognised in Germany as in Britain, bred in its turn an inferiority complex which pervaded so much of German naval thought and action. Perhaps one can allow the last words to the German Admiral Scheer, writing of the Royal Navy as he saw it in 1914. 'The English fleet had the advantage of looking back on a hundred years of proud tradition which must have given every man a sense of superiority based on the great deeds of the past. This could only be strengthened by the sight of their huge fleet, each unit of which in every class was supposed to represent the last word in the art of marine construction. The feeling was also supported by the British sailor's perfect familiarity with the sea and with conditions of life on board ship.' How, indeed, could a new and untried navy hope to win in battle against men such as these?

Further Reading
Bacon, Admiral Sir Reginald, *The Life of John Rushworth, Earl Jellicoe* (London, 1936)
Chatfield, Lord Admiral of the Fleet, *The Navy and Defence* (London, 1942)
Marder, A. J., *From the Dreadnought to Scapa Flow Vol. 1* (Oxford University Press, 1961)
Admiralty Papers
Brassey's Naval Annual (London, 1913, 1914, 1915)
Jane's Fighting Ships (London, 1913, 1914, 1915)
Public Records Office

The Russian armoured cruiser *Rurik,* a rough equivalent of the German *Blücher,* was stationed in the Baltic at the outbreak of the war. *Displacement:* 15,000 tons. *Length:* 529 feet. *Armament:* Four 10-inch, eight 8-inch, and 20 4.7-inch guns. *Armour:* Belt 6 inches, turret 8 inches. *Crew:* 899

John Batchelor

Heligoland
The First Sea Battle

The first British shot of the war was fired by the destroyer HMS *Lance* during a sweep of the North Sea as part of the British policy of distant blockade. Another sweep on August 28 resulted in the battle of Heligoland Bight — the first full scale naval fight of the war

David Woodward

No one knows who fired the first British shot in the First World War. The gun, from the forecastle of HM Destroyer *Lance* is at the Imperial War Museum in London, but the name of the gunlayer has vanished both from the records of the Admiralty and from the memories of the few men who still survive the events of the morning of August 5, 1914.

The war had started officially at 2300 hours on August 4. By that time the German auxiliary minelayer *Königin Luise* was already making her way down the North Sea from her base at Emden to lay mines at the entry to the Thames.

The *Königin Luise* was a former excursion steamer that, in peacetime, ran from Hamburg to Heligoland with holiday-makers. She had been converted into a minelayer in the space of 12 hours, so hastily that the main armament planned for her, a pair of 3.4-inch guns, had not been mounted. In addition, the windows had been left in her glass-enclosed promenade deck. With her two raked masts and two raked funnels the German ship looked very like one of the Great Eastern Railway steamers running between Harwich and the Hook, and in keeping with this impression she had been specially painted with black hull, buff upper-works and yellow funnels with black tops, the standard Great Eastern Railway colour scheme for its ships.

When minelaying began it was under the cover of a rain squall, out of which loomed long, low, dark shapes. Two of these changed suddenly into small, squat lumps as two destroyers changed course and headed for the German ship. They came out of the mist and opened fire at once.

An unknown steamer

The ships were HMS *Lance* and HMS *Landrail,* part of the British 2nd Destroyer Flotilla which, with 20 other destroyers of the 1st Flotilla, had left Harwich at dawn on the first day of the war to sweep northward towards German waters. The 1st Flotilla followed the Dutch coast and the 2nd Flotilla, led by the light cruiser HMS *Amphion,* steamed up the middle of the North Sea. A few hours after leaving port they met a British fishing vessel which reported that she had seen an unknown steamer 'throwing things overboard' about 20 miles north-east of the Outer Gabbard. When the destroyers came up with the *Königin Luise* through the mist she was still throwing things overboard, but she turned to run for home. The only guns which there had been time to mount were a pair of pom-poms and to reinforce these, as the British drew close, the Germans opened fire with rifles and revolvers. Once her mines had been laid there was nothing for the *Königin Luise* to do except scuttle herself, for her tiny armament was too weak to harm the enemy. Within a few minutes the German ship lay over to port with steam and smoke trailing from her funnels.

The British ships stopped and picked up survivors who were, according to the German Official History, 'chivalrously treated'. The destroyers then continued their sweep and very soon sighted another ship resembling the *Königin Luise,* at which they steamed full speed to attack. Fortunately, although the ship was flying a huge German flag, Captain Cecil H. Fox of the *Amphion* recognised her as a genuine Great Eastern Railway steamer, the *St. Petersburgh,* carrying the German ambassador to Britain back to Germany—hence the huge German flag.

At first the excitement of the chase was too much for the British destroyers and, failing to heed the signals, they pressed home their attack until Fox took the *Amphion* between the destroyers and the *St. Petersburgh,* deliberately fouling the range. The British ships withdrew but, next morning, on her way back to Harwich the *Amphion* struck one of the *Königin Luise's* mines. The first explosion broke her back forward, killing members of the British crew and their German prisoners, and then, a little later, there was another explosion of a ghastly lemon colour and the ship sank. The total number killed was one British officer and 150 ratings, together with 18 Germans.

On the same day, August 6, the Cabinet in London authorised the despatch of four divisions of the British Expeditionary Force (BEF) to France. They were to sail from United Kingdom ports, covered by the Channel Fleet, a force of elderly battleships commanded by Vice-Admiral Sir Cecil

HMS *Arethusa*, the British light cruiser commanded by Commodore Tyrwhitt. *Length* 450 feet. *Beam:* 39 feet. *Displacement:* 3,520 tons. *Main armament as built:* Two 6-in., six 4-in. *Armour:* Belt 3-in., Deck 1-in. *Speed:* 30 knots

The *Königin Luise* in her peacetime garb. She was sunk while minelaying off the Thames.

Staatsbibliothek/Berlin

Burney. This fleet was judged strong enough to deal with any German surface ships which might be risked so far from home as the English Channel, while the British main force, the Grand Fleet under the command of Vice-Admiral Sir John Jellicoe, was to cruise in the North Sea, in case the High Seas Fleet intervened.

The old battleships of the Channel Fleet faded away as it became clear that the German surface ships would present no real threat to the movements of the BEF, but two forces of British light craft were formed at the time of mobilisation which were to serve throughout the war and to become famous. One was the 'Harwich force' of light cruisers, destroyers and submarines, and the other was the 'Dover Patrol' consisting of destroyers and small craft.

There were many surprises on both sides during the early weeks of the war, and one of the first was the failure of the German navy to interfere with the movement to France of the BEF. No one seems to have expected a fleet action but it did seem possible, even probable, that German light surface craft and U-boats would make an attempt on the troop convoys which had consequently been routed across the central and western part of the English Channel, the principal route being that from Southampton to Le Havre. The main reason why the Germans did not attack, according to the German Official Naval History, was that the German army was completely confident of victory over the Allied armies on the Western Front, so that it did not matter to them whether the BEF was attacked on its way to France or defeated in battle after it had arrived there.

The first submarine operations

With the exception of a few fruitless cruises by a pair of Greek submarines off the Dardanelles during the First Balkan War in 1912, the operations of August 1914 were the first occasion in which submarines, as we know them, were used in warfare. The submarine was an untried weapon and, compared with the submarines of today, they were very primitive. When submerged their speed and radius of action were very small, so that their passage to the positions where they hoped to meet the enemy was made on the surface. Until the anti-submarine measures of their opponents were much better developed they preferred to wait on the surface in daylight, diving only when a possible enemy came in sight. The early U-boats had a great capacity for attracting attention to themselves, during daylight by the smoke from the exhausts of their Körting petrol engines, while at night these same exhausts gave forth brilliant flames, and at all times the noise of the engines served as a warning to any foe for miles around. In addition, at the beginning of the war these boats were without the chronometers essential for accurate navigation.

From the very beginning of the war it was clear that submarines were first rate scouting craft although British submarines were hampered for a long time by the very short range of their wireless sets. Within two days of the outbreak of the war both the British and the Germans had submarines in enemy waters seeking information.

On August 5 two British submarines, *E6* and *E8*, left Harwich for the Heligoland Bight. Their captains were, respectively, Lieutenant-Commander C. P. Talbot and Lieutenant-Commander F. H. H. Goodhart. On the first day of their patrol the area seemed full of small craft, but orders to remain submerged throughout the day and watch shipping through their periscopes, restricted them to a very small area of the Bight. On the next day, therefore, they decided to surface but by that time the German ships had withdrawn and the British submarines returned to port. In those days a patrol lasting between five and seven days was considered the maximum that could be carried out.

The German submarines were soon engaged on a similar enterprise. From July 30, when a state of 'War imminent (*drohende Kriegsgefahr*)' had been proclaimed in Berlin, they had been disposed as a reconnaissance screen across the Heligoland Bight, escorted out to sea every morning by the light cruiser *Hamburg* which, rather like an anxious mother taking a large family out to play, saw them to their stations and then watched them submerge—a lengthy process which took between five and seven minutes.

On August 6, the 1st U-boat Flotilla of

John Batchelor

ten boats, strung out in line abreast over 70 miles, headed in a north-westerly direction up the North Sea, hoping to find the British Grand Fleet, whose location was unknown at that time. One boat broke down and returned to port, one disappeared apparently as the result of an accident (U13), and a third (U15) was sunk. She alone found the Grand Fleet and, early on the morning of August 9, was spotted on the surface in hazy weather by the British light cruiser HMS *Birmingham* and sunk by ramming.

This was the first encounter between ships of the Grand Fleet and a U-boat. From the beginning of the war the Grand Fleet was very U-boat conscious. The Fleet's base at Scapa Flow in the Orkneys was almost ideally placed for the first tasks of the British navy, to blockade Germany and cut off her warships from the Atlantic. But, at the beginning of the war, Scapa Flow possessed no anti-submarine defences of any sort and at any moment a U-boat could have entered the Flow and carried out an attack. Under these circumstances, there were many false alarms that caused picket boats, destroyers and trawlers to be sent to search a suspected area in all weathers, while the entire fleet raised steam and gun crews were called to action stations. In August 1914 U-boats continued to be one of Jellicoe's greatest worries. On an early occasion he felt obliged to move the Grand Fleet out of the North Sea to Loch Ewe on the west coast of Scotland, only to bring it back almost immediately as there was a false alarm of a German invasion attempt.

Since the Grand Fleet was in northern waters, and the High Seas Fleet lay in the estuaries of the Elbe, the Jade and the Ems, the southern part of the North Sea became a non-man's land, though the British were able to protect ships trading between the United Kingdom and Holland and those conveying the BEF.

'A certain liveliness'

In search of this traffic there were U-boat reconnaissances as far south as the line from Harwich to Rotterdam, and on August 17 two German light cruisers, *Stralsund* and *Strassburg,* with two more U-boats, were sent south to try to get a clearer idea of what was going on. There was a brief

Above: U35, a German ocean-going submarine
Below: **SMS Stettin,** a German light cruiser.
Length: 385 feet. *Beam:* 44 feet. *Displacement:* 3,550 tons. *Main armament:* Ten 4.1-in guns. *Speed:* 23 knots

A German light cruiser had put 16 destroyers and *Fearless* to flight

exchange between the German light cruisers and the British light cruiser *Fearless* with accompanying destroyers. These operations were described in an Admiralty communique as representing 'a certain liveliness'.

To Commodore Keyes, however, the action was not to be dismissed with a phrase. He wrote to the Director of the Operations Division of the Admiralty a private and nearly insubordinate letter: 'I feel sore and sick. Owing to our scattered destroyer disposition a German light cruiser, equal in offensive power to the *Fearless,* had put 16 destroyers and the *Fearless* to flight. It is not by such incidents we shall get the right atmosphere.'

Two days later Keyes followed up this letter with a plan of his own for creating the 'right atmosphere'. Reconnaissance by Keyes' submarines since the beginning of the war had made clear the routine of the German patrols by day and by night around Heligoland. On this knowledge Keyes proposed that a force of British destroyers should infiltrate the German positions, just as the night patrols were relieved by the day patrols, slip in behind the latter and, turning back westward, get between them and their base. As a bait to lure the Germans farther out to sea three British submarines were to show themselves on the edge of the German patrol area.

The plan was adopted, although Keyes' proposal that the battle-cruisers under Vice-Admiral Sir David Beatty should take part was rejected. Commodores Tyrwhitt and Keyes accordingly sailed from Harwich in the light cruiser HMS *Arethusa* and the destroyer HMS *Lurcher* respectively, convinced that any big ships they met would be German. After they had sailed, however, the Admiralty changed its mind.

The BEF and the French armies were being forced out of Belgium by the advancing Germans and the Belgian coast would soon be open to attack by German forces from the direction of Brussels. Accordingly it was decided to send some 3,000 Royal Marines to Ostend.

To protect the ships carrying them the Admiralty now decided that Beatty's battle-cruisers should, after all, take part in the Heligoland operation but, because of the need for wireless silence, Keyes and

Tyrwhitt were left in ignorance of this change of plan. Accordingly when they met Beatty's ships early on the morning of August 28 there were a few tense moments, during which fatal mistakes might have been made.

As the sun rose on that day there were patches of white mist scattered all over the sea. On occasion, visibility from the decks of the ships was reasonably good, while the lookouts at the mastheads could see little or nothing. At other times, ships' masts could be seen sticking out of banks of mist, while their hulls were invisible below.

Meanwhile, the Germans guessed that the British attack was about to develop, although they did not expect that heavy British ships would be involved. Their own heavy ships were in harbour, for the most part behind the sand bar at the mouth of the river Jade, which could only be crossed near high tide. The British striking force, made up of the two light cruisers *Arethusa* and *Fearless* and 31 destroyers of the 1st and 3rd Flotillas arrived at first light in the area from which it was to begin its raid into the Bight. Here they were joined by six vessels of Commodore Goodenough's command which were to follow Tyrwhitt into the Bight.

The raid began: Tyrwhitt's force was to steam south until Heligoland lay 12 miles on its port beam, then turn westward between the German outpost vessels and their bases and roll up the line. There was an excessive amount of wireless traffic between the British ships so the Germans were soon on their guard and they despatched light cruisers and torpedo craft to investigate.

At 0650 hours Greenwich Mean Time Tyrwhitt's force sighted one group of German destroyers on the port bow and, shortly afterwards, another to starboard. Both groups turned for home, with the British in chase. The first serious opposition encountered was from the light cruiser *Stettin*, which had been lying at anchor off Heligoland. Today it may seem almost unbelievable that a light cruiser on patrol duty expecting an enemy attack and exposed to submarines, should have been at anchor in the open sea.

The action between the *Arethusa* and the *Stettin* lasted about 25 minutes. The two ships steamed south at full speed. The

Commodore Sir Reginald Tyrwhitt *(right)* with Flag-Lieutenant Floyer

Stettin was a coal-burning ship and sent up great rolling clouds of smoke, while the three funnels of the oil-fired *Arethusa* was crowned by a slight heat haze and nothing more. Both ships had great waves of spray like a pair of glistening wings at their bows and tumbling white wakes behind. The *Stettin* was joined by another light cruiser, the *Frauenlob*, and the *Arethusa* soon began to suffer. The range fell from 9,000 yards to 3,400 yards and the British and German ships settled down on a severe and parallel course. The brand new guns of the *Arethusa* gave trouble. Three jammed and a fourth was put out of action when its ammunition was hit and the cordite began to blaze. Soon she had only one gun in action, the forecastle 6-inch. On her bridge the signals officer was killed by Tyrwhitt's side. With her single gun the *Arethusa* in turn got a hit on the *Frauenlob*'s bridge and both Ger-

man ships hauled away. It was high time, as far as the *Arethusa* was concerned. Her forward engine room was flooded to a depth of three feet, her speed dropped, her wireless was out of action and her signal halliards shot away.

After the Germans had disappeared into the mist, the *Arethusa* and *Fearless* came up from astern, lay stopped side by side while they communicated by semaphore and Tyrwhitt tried to reassemble his scattered destroyers. Within a short time this was done, the *Arethusa* managed to raise steam again, and with *Fearless* and the combined destroyer force Tyrwhitt started westward to roll up the German patrol line. A new and much bigger destroyer, *V 187*, was now sighted. Dodging the British destroyers she ran into two of Goodenough's light cruisers which, after following the *Arethusa* and *Fearless* into the Bight, had now come up with them. *V 187* altered course violently once again, only to run into more British destroyers. She had got to within 2,000 yards of a division of four boats before their 4-inch shells stopped her, set her on fire, killed most of her crew and tore her hull to pieces. She slowly sank, in clouds of black smoke and escaping white steam.

The spirit with which men had gone to war in August 1914 then showed itself, for some of the British destroyers stopped and lowered boats to pick up survivors. While they were doing this the *Stettin* reappeared and opened fire, so the destroyers, collecting their boats as best they could, made off, leaving two belonging to HMS *Defender* behind for rescue later in the morning by the British submarine *E4*. This took the British officer and seamen from the boats, together with a few German prisoners— 'as a sample' said the submarine's commanding officer later—and gave the remaining Germans water, biscuits, a compass and the course to steer for Heligoland.

During this time the British steamed westward, departing from their course from time to time to chase reported enemy ships, or to attack those actually sighted. Much confusion and, to quote an official report 'a distinct element of excitement' was added to the operations by the signals of Keyes, who had sighted Goodenough's light cruisers, taken them to be enemy and reported them as such.

The British submarine *E4*, which was completed in 1913, rescued survivors after the German destroyer *V187* sank at Heligoland

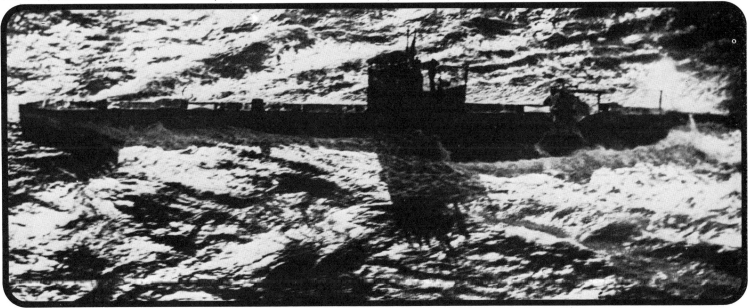

Meanwhile, Goodenough realised that there was great danger of British light cruisers and submarines attacking each other and accordingly withdrew his light cruisers from the scene and waited in the hope that the situation would soon clear itself up.

Mistaken identity

There were other cases of mistaken identity as the British ships, seeing brief and shadowy manifestations of ships appearing and disappearing in the mist, reported them as enemy and then proceeded to chase. These chases sometimes ended with the recognition of each other as British, but sometimes the chaser lost the chased in the mist without realising that he had been chasing a friend.

However, by about 1010 hours the situation, so far as the British destroyers were concerned, was much clearer, and Tyrwhitt's force, more or less reconcentrated, started westward again. The *Fearless* and *Arethusa* were in company and steaming at 10 knots, which was now the latter's maximum speed.

The morning had not been as successful as the British had hoped. True, they had sunk one destroyer, but, on the other hand,

it was by no means certain that the *Arethusa* would be able to get home. The Germans were recovering from the surprise of the British attack, and their light cruisers, which had been on guard duty close under the coast, were now putting to sea, although the battle-cruisers were still penned up behind the bar at the mouth of the Jade.

The first of the German light cruisers on the scene was the *Strassburg*; the British destroyers, on their way westward and homeward, turned back to engage her and at this providential moment Commodore Goodenough's light cruisers came down from their waiting position to the north, in answer to a call for help from the *Fearless*. The *Strassburg* was driven off, but almost at once another light cruiser, the *Mainz*, appeared, having hurried up from the Ems where she had been lying.

Tricks of light and fog had greatly magnified the size of the *Strassburg*, so that she appeared to be a cruiser of the *Roon* class of about twice her displacement. It seemed likely that a ship of that size would be scouting in front of the big ships of the High Seas Fleet so that when the message reporting her supposed presence was received by Beatty, who had been steaming backwards and forwards some 40 miles

away waiting for his chance, it seemed to him that the time had now come for the battle-cruisers to be committed. Tyrwhitt signalled 'Respectfully request that I may be supported. Am hard pressed.' The *Arethusa* and the other British light craft would stand no chance if, by themselves, they were to encounter the big ships of the High Seas Fleet, and Beatty took his ships into the Bight. At least one of the dangers which confronted them, that of submarine attack, was much reduced by the still calm which kept the sea in a state of glassy calm, thus making it comparatively easy to spot an attacking submarine and avoid it.

By now the destroyers, which had started out at dawn into the Bight with *Arethusa* and *Fearless,* had begun to head for home, but they were ordered to return to the battlefield. Captain Blunt in the *Fearless* signalled those short of ammunition to return home at once; no one did so and the destroyers were soon in action against the *Mainz*. For 15 minutes, from 1135 to 1150, they engaged the German ship without hits by either side. Then, when the destroyers closed it could be seen what was implied when unarmoured ships were engaged at ultra short range. The destroyer HMS *Laurel* was hit amidships; the ready-

Imperial War Museum

The British light cruiser *Fearless,* leader of the 1st Destroyer Flotilla during the battle at Heligoland

use ammunition of No. 2 gun exploded and put the gun and its crew out of action, blowing away half the after funnel. Beams in the engine room were twisted and the captain seriously wounded. Another shell from the *Mainz* hit the forward funnel and exploded inside, causing a back draught in the boiler which set fire to the oil fuel. This fire was soon put out with sand, but a third shell cut the main steam pipe, the fire main and the electric wires taking light to the stokeholds which were thus suddenly plunged into total darkness. A fourth shell passed straight through the ship, exploding outboard. *Laurel's* crew then rigged emergency oil lighting in the stokeholds, only to find that forced draught blew out the lamps.

Nevertheless, the ship managed to steam slowly away, amid great clouds of smoke that partially hid her from the enemy. *Laurel's* sister ship, HMS *Liberty,* was hit in a number of places, her mast and bridge shot away and her captain killed. At 4,000 yards a single salvo of four shells hit HMS *Laertes* in the bows, in No. 2 boiler room, at the base of her centre funnel and also aft. There was no water left in her boilers and she stopped dead.

The *Mainz* was now attacked by Good-enough's light cruisers, only half visible through the mist until they fired their broadsides, when the gun flashes glowed bright. The first salvos fell close to the German ship and the yellow smoke and fumes of the British shells drifted across her deck, mixed with white steam from a broken steam pipe. A hit killed or wounded the crews of the two quarter-deck 4.1-inch guns and their places were taken by others.

Another hit aft damaged the *Mainz's* rudder and she began to circle round to starboard, a circle interrupted by a crash heavier and louder than that of her 4.1-inch guns. A huge column of dirty grey water leaped out of the water alongside, the ship rocked and then settled down on an even keel, torpedoed and rapidly losing speed.

Firing by clockwork

Mainz was now surrounded by British light cruisers and destroyers. A German survivor afterwards described the light cruisers as firing as if by clockwork. Her main mast came down with a run and the midships and after funnels crashed down on the deck. Smoke and flames drifted across the ship, and all the time shells were whistling overhead or exploding in the ship or in the water and huge splashes of water were leaping up in the air and slowly falling back again.

There was a sudden silence; only one of the German's twelve 4.1-inch guns was still in action. *Kapitän* Paschen, the commanding officer of the *Mainz,* gave the order to sink his ship then but the order miscarried. The pause in the action ended as the British opened fire once more, and it was at once clear that these shells were much heavier than the 6-inch guns of the 'Town' class cruisers which had done the damage so far. Close at hand, through the mist and smoke came Beatty's battle-cruisers, HMSs *Lion, Princess Royal, Queen Mary, New Zealand* and *Invincible,* five times the size of the *Mainz* and looking even more impressive because they were neat and tidy, in order, undamaged, steaming fast and firing as if at exercise.

The *Mainz* was in her great and final agony, but she managed to get out a signal telling the High Seas Fleet and Hipper's battle-cruisers that the British heavy ships were actually in the Bight.

The last gun of the *Mainz* was now still: the order to sink the ship was given once more and the necessary preparations were made. Members of the crew began to jump

Bibliothek für Zeitgeschichte

The German cruiser *Mainz* was attacked by British destroyers, light cruisers and battle-cruisers and sunk at Heligoland

SMS *Seydlitz,* one of the three German battle-cruisers penned up behind the Jade Bar during the action of the Heligoland Bight

The German light cruiser *Köln* — badly damaged by two salvoes from HMS *Lion* and then shot to pieces by the British battle-cruisers

into the sea and were picked up by the British. But this rescue work took time so Keyes brought the *Lurcher* alongside the quarter-deck of the German ship so that many of the Germans were able to climb on board and save their lives. Other destroyers helped and every living person was brought to safety except for one young officer who stood apart and watched the proceedings. Keyes shouted to him that everything possible had been done and urged him to come over to the *Lurcher.* The young man stood to attention, saluted and refused. The *Lurcher* backed away, her upper deck crowded with survivors, and the *Mainz* sank. One of those rescued was Lieutenant von Tirpitz, son of the German Minister of Marine. He was brought to England as a prisoner of war. Churchill, on learning of this, at once sent a personal message through the International Red Cross to young Tirpitz's father, reassuring

him as to the fate of his son.

The *Mainz* sank at 1310. The German officer who had refused Keyes' offer of rescue, and another officer who had also stayed with the ship until she sank, were both picked up by the Germans. The last act of the crew of the *Mainz* had been to throw overboard the confidential books in a bag weighted with a 4.1-inch shell. When the bag was thrown the shell fell out and the bag floated away, spreading secret papers on the waters of the Bight. Horrified, even in those moments which might have been their last, the Germans threw used cartridge cases at the contents of the bag as they drifted by and succeeded in sinking them. Their work was in vain, for two days previously the Russians had recovered from the wreck of the light cruiser *Magdeburg,* at the entrance to the Gulf of Finland, the vital German cyphers which were handed over to the British. For months the

Admiralty in London was able to read the secret German messages.

By the time that the *Mainz* had sunk, Beatty's battle-cruisers had been in action with two other German light cruisers, both of which sank as the result of the damage they had received during a brief blasting from the heavy guns of the British ships.

Fog and confusion

The *Köln* was making her way through the confusion of the misty sea when suddenly from out of the mist there emerged, vast and terrific, the form of a great cruiser steaming at full speed. This was the *Lion* and two salvoes from her settled the fate of the *Köln.* Yet another of the German light cruisers, the *Ariadne,* then appeared. Engaged, she at once caught fire. She was an old ship, painted and repainted time and again, so that the paint on her hull was at least a quarter of an inch thick. This

HMS *Lurcher (left)* backing away from the sinking German cruiser *Mainz* after picking up survivors

caught fire and blazed away, so that the very steel plates of the ship's hull seemed to have burst into flames. She staggered back into the mist from which she had come and, some two hours later, sank.

Meanwhile the British battle-cruisers, steaming very slowly, undertook the destruction of the *Köln*. She was the flagship of *Konteradmiral* Leberecht Maass commanding the destroyers and torpedo boats in the Bight, and of her company of 380 men only one survived that afternoon. He was a leading stoker, stationed as a messenger on the 'tween decks', where he was protected from the worst effects of the enemy fire until smoke and flames drove him into the open. Here he saw *Lion* and the other British battle-cruisers steaming slowly by and deliberately shooting the *Köln* to pieces. Maass had been killed, presumably when the bridge was shot away. The *Köln*'s funnels were full of holes, the deck was littered with half-burnt bits of boats, woodwork, life-jackets and tangled bits of aerials and signal halliards which had been shot away. The whole of the deck seemed to be glazed with green and yellow stuff from the incomplete explosion of the British lyddite shells that gave out a suffocating smell.

The ship lay for a while sinking on an even keel. When the order came to abandon ship the leading stoker and a handful of men clung to the remains of a lifeboat, but 76 hours later he was the only man left alive of the entire ship's company.

At about 1310 hours, having sunk the *Mainz* and the *Köln* and with the *Ariadne* sinking, Beatty considered his position. There were still a number of German light craft scattered around in the mist patches of the Bight—in fact there were now no fewer than seven light cruisers in the area, *Stralsund*, *Strassburg*, *Stettin*, *Frauenlob*, *Kolberg*, *Danzig* and *Hela*. Beatty's force was scattered, the *Arethusa* was still in a critical condition and, most important of all, at 1200 hours it would have been possible for the German battle-cruisers to begin to cross the Jade Bar. In fact orders for them to do so had been given at 1207 hours, which meant that all three, *Seydlitz*, *Moltke* and *Von der Tann* would be on the scene of the battle at about 1500 hours to snap up detached British light cruisers and destroyers. Accordingly Beatty ordered the recall to be sent out. Just then the *Arethusa*'s hard-pressed engines finally broke down and she had to be taken in tow by the armoured cruiser *Hogue*. Altogether she had lost one officer and ten men killed, and one officer and 16 men wounded. The total British losses were 35 killed and about 40 wounded. No British ships had been sunk, while the Germans had lost three light cruisers and a destroyer, together with over 1,000 men killed, wounded or taken prisoner.

It had been a notable British success— perhaps too well celebrated since in the excitement and pleasure of the moment nobody seems to have considered how poor communications between the various groups of British ships had been and how disastrous that might have proved. Poor communications were to dog the British navy throughout the war, but the Germans too suffered from a notable failure of communications. During this battle the weather in the Jade was fine and clear; no one reported mist around the sea of battle so the German command imagined that

A notable British success, but ominous weaknesses began to reveal themselves

The damaged German light cruiser SMS *Frauenlob* is inspected after the battle

the cruisers reporting from around Heligoland could see everything which was going on, and that when they reported sighting individual enemy units these units were all there were to see. Nobody mentioned the mist which was concealing powerful enemy forces.

The effect of the battle on the Germans was immediate and conclusive. The success of the British attack was a tremendous shock and made the Kaiser even more determined than before to protect the High Seas Fleet from damage, for he considered that an undamaged German fleet would be a card of first-class importance for him to play when the time came to discuss peace terms. At the end of August 1914 it seemed to the Germans this time was close at hand, for the Russian invasion of Germany had been repelled, and the success of the German invasion of France and Belgium looked as though it would bring the Germans to Paris very shortly.

In the meantime, the Germans decided to lay mines in the Bight to keep British ships out instead of risking precious warships.

For the British, the first month of the war at sea had ended well. German merchant shipping had disappeared from the sea, Allied merchant shipping was moving almost unchecked all over the world, and so were Allied troops on their way to the various battlefields of the war. Only in the Baltic was the British navy unable to support the armies of its Allies.

Further Reading
Chalmers, Rear-Admiral W. S., *The Life and Letters of David, Earl Beatty* (Hodder and Stoughton, 1951)
Chatterton, E. Keble, *The Sea Raiders* (Hurst and Blackett)
Corbett, Sir J. S., *History of the Great War, Naval Operations, Vol. 1* (Longmans, Green & Co., 1920)
Groos, O., *Der Krieg zur See 1914-18. Der Krieg in der Nordsee, Vol. 1* (E. S. Mittler & Sohn, Berlin, 1920)
Jellicoe, Admiral Viscount, *The Grand Fleet, 1914-16. Its Creation, Development and Work* (Cassell & Co., 1919)
Knight, E. F., *The Harwich Naval Forces* (Hodder and Stoughton, 1919)
Marder, A. J., *From the Dreadnought to Scapa Flow, Vol. 2* (Oxford University Press, 1965)
Niezychowski, Count Alfred von, *The Cruise of the Kronprinz Wilhelm* (Doubleday, Doran, Garden City, New York, 1929)
Scheer, Admiral R., *Germany's High Sea Fleet in World War* (London, 1920)
The Naval Memoirs of Admiral Sir Roger Keyes (Eyre and Spottiswoode)

DAVID WOODWARD was born in 1909. From 1932 to 1940 he was a foreign correspondent, first with Reuters and then with *News Chronicle*. From 1932 to 1937 he was stationed in Geneva, from 1937 to 1939 in Rome, in 1939 in Berlin, and in Amsterdam from 1939 to 1940. As *News Chronicle* war correspondent, he travelled in the Middle and Far East from 1940 to 1942, and was *News Chronicle* naval correspondent from 1942-43. Attached to the Psychological Warfare Branch of the US Office of War Information from 1943-44, he covered the campaigning from Normandy to Berlin as combined service war correspondent to *Manchester Guardian* and *The Times* from 1944-46. He was Press Officer to UNESCO from 1946-48; First Secretary (Information) to the British Legation, Tel Aviv, from 1949-52; and joined the BBC in 1952, where he became producer and script writer, Sound. His publications include *The Tirpitz* (1952), *The Secret Raiders* (1955), *Ramsey at War* (1957), and *The Russians at Sea* (1965).

Imperial War Museum

Revenge at Sea

The unthinkable had happened. The Royal Navy had been beaten in a naval battle. Reaction in Great Britain was immediate and drastic, and within a few days the powerful battle-cruisers Inflexible *and* Invincible *were heading into the south Atlantic—to seek revenge*

At the outbreak of war, the German East Asia Squadron under Vice-Admiral Graf Maximilian von Spee had been widely dispersed; but by 12th October all the most powerful ships, the *Scharnhorst, Gneisenau, Nürnberg* and *Leipzig* were gathered at Easter Island where they were joined by the light cruiser *Dresden*, which brought news of the British reaction to Spee's exploits to date, and thus gave him some idea of the forces being ranged against him.

These did not amount to much. If what *Dresden*'s captain told Spee was correct, the only British ships west of Cape Horn were the old armoured cruiser *Monmouth*, the modern light cruiser *Glasgow*, and the armed merchantman *Otranto*, while just east of the Horn at the British coaling base at Port Stanley on the Falkland Islands, the admiral commanding this tatterdemalion collection of ships, Vice-Admiral Sir Christopher Cradock, waited—presumably for more effective reinforcement—in the armoured cruiser *Good Hope*.

If this were all the naval opposition ranged for the moment against him, there was obviously no point in further delay; Spee coaled his squadron from colliers carefully collected beforehand at Easter Island, and on 18th October left—first for Más Afuera and then for the Chilean coast. He and his ships were forty miles off Valparaiso late on the afternoon of 30th October, and the following evening he learned that the British light cruiser *Glasgow* was at Coronel, 250 miles to the south.

Bravely Gneisenau *and* Scharnhorst *fought their more powerful enemies in the battle of the Falkland Islands. But they were doomed. This picture painted by W.L.Wyllie, shows* Scharnhorst *and* Gneisenau *in action.* Scharnhorst *is sinking and* Gneisenau *will soon follow her. The British had taken their revenge for Coronel*

Detaching *Nürnberg* to pick up mail in Valparaiso, Spee took his squadron south in order to cut off the British cruiser, and perhaps to meet other British ships in company. By 1600 on Sunday, 1st November 1914, his ships were off Coronel, and at 1625 his lookouts sighted two ships away to the south-west; they were *Glasgow* and *Monmouth* and shortly afterwards these two were joined by *Good Hope* flying the flag of Admiral Cradock, and the armed merchantman *Otranto.* The two forces had found each other at last, and the first battle began in which ships of the German navy were ranged in line of battle against ships of the Royal Navy.

Everything favoured the German ships.

By 1800 the two battle lines were formed, and briefly there did appear some small advantage for the British: the setting sun was behind them, blinding the German gunners but lighting up the German ships into perfect targets. But the range was not close enough for the out-dated British guns,

so at 1804 Cradock turned his ships four points towards his enemy—who with superior speed and room to manoeuvre turned away and kept out of range. Grimly, the British re-formed their battle line and assessed the odds against them—now shown up with ominous clarity; *Scharnhorst* and *Gneisenau* riding powerfully over the seas, the details of their high-placed heavy armament picked out by the westering sun, the seas racing along the towering sides and occasionally sweeping the foredecks.

Behind them came the light cruisers *Leipzig* and *Dresden,* and radio signals warned that *Nürnberg* was coming down fast from the north—but most fatal of all for the British, evening slowly crept over the sea from the east and touched the German battleline, greying it into the sea and the sky beyond. As twilight thickened, the moon came up behind heavy clouds, to show fleetingly through them, briefly outlining the German ships—and at last it

seemed that *Scharnhorst* and *Gneisenau* were closing in. To the west, the afterglow of the sun made a fiery, yellow-shot tapestry of the windswept sky, against which the British ships now stood out in black, hard-edged clarity; nothing would help them tonight but their courage and the long tradition of the Royal Navy.

The massacre begins

At 1904 on Sunday, 1st November 1914, the 8·2-inch guns of the German East Asia Squadron at last opened fire on the British ships, at a range of 12,000 yards.

From the bridge of *Glasgow* were seen two lines of orange flashes from *Scharnhorst* and *Gneisenau,* and as the thunder of *Good Hope*'s 9·2s answered, grey-white mushrooms blossomed from the sea 500 yards short of the British ships, beautifully aimed, beautifully grouped.

Glasgow's pair of modern 6-inch guns fired experimentally into the darkness, but even while the gun controller was

27

vainly searching the east for fall of shot, the orange lines sparkled again and then again—lengthened now as *Leipzig* and *Dresden* opened fire. Shell splinters whined shrilly overhead, the seas erupted around the British ships, *Monmouth* steamed ahead through a forest of water and *Good Hope*'s foredeck exploded in a sheet of flame which twisted the forward 9·2-inch gun into a hopeless knot of steel protruding from a turret like a blazing cauldron, and abruptly halved the British chance of harming the enemy at anything but short range. Before the mind could react, the next salvo arrived.

Monmouth's foredeck flared in hard-edged flame and black smoke billowed from sudden, sharp fires along her starboard side; *Good Hope*'s deck amidships threw up a fan of sparks, her upper bridge, mast-head, and foretop glowed redly as *Scharnhorst*'s high-explosive burst between them, and as the glow faded cordite flared on the deck, and stacked ammunition exploded whitely along the gun-flats.

Intent on closing the range and thus bringing his secondary armament into action, Cradock now led the British ships directly towards the German line—but Spee expertly held the range to his own advantage so that his ships remained unscathed while Cradock's took a dreadful punishment. *Monmouth*, especially, received the full attention of the guns of the *Gneisenau*—which had won the Kaiser's Gold Cup only months before—and began slowly to sag out of line as though beaten away by sheer weight of metal. Flames belched from her quarterdeck, water flooded through gaping holes in her bows, she listed badly to port and as darkness increased she disappeared to the south and her guns lapsed into silence.

Except for the endless flashes from their batteries, the German ships were now quite invisible from the British decks. Not so *Good Hope*; she flared like a beacon.

Since action had commenced the British flagship had received the undivided attention of the gunners aboard *Scharnhorst*, who were to prove as efficient as their colleagues aboard *Gneisenau*. At 1940, *Good Hope* was seen to slow and stagger under the rain of blows; her foredeck was ablaze, clouds of steam and smoke billowed around her, glowing sullenly, and her ports glowed redly from the fires in her crowded flats.

Then at 1942, as if in contempt for her own condition, *Good Hope* seemed to gather up her remaining strength, turn directly towards her antagonists and charge them. Abruptly, *Scharnhorst* and *Gneisenau* changed course slightly and shortened range to bring their full broadsides to bear—and, blanketed under a dreadful fire, *Good Hope* was at last brought to a halt and her last desperate throw defeated.

As though stunned, she drifted down silently between the lines.

Then the fires reached a main magazine and at 1953—fifty minutes after the first salvo had been fired at her—*Good Hope* was shattered by an explosion which still lives in the memories of those who witnessed it. A broad column of flame rose upwards from between her main and after funnels until it towered two hundred feet above her decks, and in its awful light jagged and incongruous shapes soared up and away into the darkness, twisting and weaving in the blast, tumbling in the sudden vacuums.

Then the waves took the blazing hulk farther off into the darkness, the flames dwindled and all that remained of Cradock and his men drifted out of the battle.

A net of steel

This was virtually the end of the battle of Coronel. *Otranto* had already left the battle-line—ordered away by Cradock—and now *Glasgow*, after a vain attempt to succour *Monmouth*, fled to the south. At 2035, *Nürnberg* found *Monmouth* painfully making her way towards the Chilean coast and as the British ship made no attempt to strike her colours, had little choice but to reopen the action and finally sink her. At 2058 the waves finally closed over the stern of the British cruiser. There were no survivors—and none from the *Good Hope*, which was never seen again after she drifted from the battle. In two hours the Royal Navy had lost two ships and over 1,000 men and boys.

When the news reached Great Britain, the reaction was immediate and drastic. The first lord of the Admiralty, Winston Churchill, learned of the disaster at 1900 on 4th November, and immediately convened a meeting with the sea lords. As it happened, the position of first sea lord had just been taken over (for the second time) by Lord Fisher, and this doughty old man had no time for half measures—a characteristic which endeared him to Churchill.

Within a week the two battle-cruisers *Invincible* and *Inflexible* (as superior in speed and armament to *Scharnhorst* and *Gneisenau* as the German ships had been to *Good Hope* and *Monmouth*) had sailed from Devonport for the Falkland Islands, and they were joined on their voyage south by the County Class cruisers *Carnarvon*, *Cornwall*, and *Kent*, and the light cruisers *Bristol* and *Glasgow* (hurriedly patched up after her escape from Coronel in the dry dock at Rio). The squadron was under command of Vice-Admiral Sir Frederick Doveton Sturdee, and as it moved farther and farther south—searching all the time for Spee's ships in case they had already come around the Horn—his search line was lengthened every day by the addition of a

host of colliers together with the armed merchantman *Orama*, and eventually by another cruiser, *Macedonia*.

Sturdee's augmented squadron reached the Falkland Islands on 7th December, and he ordered concentration in Port Stanley and the outer bay at Port William for coaling. After their long voyage, some of the ships needed to draw their fires for boiler examination, but *Glasgow* and *Carnarvon* coaled through the night, *Macedonia* patrolled outside the harbour, and at dawn on 8th December the colliers went alongside the battle-cruisers to begin filling their enormous demands for fuel.

To Sturdee, it thus seemed that within ten or twelve hours—twenty-four at the most—his entire squadron would be ready for sea again, to take up the search for the elusive German ships. This, of course, was his great problem, for with the enormous power at his disposal, there could be no doubt as to the outcome of a battle with the East Asia Squadron, once they were sighted. It was a problem rapidly solved.

Shortly after 0830 on the morning after his arrival at Port Stanley—while his capital ships were still coaling and two of his cruisers carrying out boiler examination—Sir Frederick was interrupted while shaving with the news that *Gneisenau* and *Nürnberg* were approaching the island and about twenty miles off, and the smoke from the other ships of Spee's command was visible on the horizon astern of them. It says much for the Vice-Admiral's *sang-froid* that his only comment was the classic 'Then send the men to breakfast'.

Spee's critical error

There is no way of being certain why Spee chose to attack the Falkland Islands, but there is little doubt about the fact that had he ordered an immediate attack on the British squadron as they lay at anchor in the two bays, he could have inflicted on them a defeat of staggering proportions—though probably at the cost of his own ships and certainly at the cost of using up all his remaining ammunition.

Fortunately for Sturdee, however, as soon as the captain of the *Gneisenau* reported the presence of a large number of British warships, Spee issued the order: 'Do not accept action. Concentrate on course east by south. Proceed at full speed.'

In doing so, the German admiral signed his own death-warrant and condemned his squadron to annihilation—though this fact did not become apparent to him or his men until 1000 when, to the dismay and astonishment of the observers aboard *Leipzig*, two pairs of tripod masts—the recognition mark of battle-cruisers—were seen above the low-lying spit, proceeding towards Port William harbour.

From the British point of view, every

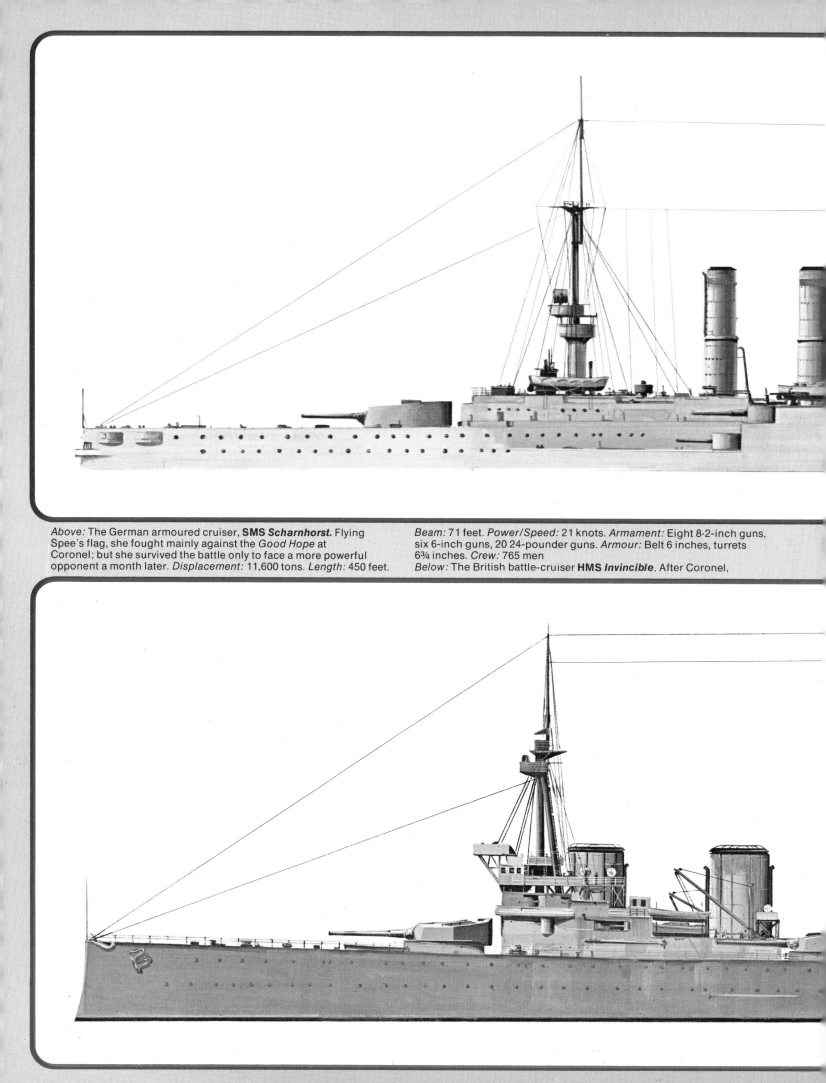

Above: The German armoured cruiser, **SMS Scharnhorst.** Flying Spee's flag, she fought mainly against the *Good Hope* at Coronel; but she survived the battle only to face a more powerful opponent a month later. *Displacement:* 11,600 tons. *Length:* 450 feet.

Beam: 71 feet. *Power/Speed:* 21 knots. *Armament:* Eight 8·2-inch guns, six 6-inch guns, 20 24-pounder guns. *Armour:* Belt 6 inches, turrets 6¾ inches. *Crew:* 765 men

Below: The British battle-cruiser **HMS Invincible.** After Coronel,

the need to send a more powerful squadron against Spee in the Pacific dictated the Admiralty's decision to withdraw her and her sister ship, HMS *Inflexible* from the Grand Fleet and prepare them hurriedly for the journey to South America. During the Battle of the Falkland Islands she received 23 hits which caused only slight damage. *Displacement:* 17,250 tons. *Length:* 562 feet. *Beam:* 78½ feet. *Power/Speed:* 28·6 knots. *Armament:* Eight 12-inch and 16 4-inch guns. *Armour:* Belt 7 inches, turrets 10 inches. *Crew:* 750 men

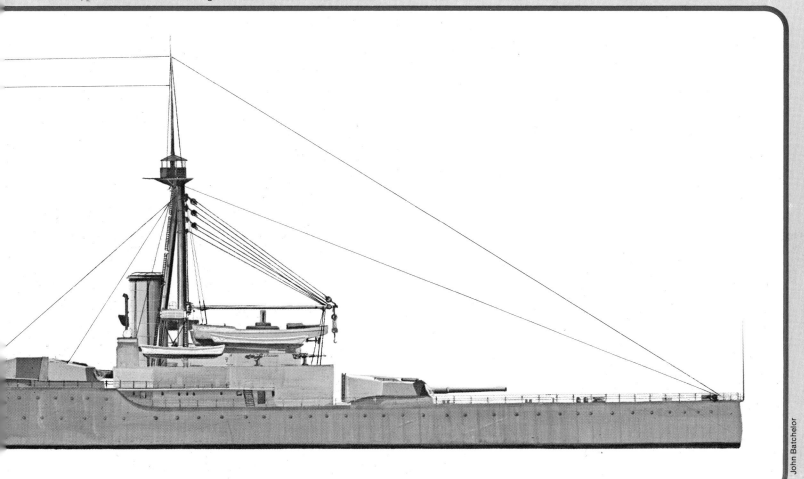

John Batchelor

advantage favoured them. A long summer day stretched ahead, visibility was at its maximum, the sea calm, the sky clear and pale. By 1048 the whole squadron was at sea in a long line stretching eastwards from Port William — *Glasgow* in the lead, *Inflexible* and *Invincible* three miles astern, *Kent* two miles astern of them and *Cornwall* and *Carnarvon* as much again. The squadron's speed was 19 knots, the enemy were some twelve miles ahead and their calculated speed was only 15 knots.

The distance between the two adversaries inexorably lessened and at 1257 *Inflexible* fired the first shot of the battle of the Falkland Islands — at *Leipzig,* the lame duck of the German squadron. The shell fell well short, and only occasional sighting shots were fired during the next thirty minutes; then at 1320, Spee hoisted the signal: 'Light cruisers part company and endeavour to escape.' And the two armoured cruisers bravely turned to accept action from their formidable opponents.

As at Coronel by six o'clock in the evening, the main forces were now ranging broadside against broadside — but this was half past one in the afternoon, there were still eight hours of daylight left, and no mounting seas or storm clouds to complicate the hazards of war. *Invincible* opened fire against *Gneisenau*; *Inflexible* against *Scharnhorst.*

By this time, the British light and County Class cruisers had swung away from the main battle to chase the escaping German light cruisers, and Captain Allen aboard *Kent,* later wrote this description of the scene:

'With the sun still shining on them, the German ships looked as if they had been painted for the occasion. They fired as if they had but eight minutes in which to make a record battle-practice score and never have I seen heavy guns fired with such rapidity and yet with such control. Flash after flash travelled down their sides from head to stern, all their six and eight-inch guns firing every salvo.

Of the British battle-cruisers less could be seen as their smoke drifted from them across the range and not only obscured" their own view but also the spectator's view of them. Nevertheless, they seemed to be firing incessantly, their shells hitting the German ships at intervals whereas all that could be seen of the German fire was that it straddled the British ships. Four or five times in the first twenty minutes the white puff of bursting shell could be seen among the clouds of brown cordite smoke in Gneisenau, and she was seen to be on fire near her mainmast, but this soon disappeared. (By permission of *Naval Review.*)

In addition to the greater weight of broadside and greater range of guns, the battle-cruisers had a further advantage — they were firing, for the first time in a naval battle, lyddite shell, and this new explosive wreaked dreadful havoc aboard the German ships. However Spee might seek to twist and turn, hoping for some sudden squall or mist patch in which to escape, the British battle-cruisers hung grimly on, unhurried but implacable, inexorably smashing his ships to pieces. All through the afternoon the battle continued, and aboard the British ships great admiration was felt for the perfect timing and grouping of the German gunnery, despite the chaos visible on the German decks.

By 1545 clouds of steam gushed upwards from *Scharnhorst's* decks, the first and second funnels were leaning against each other, an enormous livid rent had been torn in the side plating below her quarter-deck and she was blazing fore and aft — but still her starboard batteries fired.

Her masts were gone, her bridge was wrecked, her magazines must have been almost empty, but still her ensign fluttered from a jury mast above the after control station. Then suddenly, just before 1600 her batteries ceased fire as though they had been switched off, and she was seen to turn eight points to starboard and come staggering across the seas towards her powerful antagonists. Behind her, *Gneisenau* swung across still firing rapidly, and as *Inflexible* re-engaged the farther ship, *Invincible* turned and headed for Spee's flagship. Less than 10,000 yards separated the two admirals, but it was soon evident that they would never meet, for *Scharnhorst's* decks were a sea of fire, her speed fell away and she listed badly.

Just before 1610 her list took her deck-rails under, water flooded inboard to quench the flames and she rolled on to her beams end. Through rents in her plating a few figures climbed laboriously and stood on her side-plates watching the battle-cruisers and the cold, impartial sea. Seven minutes later, *Scharnhorst's* bows suddenly dipped, her stern came up, steam and smoke wreathed about her and with her flag still flying, she slid quickly under water and was gone, leaving only a huge yellow patch on the surface of the sea.

Fifteen minutes later, *Carnarvon* reached the spot and steamed directly through the stained waters. Neither survivors nor wreckage were visible.

By this time, *Invincible* had rejoined *Inflexible* and the two battle-cruisers turned their attention on *Gneisenau.*

The end was now a foregone conclusion, and as Sturdee had no intention of sustaining avoidable damage to either of his ships, he ordered them to stand off and take their time. Thus *Gneisenau's* agony was protracted for another hour, by which time the destruction aboard *Gneisenau* beggared description.

Between the masts, her decks were beaten down to the armoured deck, and soon even this was torn open by plummeting shells. Her after-turret was jammed at ninety degrees, all the starboard casemate guns blown into the sea or pounded into shapeless masses of metal. Half her crew were dead or wounded, and shells had ended much suffering by exploding in the sick-bay and in the stokers' bathrooms where an emergency bay had been set up.

Then a shell from *Carnarvon* caused jamming of *Gneisenau's* helm so that she slowly came round and, almost for the first time, the port batteries could come into action — though there was little enough ammunition left to fire. But there was some — enough to sting the battle-cruisers into re-opening fire and finishing *Gneisenau* as a fighting ship. Just before 1730 she lay almost motionless in the water, listing so badly that the seas flooded inboard through the lower gun ports.

Yet she was not sinking — and in order to ensure that nothing of value would fall into British hands, her captain gave the order for explosive charges between the inner and outer hull skins to be blown, and the stern torpedoes to be fired with the sluice gates left open. At a few minutes to six in the evening, *Gneisenau* seemed to shake herself and come fractionally out of the water; then she lay over at about ten degrees and began to settle. Her crew — what was left of them — gave three cheers for the Kaiser and then clambered across the decks to drop down into the icy waters alongside; and at two minutes after six, *Gneisenau's* bows came up, keel uppermost, then slid down out of sight, leaving the seas littered with debris and struggling men. Only 187 of these, including seventeen officers but not *Gneisenau's* captain, were picked up by British boats.

Of the remaining ships of Spee's command, *Nürnberg* was chased, caught, and sunk by *Kent* at 1927, *Leipzig* fought gallantly until 2123, against both *Cornwall* and *Glasgow*; and *Dresden* escaped for the moment. She reached Punta Arenas three days after the battle, passed through the Magellan Straits and played hide and seek with British pursuers until the morning of 14th March 1915, when she was found by *Glasgow* and *Kent* sheltering in Cumberland Bay on Juan Fernández Island.

But there was no battle. Tamely, her captain ran up a white flag, evacuated the crew ashore and then blew up the main magazine — and *Dresden's* wreck still lies in the bay. After the fire and fury of the two battles, this was something of an anti-climax, but it should be remembered that *Dresden* was not an original member of the East Asia Squadron. Spee's captains all fought to the end, and went down with their ships.

THE CRUISE OF THE
EMDEN

Leaving Vice-Admiral von Spee's East Asiatic Squadron early on the morning of August 13, 1914 the German cruiser *Emden,* accompanied by her collier *Markomannia,* set course for the Indian Ocean, then virtually a British lake. During the next three months she cruised 30,000 miles, sank or captured 23 merchant ships, disposed of a cruiser and a destroyer, inflicted £15 million worth of damage and occupied the attention of a combined Allied naval search force involving at one time or another nearly 80 vessels. Not surprisingly, she and her captain rapidly became a living legend in Germany, where she was seen as the epitome of German superiority. In Britain her captain's chivalry, daring and humanity were applauded by the public as romantic examples of what they thought war should be like. A formidable ship in her own class, the *Emden* was outclassed by the Australian cruiser *Sydney,* and her adventure ended in 'grim and bloody tragedy'. *Below:* SMS *Emden*; soon she added an oval fourth funnel in simulation of HMS *Yarmouth.*
Lionel Fanthorpe

On the afternoon of August 12, 1914, Vice-Admiral Maximilian von Spee, commander of Germany's East Asiatic Squadron, gathered his five senior captains around the chart table of his flagship, SMS *Scharnhorst*, anchored off Pagan Island. During their discussion it became clear that Spee favoured a 'fleet-in-being' policy. This entailed keeping the Squadron united and its whereabouts a secret—a sinister, tenebrous but formidable threat. Like a chess player, Spee calculated that a threat was often more effective than its implementation. He also envisaged a move eastwards and operations against the Pacific coast of America.

The Indian Ocean—tempting hunting ground for the German Squadron—was virtually a British lake in the summer of 1914, and coaling problems made it impracticable for Spee's vessels to enter it. The 11,420-ton *Scharnhorst* and her sister ship, the armoured cruiser SMS *Gneisenau*, each used 93 tons of coal a day at an average speed of 10 knots; at an action speed of 20 knots consumption rose to 375 tons a day. Without ports and agents coal would be unobtainable.

Captains Maerker of the *Gneisenau*, Schönberg of the light cruiser SMS *Nürnberg* (3,400 tons) and Thiereken of the auxiliary cruiser SMS *Prinz Eitel Friedrich* agreed with Spee. Captain Schultz of the *Scharnhorst* agreed in principle with a move east but suggested a preliminary squadron raid on an enemy port. Captain Karl von Müller of the light cruiser SMS *Emden* disagreed. He argued in favour of activity in the Indian Ocean. Coal supplies were impossible for the entire squadron or the heavy armoured cruisers, but not for one light cruiser, which could, in an emergency, coal at sea. Captain Fieltiz, Spee's Chief-of-Staff, agreed with Müller's arguments that British naval strength would be diverted to Europe if there were no active German warships elsewhere. Müller returned to the *Emden* to await Spee's decision.

Coaling was still in progress aboard the *Emden* when a cutter arrived with a message from the Vice-Admiral. Müller was granted permission to detach his ship and operate as an independent unit. At 1730 hours on August 12 the Squadron steamed almost due east from Pagan, warships to port, *Scharnhorst* leading, merchantmen and auxiliaries to starboard led by *Prinz Eitel Friedrich*. Early next morning *Emden* detached and, accompanied by her collier, *Markomannia*, headed SSW at 12 knots along the eastern side of the Marianas.

The *Emden* carried ten 10·5-cm rapid fire guns and two torpedo tubes. She was 395 feet long by 43⅓ feet wide and her bow projected further at the waterline than at deck level. Her twin steam engines could propel her 3,650 tons at a top speed of 24·5 knots, and cruising economically she could cover 6,000 miles.

The *Emden*'s 10·5-cm (4·13-in) guns were 40 calibre ones (that is to say the barrel length was 40 times the barrel diameter). This gave them a high muzzle velocity of 2,835 feet per second, and, with a shell weighing 30·86 pounds and a rate of fire of eight rounds per minute, made her a formidable ship in her own class.

Most of the *Emden*'s men were young, enthusiastic, dedicated and efficient. *Korvettenkapitän* Karl von Müller, born June 16, 1873, had a long Prussian military fam-ily tradition and his uncle, Rudolf von Bennigsen, had led an early German nationalist movement. Müller was quiet, withdrawn, lonely and conscientious. Trained on SMS *Stosch* and *Gneisenau*, he had been signal officer on SMS *Moltke* and officer of the guard on the cruiser SMS *Gefion*. He had also served aboard SMS *Schwalbe* and the torpedo school ship SMS *Blücher*.

After a day and a half's cruising from Pagan, the *Emden* was unable to establish contact with the German radio station at Yap, north-east of the Palau Islands, and sent a cutter to investigate. Herr Schmidt in charge of the Jaluit Trading Company on the island showed the shore party the wreckage of the radio installation—shelled by three British cruisers: HMS *Hampshire*, *Yarmouth* and *Minotaur*. The *Emden*'s next objective was Angaur Island in the Palau group, leased by a German phosphate company. Here a hoped-for rendezvous with the collier *Choising* failed to materialise but the *Emden* encountered *Prinzessin Alice* instead. When war was declared she had been carrying 4,000,000 dollars in gold for the Indian government, but she had promptly changed course and delivered it to the German Consul in the Philippines. Müller took on extra men from this vessel and *Markomannia*. He put a letter to his mother aboard *Prinzessin Alice*, which was then directed to Cebu, a neutral port in the Philippines.

A floating coffin

The *Emden* now steamed towards the Moluccas with the idea of entering the Indian Ocean via Mindanao and the Dutch East Indies. On the night of August 20 Müller was attempting to contact Tsingtao in the German colony of Kiaochow, the *Emden*'s last home port, when he received a radio message from the old German light cruiser SMS *Geier*. During the British bombardment of Yap, *Korvettenkapitän* Grasshof had hidden *Geier* and her collier *Bochum* in a cove. On August 21, Müller met him and advised him to take the ship to Honolulu to be interned. The *Geier* was too old, too lightly armed and with her maximum speed of 12 knots too slow to be anything but a floating coffin in action.

The *Emden* steamed on again. On August 22 she crossed the equator, and on August 23 she established radio contact with the German steamer *Tannenfels* and arranged a rendezvous with her at Timor to replenish coal and food. *Emden* and *Markomannia* reached the rendezvous and waited half a day on August 25 for *Tannenfels*, which did not appear. In desperation Müller took 470 tons of coal from *Markomannia*, seriously depleting her reserves.

While coaling was in progress a small party went ashore for fodder for livestock kept aboard the *Emden* as a dietary supplement. A machine gun guard accompanied the party because of stories of Timor's head-hunters, but there were no incidents. Shortly afterwards the Dutch battleship *Tromp* arrived and prevented further coaling because it contravened the neutrality laws. It transpired that *Tannenfels* had kept her appointment but *Tromp* had driven her away.

Emden was escorted to the edge of the three-mile limit and made off eastwards in the direction of the Pacific. As soon as he had lost sight of the Dutch battleship, however, Müller turned west again and steamed for Bali. While they cruised slowly and waited for darkness to cover their passage through Lombok Strait, Mücke (Müller's second in command) had an ingenious idea for disguising the *Emden*. Her three funnels were the trademark of a German light cruiser. British light cruisers had four. Mücke knew that the British *Yarmouth* had three round and one oval, and he produced a very fair simulation of this style. With her false stack in position, *Emden* passed through the Sunda Straits off Batavia, between the Indian Ocean and the Java Sea. From time to time Müller intercepted heavy wireless traffic among Allied warships searching for German raiders. One shore station even asked, '*Emden*, where are you?'

Narrow escape

On September 3 *Emden* was approaching Simalur Island off Sumatra when she came within sight of the *Hampshire*—big enough to blow her to pieces at long range. Despite this narrow escape, Müller carried out his coaling and had succeeded in loading nearly 1,000 tons aboard before he was interrupted by a Dutch government yacht. During the coaling two spare five-pounder guns had been transferred from *Markomannia*'s storage lockers to *Emden*'s wardroom.

At 1100 hours on September 8, *Emden* encountered the 4,094-ton Greek steamer *Pontoporos* commanded by Captain D. Polemis and carrying 6,500 tons of coal from Calcutta. Müller gave careful thought to their legal position. Technically the ship was neutral but the cargo was contraband. Prize Officer Lauterbach studied the recent Calcutta newspapers discovered aboard *Pontoporos* and they enabled him to calculate approximate positions of the ships whose sailing notices were published. On the strength of this *Emden*, *Markomannia* and the captive *Pontoporos* headed for the Colombo-Calcutta steamer lane.

At 0900 hours on September 10 *Emden* intercepted SS *Indus*, a British passenger-freighter en route from Calcutta to Bombay. Technically under charter to the British government, legally *Indus* was undoubtedly an enemy vessel intended to transport men and horses from India to the European theatre of war. Her captain had assumed *Emden* was a British cruiser until too late. *Markomannia*'s mate was now placed in charge of *Pontoporos*, assisted by Vice-Steerman Meyer, *Emden*'s senior NCO, while Lauterbach took over the *Indus*. The personnel from *Indus* were sent aboard *Markomannia* where an armed guard under *Kapitänleutnant* Klöpper ensured that the prisoners did not seize the collier. Having taken what he could from *Indus*, Müller ordered her to be sunk, and a sinking party from the *Emden* (consisting of an engineer officer, a petty officer and three stokers) boarded *Indus*, removed the doors from the bulkheads between the boiler rooms and engine room and opened the sea cocks. Later four shells were fired into her at the waterline, but she took almost two hours to go down.

During the morning of September 11 *Emden* encountered *Lovat*, an English ship bound for Bombay to pick up troops. Lauterbach was mildly embarrassed because her captain was an old friend. He and his crew were put aboard *Markomannia*, but *Lovat* sank as stubbornly and reluctantly as *Indus*.

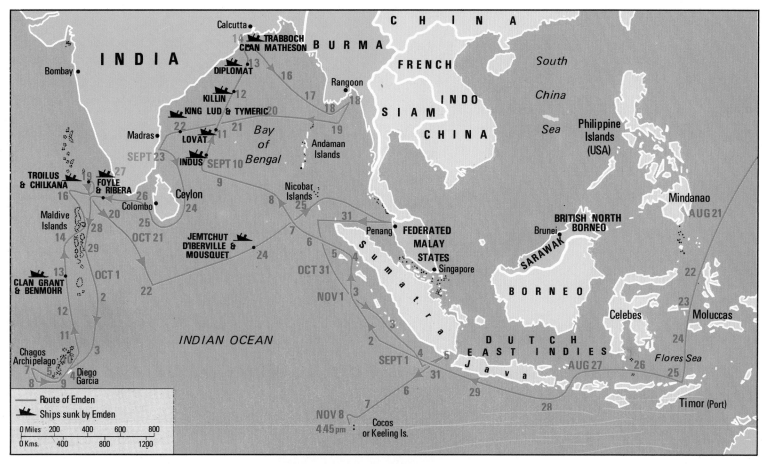

Map labels:
CHINA
BURMA
INDIA
Bombay
Calcutta
TRABBOCH
CLAN MATHESON
DIPLOMAT
KILLIN
KING LUD & TYMERIC
Madras
LOVAT
INDUS
Rangoon
FRENCH
INDO
SIAM
CHINA
South
China
Sea
Philippine
Islands
(USA)
Bay
of
Bengal
Andaman
Islands
Nicobar
Islands
TROILUS
& CHILKANA
FOYLE
& RIBERA
Ceylon
Colombo
Maldive
Islands
JEMTCHUT
D'IBERVILLE &
MOUSQUET
Penang
FEDERATED
MALAY
STATES
Singapore
BRITISH NORTH
BORNEO
Brunei
SARAWAK
Mindanao
AUG 21
CLAN GRANT
& BENMOHR
OCT 21
OCT 1
SEPT 23
SEPT 10
OCT 31
NOV 1
Sumatra
BORNEO
Celebes
Moluccas
INDIAN OCEAN
DUTCH
EAST
INDIES
Java
Flores Sea
AUG 27
Chagos
Archipelago
Diego
Garcia
SEPT 1
Timor (Port)
NOV 8
4.45pm
Cocos
or Keeling Is.

Route of Emden
Ships sunk by Emden
0 Miles 200 400 600 800
0 Kms. 400 800 1200

The elusive *Emden* kept 14 major Allied warships occupied. One radio message even asked '*Emden*, where are you?'

Above: The *Emden's* 30,000-mile cruise, during which she twice only narrowly escaped detection by superior Allied warships.
Right: Tanks of the Burmah Oil Company in Madras burning fiercely after shelling by the *Emden* from a range of two miles

At 1100 hours on September 12 *Emden* intercepted the 4,657-ton *Kabinga*, an English vessel belonging to the Ellerman and Bucknell Steamship Company of London. *Kabinga* was carrying jute to New York, and sinking her would render the German government liable for the cargo. In any case, Müller was looking for a *lumpensammler* (junkman or prisoners' repatriation ship). The crews of *Indus* and *Lovat* were placed aboard *Kabinga,* and with a German prize crew in command she steamed in *Emden's* wake.

Three unexpected cheers
During the night, *Killin,* a Glaswegian collier heading from Calcutta to Bombay with 6,000 tons aboard, was captured and sunk. At 0300 hours on September 13 the 7,600-ton Harrison liner *Diplomat,* loaded with 1,000 tons of tea, was also intercepted and sent to the bottom. At 1630 hours that afternoon the Italian *Loredano* was encountered. Despite the prewar Triple Alliance between Italy, Germany and Austria-Hungary, her captain broadcast the *Emden's* position as 86 degrees

24 minutes east, 18 degrees 1 minute north and this information was duly relayed to shipping from the Calcutta lightship. The 4,000-ton collier *Trabboch,* in ballast, was encountered and sunk at 1800 hours on September 14. Later that afternoon, with the crews of *Killin, Diplomat* and *Trabboch* also aboard the *Kabinga,* the *lumpensammler* was escorted safely to within 75 miles of the sandheads off the mouth of the River Hooghly, where those aboard unexpectedly gave three rousing cheers for the *Emden.*

Emden's men were now becoming adept at boarding and sinking techniques. Their next encounter was with the *Clan Matheson,* another Glaswegian, heading from Southampton to Calcutta with a cargo of Rolls-Royce cars, locomotives, typewriters and thoroughbred racehorses. The horses were shot before the ship was sent down, and yet the whole process was over in less than an hour. Next morning Captain W. Harris and his crew were transferred to a small Norwegian freighter. Harris shook hands with the German captain before leaving and told Müller to his face that at

least he appreciated the courtesy he and his men had been shown.

On September 15, *Emden, Markomannia* and *Pontoporos* were cruising and coaling in the deserted ocean south of Calcutta. The Greek collier was then sent off to a rendezvous at Simalur Island. Two days later the *Emden* searched the upper Bay of Bengal and crossed the Madras-Rangoon and Calcutta-Singapore routes, but sighted no vessels. Müller began to consider a fresh line of attack.

A raid on Madras commended itself to him for four basic reasons: it was a long way from the location given by the *Loredano*; it would disturb British supremacy in India, unchallenged for a century; the Madras port installations were easily accessible from the sea; and one of the *Emden's* crew had once worked in the city and knew its geography well. The harbour was protected by Fort St George with a 30-year-old battery of 5·9-inch guns. At 2145 hours on September 22 *Emden* fired the first of 125 shells from a range of two miles. Hits included the prominent white and red striped tanks of the Burmah Oil

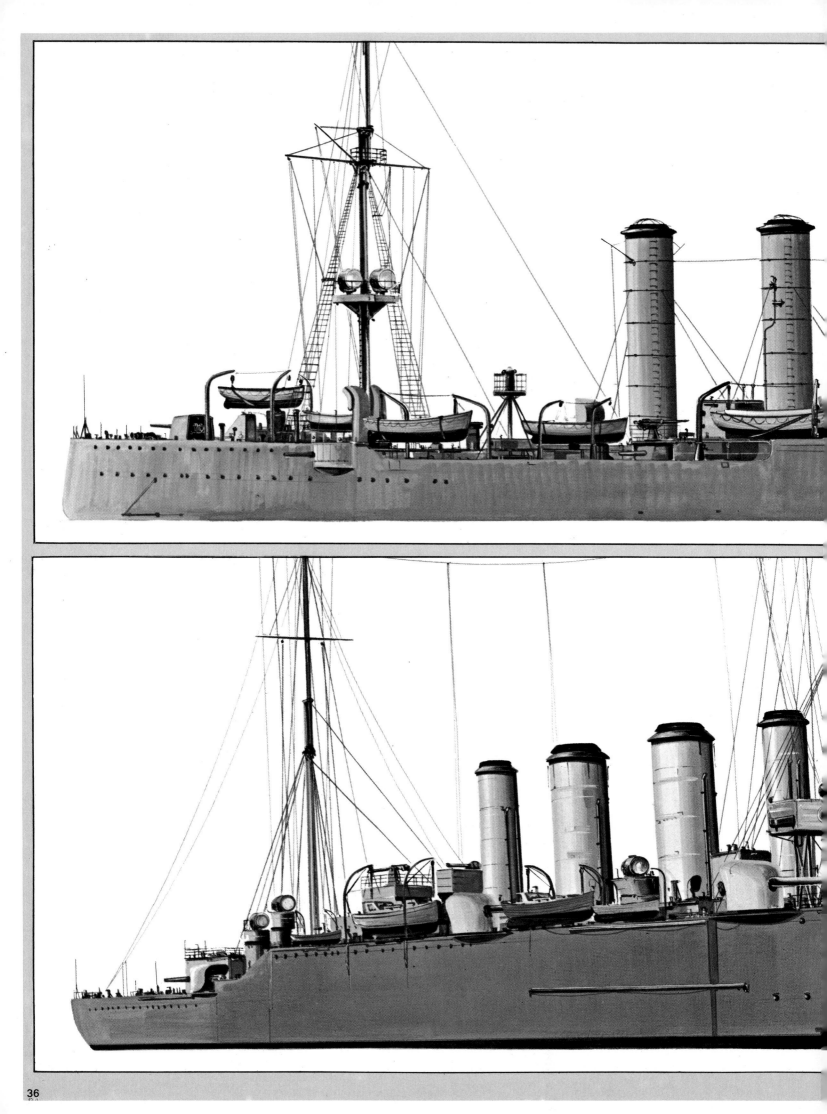

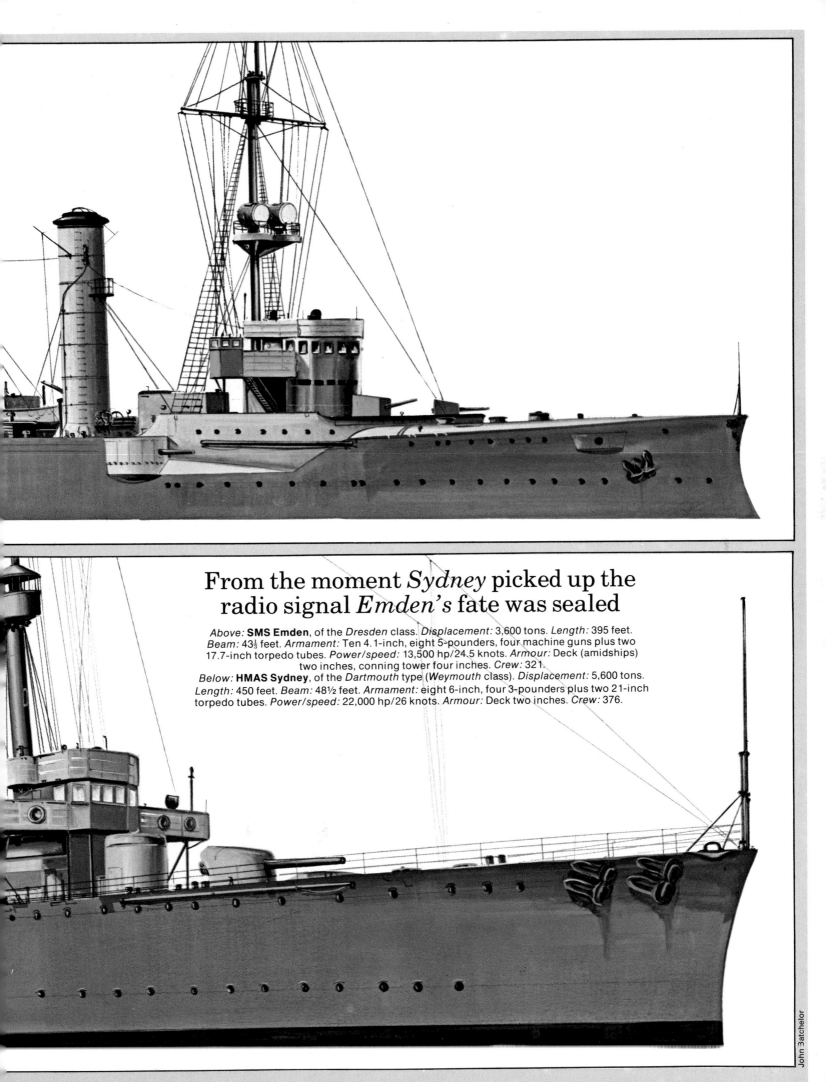

From the moment *Sydney* picked up the radio signal *Emden's* fate was sealed

Above: **SMS Emden**, of the *Dresden* class. *Displacement:* 3,600 tons. *Length:* 395 feet. *Beam:* 43⅓ feet. *Armament:* Ten 4.1-inch, eight 5-pounders, four machine guns plus two 17.7-inch torpedo tubes. *Power/speed:* 13,500 hp/24.5 knots. *Armour:* Deck (amidships) two inches, conning tower four inches. *Crew:* 321.
Below: **HMAS Sydney**, of the *Dartmouth* type (*Weymouth* class). *Displacement:* 5,600 tons. *Length:* 450 feet. *Beam:* 48½ feet. *Armament:* eight 6-inch, four 3-pounders plus two 21-inch torpedo tubes. *Power/speed:* 22,000 hp/26 knots. *Armour:* Deck two inches. *Crew:* 376.

Company, which burned fiercely. Answering shells failed to find *Emden* and she steamed away from Madras unscathed.

Müller now cruised south past the old French colony of Pondicherry, but finding no ships there he pressed on towards the Singhalese port of Colombo. No fewer than 14 major Allied warships were now searching for the German raider: HMS *Empress of Asia, Empress of Russia, Gloucester, Hampshire, Minotaur, Weymouth* and *Yarmouth;* the Australian ships *Melbourne* and *Sydney;* the French *Montcalm;* the Japanese *Chikuna, Ibuki* and *Yakagi;* and the Russian *Askold*. Despite them all *Emden* sank the 3,600-ton *King Lud* and the sugar-laden *Tymeric* before apprehending the 4,000-ton *Gryfevale* to serve as *lumpensammler* for their crews.

The world could scarcely fail to react to these exploits. Macaulay records Lars Porsena's grudging praise of Horatius when 'e'en the ranks of Tuscany could scarce forbear to cheer'. The Allied reaction to Müller was very similar. His chivalry was respected, his daring admired, his humanity applauded. He appealed strongly to British sporting instincts, but this did not lessen their determination to hunt him down. In Germany he was rapidly becoming a living legend, an almost mystical epitome of that superiority of the fatherland which Kaiser Wilhelm frequently preached.

Emden needed good quality coal and found over 6,000 tons aboard *Buresk,* destined for Admiral Jerram's ships at Hongkong. The collier was added to

Müller's retinue. Before October 3 *Foyle* and *Ribera* were captured and sunk. The raider then proceeded to the Maldive Islands and Chagos Archipelago where boiler tubes were changed and condensers overhauled. Her next call was Diago Garcia where the Germans were welcomed by the assistant manager of the island's oil company (a septuagenarian French Madagasque) who had heard no news for three months and knew nothing of the war. The *Emden's* men took care not to enlighten him.

The ship was canted, scraped clear of barnacles and repainted. Müller then headed back towards his hunting area in the Indian Ocean where his next prizes included *Clan Grant* on October 13, with a miscellaneous cargo including live cattle,

The beginning of the end: Direction Island —*Emden's* last raid

Top left: A lifeboat from the captured collier *Buresk* supports the severed Perth-Cocos cable salvaged after the German raid on the British radio and telegraph installation on Direction Island in the Cocos group. *Top right:* The instrument room after the Germans had gone. However, before it was wrecked the telegraph station had managed to signal tne *Emden's* presence to the nearby Anzac convoy. *Below:* Mucke's landing party leaving Direction Island — surprised by the *Sydney's* arrival, Müller had been forced to abandon the landing party and head out to sea

ROYAL AUSTRALIAN NAVY

H.M.A.S. "Sydney".
at sea,
9th November 191 4.

Sir,

I have the honour to request that in the name of humanity you now surrender your ship to me. In order to show how much I appreciate your gallantry, I will recapitulate the position.

(1) You are ashore, 3 funnels and 1 mast down and most guns disabled.

(2) You cannot leave this island, and my ship is intact.

In the event of your surrendering in which I venture to remind you is no disgrace but rather your misfortune I will endeavour to do all I can for your sick and wounded and take them to a hospital.

I have the honour to be,

Sir,

Your obedient Servant,

John C.T. Glossop

Captain.

The Captain,

H.I.G.M.S. "Emden".

'Müller and *Emden* seemed romantic survivals in a world sliding rapidly into the ruthless realities of total war'

Top, left to right: The *Emden's* captain, Karl von Müller—'quiet, withdrawn, lonely and conscientious', his chivalry and daring caught the imagination of the world; the letter from Captain Glossop requesting Müller to surrender his ship—sporting and polite, it reads rather like the winning captain's speech after a game of cricket; Captain John Glossop of HMAS *Sydney*; the *Sydney* immediately after action against the *Emden*—the latter's fourth salvo knocked out the *Sydney's* fire direction system, causing her to withdraw out of the *Emden's* range.

Below: The wreck of the *Emden* aground on a coral reef south of North Keeling Island—placed at a disadvantage by *Sydney's* greater range, her guns and torpedoes no longer operable, Müller decided that he should run her aground

the 4,800-ton *Benmohr* carrying machinery, and the 7,500-ton Blue Funnel *Troilus* on October 19, laden with valuable metals and rubber. But even while Müller was making these captures, *Markomannia* had been sunk. *Markomannia* was actually coaling from *Pontoporos* off Pulo Topak, an island on the west coast of Sumatra near the south end of Simalur on October 12. When *Yarmouth* appeared *Markomannia* was sunk with 1,300 tons of coal aboard and *Pontoporos* was taken in prize with 5,000 tons aboard. *Buresk* was therefore *Emden's* last remaining source of coal.

The 473-ton British ocean-going dredger *Ponrabbel*, bound for Tasmania, probably qualified as Müller's most unusual victim. She was captured and sunk on October 16.

The sheer volume of prisoners was now causing problems which Müller solved by intercepting *St Egbert*, an English ship bound for New York, to use as another *lumpensammler*. He also picked up the collier *Exford* and disposed of the 5,000-ton *Chilkana*.

Early on the morning of October 20 *Emden* ran dangerously close to *Hampshire* and her companion *Empress of Russia* but was not seen. The Germans celebrated their Kaiserin's birthday on October 22 and the three following days were uneventful. On October 26 *Emden* and *Buresk* pulled into Nancowrie in the Nicobar Islands to coal. Müller was planning a dawn attack on Penang harbour for October 28.

Entering the harbour mouth as planned *Emden* passed within yards of a pilot boat which paid her no attention. As dawn broke the Germans saw the Russian light cruiser *Jemtchug*. At 0518 hours the first torpedo from the *Emden* struck the *Jemtchug* amidships causing severe damage. It was followed by heavy accurate salvoes from the *Emden's* guns. *Jemtchug* was ablaze and sinking fast, but some of her men had reached action stations and were grimly returning *Emden's* fire. The French destroyer *D'Iberville* joined in. *Emden* put a second torpedo into *Jemtchug*, which finished the Russian completely, before heading towards the harbour mouth. What looked like a fast torpedo boat steamed rapidly from the open sea towards the raider. It was not until after Gunnery Officer Gaede had put a shell through her funnel that the Germans realised she was only a harmless pilot boat. Müller ceased firing and the *Emden* headed out to sea.

At 0700 hours the raider stopped the British *Glen Turret*, carrying explosives, but instead of being sunk she was sent into Penang as Müller's messenger. The German captain apologised to the survivors of the *Jemtchug* for not picking them up and to the crew of the pilot boat for unintentionally firing on their unarmed vessel.

Full naval honours

The small French destroyer *Mousquet* appeared next and prepared to attack the *Emden*, manoeuvring as though to launch a torpedo. The Germans steered hard to port and fired three salvoes at *Mousquet*. Several shells hit her stern and detonated the magazine, but even after this she launched two torpedoes which the *Emden* easily avoided. The French captain's legs were shot away during the action but lashed to the bridge he continued directing the fight until his shattered vessel took him down with her. The Germans picked up over 30 survivors, two of whom died during the night of October 29 and were buried at sea with full naval honours. Meanwhile *Fronde*, sister ship of *Mousquet*, was following *Emden*, taking care not to close with her. The following day Müller apprehended the 3,000-ton freighter *Newburn* carrying salt to Singapore and arranged for her to ship the French survivors to Khota Raja where the severely wounded could receive hospital treatment.

On October 31 *Emden* met *Buresk* near North Pageh Island in the Nassau Group at 0330 hours, and two days were spent in coaling, cleaning, carrying out repairs and resting. During coaling a cable snapped and *Emden* suffered her first casualty of the war: a torpedoman's thigh was broken. A Dutch patrol boat arrived to ensure *Emden* was outside the three-mile limit and brought the news of Portugal's entry into the war.

Having arranged a further rendezvous with *Buresk*, *Emden* set off for the Sunda Straits dividing Java from Sumatra.

Nothing offered itself as a prospective prize in the Sunda area and Müller devised an alternative plan: an attack on the British telegraph and radio installation on Direction Island in the Cocos (or Keeling) group, where the Australian, African and Indian cables met.

Early on the morning of November 9 *Emden* anchored off the island while Mücke led ashore his landing party of 50 men, threading shallow coral mazes with a steam launch towing two cutters. At 0630 hours they landed and found Superintendent D. A. G. de H. Farrant, of the Eastern Extension Telegraph Company. No resistance was offered. Farrant gave Mücke the keys and congratulated him on the award of the Iron Cross, news of which had been picked up during a German broadcast. Firearms were handed over to the raiders and the islanders assembled in the square near the telegraph building. The Germans were thorough and efficient wreckers. Even an innocuous seismometer was smashed along with the electrical equipment, but three sets of charges were needed to topple the mast and the undersea cables were difficult to locate and sever.

The *Emden's* lookout reported a vessel with a single funnel and two masts, a description which fitted their anticipated collier, the *Buresk*. An officer ascended to the crow's nest and confirmed the description, but it was either an optical illusion or the *Buresk* was accidentally obscuring another vessel. Bearing down on the *Emden* was HMAS *Sydney*, a protected cruiser of 5,400 tons carrying eight 6-inch guns and capable of nearly 26 knots. She was bigger and faster than the *Emden* and carried weapons outweighing and outranging those on the German cruiser.

Nor was it a fluke that she had arrived in so timely a manner since, in fact, the island telegraph station had managed to transmit a signal announcing the arrival of the *Emden* before the Germans could interrupt, and this signal was picked up by the great Anzac convoy nearby – of which the *Sydney* was one escort, sailing in advance of the main body of ships. From that moment the *Emden's* fate was sealed. Müller was forced to abandon his landing party and head for open sea. To be caught at anchor would give *Emden* no chance at all. At 0940 hours the first three German salvoes bracketed *Sydney*; the fourth landed, knocking out the fire direction system. The Australian ship withdrew to 7,000 yards, out of *Emden's* range but well within her own. Shells fell near the German bridge and the wireless room disappeared following a direct hit. The crow's nest and a stern gun were struck. Another shell destroyed the gunnery control system. Hits below deck ruptured *Emden's* steam pipes and drastically reduced her speed. Multiple fires were spreading rapidly. A direct hit shattered the number one gun; number four's ammunition port exploded wiping out the crew. At 1020 hours the steering and communication systems were destroyed. A hit below the waterline temporarily flooded the torpedo flat, but *Emden* kept on manoeuvring skilfully on the engines in the hope of delivering an effective torpedo. Another Australian broadside brought down the German foremast; the funnels were gone; scores of dead, dying and wounded lay among the wreckage. With guns and torpedoes inoperable Müller decided to run his ship aground. Shortly after 1100 hours she shuddered on to the coral reefs south of North Keeling Island. Throughout the heat of the day the Germans suffered considerably from heat and thirst; several were killed attempting to swim through the surf. The *Sydney* had raced off to capture the *Buresk*, and when she returned Captain Glossop reopened fire on the wreck of the *Emden* because the German battle colours still flew. Müller replaced them with a white flag and firing immediately ceased. The *Sydney* now released one of the *Buresk's* boats which she had in tow and *Leutnant* Fikentscher, who had been with the prize crew aboard the collier, crossed to the *Emden* with a handful of men to give what aid he could. The *Sydney* turned and headed for Direction Island, intending to capture Mücke's raiding party. It was nearly 24 hours before the Australians returned to the wreck and took off *Emden's* survivors. Müller was the last man to leave. Of his ship's company 141 were dead and 65 more were wounded. Only 117 men remained unhurt. Müller and *Emden* seemed to be strangely romantic, chivalrous, anachronistic survivals in a world sliding rapidly into the new ruthless realities of total war; their adventure ended in grim and bloody tragedy.

But what had been achieved? In their three-month cruise of 30,000 miles the men of the *Emden* had sunk or captured 23 merchant ships, disposed of a cruiser and destroyer, inflicted £15,000,000 worth of damage on their enemies and occupied the attention of a combined Allied naval search force involving nearly 80 vessels at one time or another.

Further Reading

Hoehling, A. A., *Lonely Command* (Cassell & Co, 1957)

Hough, R., *The Pursuit of Admiral von Spee* (Allen and Unwin, 1969)

Hoyt, E. P., *The Last Cruise of the Emden* (Andre Deutsch, 1966)

Mücke, Kapitänleutnant H. von, *The Emden* (Ritter & Co, 1917)

Raeder, E., *Der Krieg zur See,* Vol. 2 (Mittler & Sohn, Berlin, 1923)

Thomas, Lowell, *Lauterbach of the China Sea* (Hutchinson, 1939)

Witthoeft, R., *Unsere Emden* (Reimar Hobbing, Berlin, 1926)

In January 1912 a seaplane took off from an improvised staging on the forecastle of HMS *Africa,* the first time this had been done from a British warship

The eyes and teeth of the fleets, the seaplane and the big gun

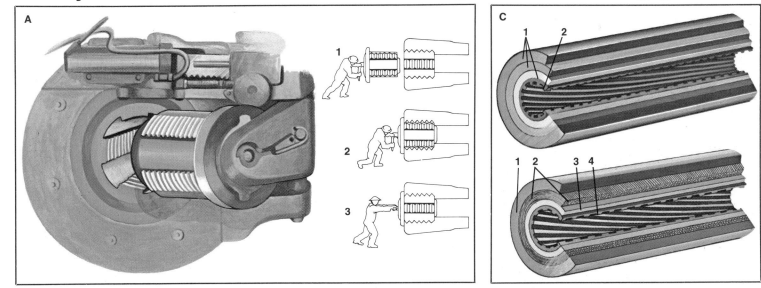

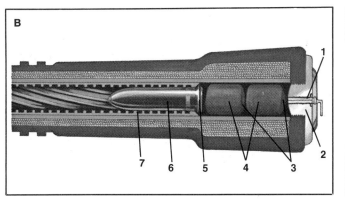

A The breech mechanism. The breech block, which swings out to allow the shell to be loaded into the breech, is a threaded block into which longitudinal slots have been cut, corresponding to threads and slots in the breech. After the breech block has been moved back into the breech, the threads of each fitting into the slots of the other (1 and 2), the whole mechanism is locked by giving the breech block a partial twist, which locks its threads with those of the breech (3). **B** The breech of a British naval gun. **1** Electric firing pistol. **2** Breech block. **3** Priming charges. **4** Cordite propellant in silk bags. **5** Soft copper driving band. **6** Shell. **7** Rifling in barrel. **C** Construction of a German (above) and a British gun (below). The German gun is made of three tubes (1) sweated together, with a liner carrying the rifling (2) inside them, while the British gun comprises an inner tube (3) carrying the liner (4), bound with wire (2), with an outer tube (1) over that

DOGGER BANK
CLASH OF THE BATTLE CRUISERS

Shortly before noon on January 23, 1915, Winston Churchill returned to his room at the Admiralty after a long talk with Admiral Fisher, who was laid up in bed with a cold. Hardly had he sat down, Churchill recounts, when Admiral Sir Arthur Wilson strode hurriedly into the room with a 'glow in his eye' and baldly announced: 'First Lord, those fellows are coming out again.' The fellows referred to were of course the Germans, and the decisions and orders which followed from this announcement were to lead to the greatest clash in the North Sea since the war began.

The movements had begun only a short while earlier at 1025 hours that same morning when Rear-Admiral Hipper, resting with his battle-cruisers off Wilhelmshaven, received orders to take them, together with some cruisers and destroyers, and to sweep into the Dogger Bank area that night. The German intentions were not very clear but it was hoped to disrupt the British fishing fleet there and to sink a few of their escorts. Moreover, the report of British scouting operations in that area, brought in by a German seaplane on the 19th, had aroused curiosity at the German admiralty and also the anticipation that some light forces of the the British might be caught unawares by a swift one-day reconnaissance mission from Wilhelmshaven. Such a sweep was in any case well in line with the Kaiser's recent decision that the battle-cruisers could sortie to harass the British, although a major fleet action was still considered to be undesirable.

It was the efficiency of its Intelligence services which enabled the Royal Navy to learn so very quickly about the planned German operation and to take steps to meet it. The chance recovery by the Russians in August 1914 of the German navy's cipher signal books and squared reference charts from the wrecked cruiser *Magdeburg* had been a boon to the British deciphering team, who, from then on, were able to decode the Germans' intercepted wireless messages. In addition, the establishment of radio direction-finder stations along the east coast of England enabled the Admiralty to pinpoint the position of German vessels when they used their radios. Thus Churchill had news of the German plans and the probable size of their forces only one hour and a half after Hipper had received his instructions.

Shortly after Hipper's ships slid out of the Jade estuary on the evening of January 23, a variety of British squadrons emerged from harbour and also proceeded towards the Dogger Bank.

Rear-Admiral Hipper's force consisted of the 1st and 2nd Scouting Groups and two flotillas of destroyers. The 1st Scouting Group had to sail without the *Von der Tann,* which was in dockyard hands, and therefore was composed of four battle-cruisers, *Seydlitz,* Hipper's flagship, *Moltke, Derfflinger* and *Blücher.* The first three vessels were similar, each carrying ten 11-inch guns, (the *Derfflinger* had eight 12-inch guns), adequately armoured and able to steam at about 25/26 knots. The *Blücher* however was an older, large armoured cruiser rather than a battle-cruiser. Her armour, main armament and displacement were consequently all much smaller than that of the rest of her squadron. Most important of all, her maximum speed was some 2/3 knots less than theirs and this tended either to slow down the whole squadron when in action or to cause the *Blücher* to gradually fall behind. Tactically she was a liability to the squadron.

The 2nd Scouting Group consisted of the four light cruisers *Stralsund, Rostock, Kolberg,* and *Graudenz,* all of which carried twelve 4.1-inch guns. These were accompanied by 18 destroyers.

In numbers the balance of strength clearly lay with the British, but in gun-power there was less of a discrepancy since the German 11-inch gun was superior to the British 12-inch gun. Hipper's main opponents were to be Vice-Admiral Beatty's powerful battle-cruisers *Lion, Tiger, Princess Royal, New Zealand* and *Indomitable,* all based on Rosyth. Although the last two ships were smaller and not as well armoured as their German opposite numbers and the *Indomitable,* constructed in 1908, was slightly slower, they both carried eight 12-inch guns as main armament. Moreover the *Lion, Tiger* and *Princess Royal* were faster than Hipper's squadron and each carried the powerful 13.5-inch guns, although the British battle-cruisers carried less armour than Hipper's three big ships.

Administrative and tactical reasons had caused the British battle-cruisers to be divided into a fast and a slow division. Thus Beatty directly controlled the 1st Battle-Cruiser Squadron which included the *Lion* (his flagship), *Tiger* and *Princess Royal,* while Rear-Admiral Moore, his Second-in-Command, directed the newly-formed 2nd Battle-Cruiser Squadron, which consisted of the *New Zealand* (Moore's flagship) and the *Indomitable*—though remaining under Beatty's control throughout. These ships were accompanied from Rosyth by Commodore Goodenough's 1st Light Cruiser Squadron, consisting of *Southampton, Birmingham, Nottingham* and *Lowestoft,* all carrying eight or nine 6-inch guns.

January 24, 1915 saw the largest naval clash of the war up to that date: four German battle-cruisers pitted against five British ones. The conflict was confused, and poor British signalling was mainly responsible for the major elements of the German squadron slipping away, leaving only the hybrid battle-cruiser *Blücher* to be finally crushed by the storm of British fire. In the battle, however, points of enormous importance for future naval operations had become apparent. Signalling had to be improved, gunnery, in the British vessels particularly, needed drastic attention, armour protection for the ships' vitals needed strengthening and a way of stopping flash travelling down to the magazines needed devising. These lessons were apparent to both admiralties, but whether or not the lessons had been learnt fully would have to wait till the next clash. *Paul Kennedy* analyses the course and lessons of this vital battle. *Below:* White plumes of spray mark the fall of British shells among the German battle-cruisers. In the foreground, emitting a cloud of black smoke, is the *Blücher*, already hit and damaged by British fire. Throughout the action she was a hindrance to the German force, and by abandoning her the rest of the German squadron made their own escape easier

Other British forces were also on the move on the evening of the 23rd. As soon as the Admiralty had received the news of an imminent German sweep, Wilson and Vice-Admiral Oliver (the Chief of Admiralty War Staff) had worked out in Churchill's office the most likely position for an interception. With professional expertise they ordered Beatty to be at a point about 30 miles north of the Dogger Bank at 0700 hours on the 24th and also ordered Commodore Tyrwhitt with his three light cruisers *Arethusa* (his flagship), *Aurora* and *Undaunted,* together with 35 destroyers, out of Harwich, to join Beatty there and provide the escort for the battle-cruisers.

Strict radio silence
Although the Admiralty was almost certain that only the German battle-cruisers would come out and that their cartographical calculations were correct, they were still not inclined to take chances. The seven pre-dreadnought battleships of Vice-Admiral Bradford's 3rd Battle Squadron, also based on Rosyth, accompanied by Rear-Admiral Pakenham's 3rd Cruiser Squadron, were ordered to a position about 40 miles north-west of Beatty, to intercept Hipper if he came by a more northerly route or to support the British battle-cruisers if they got into trouble. Much further south, Commodore Keyes was moving from Harwich to the Heligoland Bight in the hope of intercepting and torpedoing any German vessels with his 'Overseas' squadron of *Firedrake, Lurcher* and four submarines.

Finally, Admiral Jellicoe, resting at Scapa Flow with the main battleship force of the Grand Fleet, cleared harbour at 2100 hours on the 23rd with three battleship squadrons, covered by three cruiser squadrons and 28 destroyers. Further ahead of him ranged Rear-Admiral Napier's 2nd Light Cruiser Squadron. These forces, while covering the Scottish coast in the early stages of their cruise, were to sweep down to the rendezvous with Bradford's vessels by mid-morning.

During the night the various squadrons picked their way between the minefields (Beatty's force actually dashing through an area which was reportedly mined) and approached the Dogger Bank from different directions. The British ships kept a strict radio silence while the occasional German wireless traffic intercepted by the D/F stations continued to confirm the Admiralty's belief that something was afoot on the German side. The weather

was calm and the sea still. Apart from Tyrwhitt's forces, which were a little delayed by fog at Harwich, all the British ships appeared to be moving according to schedule and Churchill was thrilled with the idea of 'a beast of prey moving stealthily forward hour by hour into the trap'.

At 0700 hours on the 24th Beatty, with Goodenough's cruisers steaming parallel on his port beam, reached the rendezvous area. Ten minutes later, with the dawn breaking to give almost perfect visibility, the *Arethusa* with seven new 'M' class destroyers of the Harwich force were sighted straight ahead. The *Aurora, Undaunted* and the rest of the destroyers were then some 13 miles astern, delayed because of the early fog.

It was this latter group, still south of the rendezvous point, which first clashed with Hipper's forces. The *Aurora,* leading the 1st Destroyer Flotilla, sighted a three-funnelled cruiser and four destroyers on her starboard bow shortly after 0700 hours and moved closer to challenge, expecting to meet up with Tyrwhitt's flotilla again. The cruiser was, in fact, the *Kolberg,* which was guarding the port flank of Hipper's battle-cruisers, then steaming around the north side of the Dogger Bank. Opening fire on the *Aurora* at 0715 hours the *Kolberg* managed to get in three quick hits although they did little damage. Recovering from this surprise, the *Aurora* began to return the fire and soon scored a hit on the *Kolberg's* forebridge, which killed two men and forced her to turn away. The *Aurora,* proceeding north-eastwards again and joined by *Undaunted's* flotilla, soon sighted more German warships to starboard and then, at about 0730 hours, saw the *Southampton's* shape at the head of Goodenough's squadron, looming out of the dusk to the north. Some five miles behind the *Southampton* steamed Beatty's five battle-cruisers.

Confident that he was about to surprise a weaker enemy, Beatty had ordered his battle-cruisers to steer SSE towards the sounds and flashes of the guns and to increase speed to 22 knots, while sending the cruisers on ahead. Hipper, on the other hand, had not expected an immediate encounter and therefore had to act warily in case he came up against the Grand Fleet or a part of it. The engagement with the *Aurora* to the westward was soon followed by sightings of more destroyers and Goodenough's squadron, and then by the sight of heavy smoke further north. Although not greatly increasing his speed, Hipper therefore ordered an almost complete turn so that his forces were steaming south-eastwards by

Südd Verlag

0740 hours. By that time the heavy smoke to the north-west had resolved itself into the five British battle-cruisers, which were steadily working themselves up to full speed.

Hipper, suddenly aware of his critical position 170 miles from Heligoland without any hope of support from the High Seas Fleet, ordered his destroyers to push on ahead and his main force to increase speed to 23 knots, which was *Blücher's* maximum. The German battle-cruiser squadron then steered south-easterly in line ahead formation, led by *Seydlitz* with *Moltke*, *Derfflinger* and *Blücher* following in that order. Beatty, who had originally hoped to get to the Germans' leeward (the port side, in this instance) before engaging and thus avoid his own smoke as well as eventually cutting off the Germans from their base, was forced by Hipper's manoeuvre to follow on the starboard and fear of mines being dropped from the enemy's stern, and of loss of time, now prevented his battle-cruisers from switching over to port.

As the chase developed, the respective admiralties were being acquainted with the situation. Churchill, Fisher, Wilson and Oliver, gathered together in the War Room of the Admiralty, could do nothing but wait and hope as confused messages came flooding in. In the middle of the North Sea and about 140 miles NNW of the action, Jellicoe's great fleet of ships swung slightly more to starboard to intercept if the German battle-cruisers turned north. Further south, Vice-Admiral Bradford's force, cruising north of the Dogger Bank and joined by the 2nd Light Cruiser

Squadron, was ordered to steer eastwards to cut off Hipper if he fled to the north-east. The German admiralty, which first received the news of *Seydlitz's* sighting at about 0750 hours, ordered all ships at Wilhelmshaven to get up steam and to assemble in the Schillig Roads, but having left it so late it would be many hours before they could join in the battle.

Closing at 28 knots

Settling down to a steady pursuit and increasing speed, Beatty sent the fast 'M' class destroyers ahead to report on the exact strength of his opponent. By 0845 hours, despite the shelling which the destroyers encountered as they closed to within 9,000 yards of the *Blücher,* the composition of the German force was clear. It was also clear by then that Beatty's ships had the edge as regards speed and were gradually closing up to the German battle-cruisers. The British ships reached 25 knots, increased to 26 and then met Beatty's demand for 27 knots, although the *Indomitable* slowly began to be outpaced. Beatty afterwards stated that at one point his ships had reached the almost incredible speed of 28.5 knots, and indeed even the 'M' class destroyers found it hard work later to move ahead of the battle-cruisers.

As a result of these high speeds the *Lion* drew to within 20,000 yards of the *Blücher* shortly after 0900 hours and then commenced firing at a range hitherto had been considered impossible; (the experimental maximum in 1914 had been 16,000 yards). Shortly afterwards the *Tiger* and *Princess Royal* were also able to open fire on the *Blücher,* which began to suffer from this concentrated fire. Soon the German battle-cruisers, echeloned to enable all four of them to return the fire from their starboard side, were answering vigorously although greatly inconvenienced by the smoke from the English destroyers to the north-east.

Naturally enough the rearmost German and the foremost English vessels attracted the most attention and suffered as a consequence. The *Lion*, *Tiger* and *Princess Royal,* swinging slightly to starboard, brought their after turrets into action and began to damage the *Blücher* seriously with regular salvoes. At the third salvo the German vessel was hit on the water-line and had her speed reduced; and at the fourth, explosions shattered the after superstructure and two turrets, killing or injuring over 200 sailors. The *Lion,* being the nearest English ship and the one surrounded by least smoke, also took punishment. At 0928 hours she received a hit on her water-line, which penetrated the bunkers. Hammocks, mess-stools and anything else available were quickly used to make good the damage and the *Lion* steamed ahead unhindered, but Beatty was getting worried about the Germans' concentration on his ship. At 0935 hours therefore, seeing that the *New Zealand* had come within range of the *Blücher* and was

Above: The *Blücher* steams into her last action. *Above right:* Mortally hit, *Blücher* burns and begins to list to port. *Below:* The end for Germany's first 'battle-cruiser'. The crew scurries over *Blücher's* revolving hull as she capsizes prior to sinking, abandoned by her fellows

engaging her, Beatty gave the order to fire at opposite numbers.

Consequently, while the *New Zealand* continued to pound away at the *Blücher,* the *Lion* shifted her fire to Hipper's flagship *Seydlitz* and the third English vessel, *Princess Royal,* turned upon the third German battle-cruiser, the *Derfflinger.* However, the commander of the *Tiger,* Captain Pelly, who had begun to direct his ship's fire upon the *Seydlitz* a few minutes earlier, continued to shoot at this target in the belief that *Indomitable* was by then engaging *Blücher.* Thinking that the rear three ships of the opposing battle-lines were respectively firing at each other, Pelly felt that his task was to assist the *Lion* in crippling the German flagship. Though sound enough in theory this idea failed in practice because the *Indomitable* was still not within reach of the *Blücher.* This meant that with the existing dispositions the second German battle-cruiser, *Moltke,* was able to lob salvo after salvo undisturbed at *Lion.*

Beatty had therefore failed to divert any of the German fire from himself and all three battle-cruisers continued to shoot at his flagship. At first this did not appear to be so serious a matter since it was the English ships who were handing out the punishment. The *Lion's* salvoes had found *Seydlitz* almost at once, from a range of some 17,500 yards, and a 13.5-inch shell penetrated the working chamber of the rearmost turret. The flames roared downwards threatening the turret magazine and then along towards the magazine of the adjacent turret. The ammunition in transit exploded and killed 159 men, put both after turrets out of action and sent flames shooting up high above the ship. Only the action of the executive officer, who promptly flooded both magazines, avoided the explosion of the stored ammunition and the probable destruction of the battle-cruiser. Moreover, far at the rear of the German line, *Blücher* was also taking a battering and slowly dropping further back.

British gunnery hampered

Nevertheless, the British gunnery was greatly hampered by smoke drifting from Tyrwhitt's squadron which had moved to the north-east. The *Tiger,* a newly commissioned ship with an inefficient gunnery officer, spotted *Lion's* shells as her own in consequence of the smoke and did not realise that she was in fact firing 3,000 yards over *Seydlitz.* On the other side, however, the more efficient German gunners were making themselves felt on board the *Lion.* Shortly before 1000 hours she was hit on the roof of her foremost turret and one of the guns was disabled. A few minutes later an 11-inch shell from the *Seydlitz* pierced the *Lion's* armour, flooding the engineer's workshop and putting two dynamos, the after fire control and the secondary armament circuits out of action.

At 1018 hours the *Derfflinger,* which was on fire herself from one of *Princess Royal's* shells, managed to land two 12-inch shells on Beatty's flagship. One of these flooded the port bunkers, the other flooded the torpedo flat and adjacent compartment. The *Lion,* with speed gradually falling, was by then zig-zagging desperately while Beatty still stood on the open bridge with his staff, all drenched by the 'near-misses'.

As the German battle-cruisers continued to pour shells at the *Lion,* the battered *Blücher* was burning fiercely and dropping even further behind. At 1048 hours she sheered off to port, apparently out of control, and came under a concentrated fire from the Harwich flotillas and the *Indomitable,* which had at last caught up with the action. The *Blücher,* to all eyes, was obviously finished.

Beatty's overriding concern, however, was to catch the rest of Hipper's squadron. The prospects for this looked bright with the slower German battle-cruisers still over 100 miles from Heligoland and many hours of daylight left, but a whole series of incidents altered the course of the battle. The *Lion,* still under an intense bombardment, was hit at about 1052 hours by a shell which penetrated the boiler-rooms and flooded the feed tank, stopped the port engine and reduced speed to 15 knots. Moreover, as the ship listed 10 degrees to port, the remaining dynamo suddenly failed and cut off lighting and power. Most important of all was the fact that Beatty could henceforward only signal with flags, since the wireless and signal lights were also put out of order. Falling out

of line, Beatty was forced to watch as the *Tiger, Princess Royal* and *New Zealand* rushed past and Rear-Admiral Moore was left with the command.

It was at this point that Beatty and others on board the *Lion* thought they saw submarines on the starboard bow. In fact the nearest German submarines were many miles away, but Beatty was not to know that and anticipated a submarine trap. He therefore signalled for a sharp turn to port, which would take Moore's vessels away from the danger—a manoeuvre which enabled the *Indomitable,* by cutting the corner, to catch up with the squadron again. Since this new course also took the British battle-cruisers away from Hipper's at almost right angles it meant that they would later have to cross the enemy's wake and run the risk of mines. As it happened the German ships carried no mines on this occasion, but nevertheless Beatty soon changed his mind and modified his ships' course to the north-east.

This was not a great modification, however, and it carried Moore's vessels more towards the battered *Blücher* than towards the rest of Hipper's battle-cruisers just when they were beginning to turn back in a gesture to help the *Blücher,* and their destroyers were rushing ahead to launch torpedo attacks against the British squadron as it made its swing to the north-east. With the distance between the two forces rapidly widening, Hipper seized this chance to extricate the rest of his force and ordered a resumption of the south-easterly course. Since *Seydlitz's* after turrets were out of action and her ammunition supplies were running short, it would have been an expensive gesture in any case to have tried to recover the shattered wreck of the *Blücher.*

This temporary breathing-space afforded to the German squadron was now prolonged by confused communications on the British side. Beatty, breathing fire at his ship's disablement, was determined to make it quite clear to Moore that Hipper's main force was to be destroyed and ordered the flag signal 'Attack the rear of the enemy'. In confused circumstances such as these this message was not the clearest expression of the Admiral's intentions, but it was made even less clear when the flags for this signal were hauled down together with those for the previous signal 'Course NE' thus combining two separate messages with one executive order. As a result, the British battle-cruisers read the message as 'Attack the rear of the enemy, bearing NE', which was where the crippled *Blücher* lay. Moore, who was unaware of the reported submarine threat and thought that the earlier turns to port had been to get nearer to the *Blücher,* became convinced that this was Beatty's intention when he saw the German vessel bearing to the north-east. With no thoughts of questioning such orders, the four battle-cruisers gave up the pursuit of Hipper's force and turned towards the *Blücher.*

Beatty had indeed tried to make his intentions clearer by later hoisting Nelson's famous signal 'Engage the enemy more closely' and incidentally but perhaps symbolically found that this had been replaced in the signal book by the less inspiring phrase 'Keep nearer to the enemy'. In any case the fast-disappearing British battle-cruisers could no longer read the *Lion's* signals. Shortly afterwards, being eager to discover what was really happening and having ascertained that immediate repairs to his ship were impossible, Beatty transferred to the nearest destroyer, the *Attack,* and set off in pursuit. The *Lion* meanwhile limped slowly away towards the north-west.

Over the horizon to the south-east the *Blücher* was suffering in isolation as more and more British ships closed in upon her and as the rest of Hipper's force steamed hurriedly towards Wilhelmshaven. *Blücher* continued to fight stubbornly against the overwhelming odds. By this time she was on fire in many places and only two of her main guns were in action, trying to keep her enemies at bay. By 1120 hours the *Arethusa* and her 'M' class destroyers were also in the fray and the *Meteor* went in close to launch torpedoes. She was then suddenly hit by an 8.2-inch shell, which burst in the front boiler-room and put her out of action. *Blücher* was still a danger to those impetuous enough to get too close to her.

The other three 'M' class destroyers and the *Arethusa* were by now closing in and firing torpedoes. Tyrwhitt steered his cruiser to within 2,500 yards of the *Blücher,* blasting away at her continuously with *Arethusa's* 6-inch guns and finally let fly with two torpedoes, both of which hit. Even now the *Blücher* was not only firing her guns at the *Arethusa* but also launching torpedoes at the British battle-cruisers, which were contributing to the destruction. Overhead the whole scene was being watched by the helpless crew of a Zeppelin, who could do nothing other than chronicle *Blücher's* end.

This came shortly after noon, at about 1210 hours. Hit by seven torpedoes and over 70 shells, *Blücher* had been a blazing wreck

long before that and had her last gun put out of order about 1145 hours. Tyrwhitt again ordered the *Arethusa* to close the German ship but this time only to rescue the survivors, who cheered at her coming. Turning over completely, *Blücher* lay bottom upwards for a few minutes while *Arethusa's* small boats picked up the German seamen and then suddenly she disappeared. The *Arethusa* and her destroyers managed to rescue 260 of these gallant men, who had been under more or less continuous fire for three hours, before a German seaplane arrived and unfortunately forced an end to this rescue operation by bombing the small boats. In fact the pilot, an inexperienced flyer, was trying to attack the destroyers, but his action was later criticised by the German admiralty.

Moore's battle-cruisers had turned north a short while before. The Rear-Admiral knew that his squadron would probably be in sight of Heligoland before they could catch up with Hipper again and that the risks were therefore too great. Already Keyes had reported that the High Seas Fleet was on the move. Moreover Moore knew nothing about the condition of the *Lion* after seeing her limp away to the north-west and greatly feared for her safety.

At 1220 hours they met the destroyer *Attack* coming southwards with Beatty on board. Hastily transferring his flag to the *Princess Royal,* the Admiral rushed aboard the battle-cruiser and learnt for himself the sad news. Bitterly disappointed, he impetuously signalled for an immediate about-turn and set off after Hipper. After further enquiry, however, he also realised that their task was by then impossible. Hipper had slipped out of his net for the second time within six weeks and could not be caught. It was, as his Flag Lieutenant Seymour put it, 'like trying to win the Derby after falling at Tattenham Corner'. The British battle-cruisers therefore turned to find the *Lion* and to escort her home.

The *Lion* had in fact to be towed to Rosyth. By 1530 hours with her speed below 8 knots, she was forced to take a towline from the *Indomitable.* Surrounded by a large force of destroyers and cruisers, with the battle-cruisers and the Grand Fleet battleships providing a more distant cover in case of a surprise German attack, these two exposed vessels slowly edged their way home all that day and the next. Early on January 26 the *Lion,* whose engines had by then completely failed, was anchored in the Forth. On the other side of the North Sea, with ideas of surprise attacks on the Grand Fleet very far from their minds, Hipper's very relieved squadron had been met at about 1430 hours on the 24th and escorted back to the Jade estuary.

On the face of it, the battle of the Dogger Bank was a clear-cut British victory. They had chased Hipper's squadron from the seas and destroyed one of his larger vessels without losing so much as a destroyer themselves. The *Seydlitz* had also been seriously damaged, while both the *Derfflinger* and the *Kolberg* suffered to some extent. Against this, the *Lion* was to stay out of action for four months while the *Tiger* had trifling damages. The destroyer *Meteor* had been damaged by the *Blücher,* and the *Aurora* only scratched by the *Kolberg.* The Germans lost almost 1,000 men killed, but fatal casualties on the British side totalled only 15.

Misunderstanding or tragedy?

But if this victory appeared decisive to the British press, it was not so obvious to the professional critics. Beatty was unanimously praised for his part and Fisher's only quibble with him was that the battle-cruisers had carried enough fuel for 3,000 miles instead of the probable 500 miles, and therefore reduced their speed by a knot or two. The actions of the other officers, however, were not so well received, and with some reason. Keyes was later to admit that 'the spectacle of Moore and Co yapping around the poor tortured *Blücher,* with beaten ships in sight to be sunk, is one of the most distressing episodes of the war'. Like everyone else, he saw the lucky escape of the German battle-cruisers, due to a simple misunderstanding, as a tragedy for the Royal Navy.

Fisher criticised Moore's decision to give up the chase, calling it 'despicable' and 'absolutely incomprehensible'. While sympathising with Moore's confusion and bewilderment at Beatty's signals from the crippled *Lion,* one is forced to conclude that he did not show any of the initiative necessary in such tense encounters. Before the *Lion* was knocked out of the battle, Beatty had clearly shown that his primary concern was to catch the main body of Hipper's force and not just to finish off the already doomed *Blücher.* With the advantage in numbers, armament and speed the British had a unique chance to destroy all of the German battle-cruisers, but Moore had let the opportunity slip. Churchill and Fisher shortly sent him away to command a cruiser squadron in the Canary Islands region.

Moore's attitude was symptomatic of the rigid adherence to orders which characterised the Royal Navy's outlook at that time. Initiative and independent judgement were not encouraged. Fisher might fume that 'in war the first principle is to disobey orders. Any fool can obey orders!', but he was hardly renowned for his tolerance when subordinates ventured to cross his opinions and commands.

There was also a failure on board the *Lion* to communicate Beatty's wishes exactly. The order to engage the enemy's rear was both unnecessary and confusing, and was in any case mixed up with the flags of his previous direction. Without this ambiguous signal Moore would have continued to fire away at the *Seydlitz* and *Derfflinger,* and perhaps this was the reason why Beatty was not very eager to chastise his Second-in-Command afterwards. But it is worth remembering that Seymour, Beatty's Flag Lieutenant, had had no specialist training in signals, and had sent unclear messages during the Scarborough Raid action.

Probably Captain Pelly of the *Tiger* was the person who came in for most criticism, especially from Fisher, who thought that his failure to engage the *Moltke* was 'inexcusable', and that he was a 'poltroon' for not charging after the enemy when the *Lion* sheered out of line. The first point is worth examining. The official naval historian is to some extent correct in following Fisher and pointing out that 'the master principle was that no ship should be left unfired upon', but there is another side to the matter. Pelly's information regarding the position of the *Indomitable* was in fact incorrect but his tactics were right. After all, the leading three German battle-cruisers continued to concentrate upon the *Lion* (though the *Tiger* was also engaged and suffered six hits) and achieved great effect. Crippling the enemy's leading ship had been, and still remained, a major stepping-stone on the path to winning the battle, and the official historian was forced to admit that the German firing policy 'was all that the advocates

The battle orders were reworded so that Pelly's mistake regarding fire concentration could be avoided in the future and the signalling system was improved by the installation on each ship of an auxiliary wireless set and by further additions to the signal book which would clarify the sort of instructions which Beatty had so desperately wished to send when his flagship fell out of line.

The other innovation which Churchill and Fisher pressed for, the transfer of the battle-cruisers to the Humber and the Grand Fleet battleships to Rosyth, was abandoned after vigorous protests from both Jellicoe and Beatty. For although this move would put both forces in a better intercepting position, these two bases did not compare with Scapa as an anchorage or a practice area, were navigationally unsuitable and could easily be mined. In the field of tactics the British did not seek for, or perhaps did not think of, any answers to the threat posed by German mines and submarines during the action. Yet without such answers and in view of the Grand Fleet's super-sensitiveness to such attacks, their only reply remained that of swinging away, disengaging, temporarily at least, from the battle. Temporary disengagements, however, could swiftly develop into more permanent ones if great care were not taken.

Finally, the Dogger Bank action tended to confirm the opinion of Fisher, Beatty and perhaps others that the battle-cruisers themselves 'will finish the job'. This was a rather natural thing to say in view of their performance here and earlier at the Falklands, but in both battles the British warships had possessed a large numerical superiority and the enemy had retreated without engaging in a 'toe-to-toe' boxing match. In other words, although the *Lion* indeed took some heavy punishment, the British battle-cruisers were not yet proven in full battle, especially in their defence capabilities. In particular the weaknesses of Beatty's ships to plunging shells and to the possibility of the magazines

Survivors from the *Blücher* dot the surface of the cold North Sea as they wait to be picked up by British destroyers

of concentration on the van could wish'.

Finally, and perhaps more important still, the fuss over Pelly's decision tended to obscure the much more vital fact that the British standards of shooting were rather poor. Here indeed could the *Tiger* feel somewhat ashamed, for despite being the only British battle-cruiser equipped with a director fire-control system she had not registered a single hit. The *Southampton,* as mentioned earlier, had seen her shots regularly land some 3,000 yards over the German ships. The *Tiger* was in fact a special case, with a gunnery lieutenant who was 'villainously bad' (Fisher) and a large number of recovered deserters among the crew. Moreover, being a relatively new ship, she had not fired at a moving target!

Nevertheless she serves as a symbol for the gunnery standards of the British battle-cruisers, which, even allowing for the vast clouds of smoke often obscuring the view, was very poor when compared with that of their opponents. Apart from the *Blücher* and the *Kolberg,* which suffered at the hands of *Aurora* in the first encounter, the only hits made upon the German ships during the entire battle were the two on *Seydlitz* and the one on the *Derfflinger.* In contrast the *Lion* received 16 hits while the *Tiger* was hit six times. Had the German shells been more effective, the battle of the Dogger Bank might have had a different ending, but the British also lacked a really good armour-piercing shell.

Correcting the failures

Some, but not all, of the failures on the British side were recognised and attempts were made to correct them. The *Tiger* and the other battle-cruisers were urged to improve their gunnery, which to Jellicoe had always been suspect, and the Admiralty accelerated its programme of installing director firing systems in all ships.

being ignited by flashes in the turrets had not shown itself, as it had done in the case of the *Seydlitz,* where the Germans took the necessary corrective action.

The battle of the Dogger Bank had seen the British and German battle-cruisers engage each other and the weaker force once again evade the stronger. In that it revealed where command of the sea lay, the action justified the eulogising of the British press. But it also produced evidence of serious weaknesses on both sides. Whether this would be enough to tilt the balance of power in the North Sea in the future was another question.

Further Reading
Bennett, Geoffrey, *Naval Battles of the First World War* (Batsford)
Chalmers, Rear-Admiral W.S., *The Life and Letters of David, Earl Beatty.*
Churchill, Sir W.S., *The World Crisis. 1911-18* (Four Square)
Corbett, J., *Naval Operations Vol 11 (Official History)* (Longmans)
Jellicoe, Admiral, *The Grand Fleet 1914-18: Its Creation, Development and Work* (Cassell)
Marder, A. J., *From the Dreadnought to Scapa Flow Vol II. The War Years: to the Eve of Jutland 1914-16* (Oxford U.P. 1965)
Scheer, Admiral, *Germany's High Seas Fleet in the World War* (Cassell)

PAUL KENNEDY was born in 1945 and was educated at St. Cuthbert's Grammar School, Newcastle-upon-Tyne and at the University of Newcastle, where he obtained a first-class honours degree in Modern History in 1966. Since then he has been researching for his doctorate at St Antony's College, Oxford. From 1966 to 1969 he worked as research assistant to the late Sir Basil Liddell Hart, and contributed articles to Purnell's *History of the Second World War.*

SMS Blücher – the hybrid offspring of German ambition and British deceit

Below: SMS *Blücher* was Germany's answer to the *Invincible* class of battle-cruiser. The British had 'leaked' the information that they would be armed with 9.2-inch guns, so the Germans countered with their superior 8.2-inch weapon. The *Invincibles* did, of course, have 12-inch guns. *Displacement:* 15,500 tons. *Length:* 530½ feet. *Beam:* 80½ feet. *Power/speed:* 32,000-44,000 hp/24½ knots. *Armament:* Twelve 8.2-inch, eight 5.9-inch and sixteen 3.4-inch guns. *Armour:* Belt 6¾ inches, turrets 6¾ inches. *Crew:* 847

HMS Lion – the 'Splendid Cat' severely mauled at the Dogger Bank

Below: HMS *Lion,* Beatty's flagship at the Dogger Bank, was the first of the new class of battle-cruisers armed with 13.5-inch guns. She took a heavy pounding during the battle. *Displacement:* 29,700 tons. *Length:* 700 feet. *Beam:* 88½ feet. *Power/speed:* 70,000-80,000 hp/28-32 knots. *Armament:* Eight 13.5-inch and sixteen 4-inch guns. *Armour:* Belt 9 inches, turrets 9 inches. *Crew:* 1,061

John Batchelor

NAVAL WAR IN THE MEDITERRANEAN

The blockade of the Austrian fleet in the Adriatic countered one of the threats to the Gallipoli supply route, even if it did make the Italian coast the target of Austrian wrath. Another threat, that of German submarines operating from Adriatic ports, was not solved by the blockade, and the U-Boats continued to prey on Allied shipping. *Peter Kemp.* *Below:* The Italian cruiser *Giuseppe Garibaldi* sinking after she had been torpedoed by a German U-Boat, July 1915

53

The naval war in the Mediterranean in 1915 was one of vast complexity. At the far end of this huge inland sea was being waged the campaign in the Dardanelles under entirely British control and command. Over the rest of the Mediterranean the war at sea followed a somewhat spasmodic course dictated partly by the moves of the enemy and partly by the difficulty of bringing together the operations of three separate allies each with different anxieties which dictated the movements of their ships and squadrons.

The immensity of the task can perhaps best be realised by the recollection that the Mediterranean Sea covers an area of more than 1,000,000 square miles. Across this vast expanse of sea had to be carried all the supplies and logistic support for the army engaged in Gallipoli, for considerable British forces stationed in Egypt and the Suez Canal zone, and for the struggling Serbian army trying to hold at bay, on the line of the River Danube, the attacking troops of Germany and Austria. Grand Admiral von Tirpitz, Minister of Marine in Germany, had been quick to appreciate the length and vulnerability of these lines of supply, and on April 25, 1915 had ordered the first German U-Boat to proceed into the Mediterranean. It was no coincidence that this was *U21,* commanded by Korvettenkapitän Hersing. Tirpitz chose his best submarine commanders for the Mediterranean, and at this period Hersing was outstanding. He was followed by five others—Forstmann, Valentiner, Rücker, Gansser, and Kophamel —the pick of the German U-Boat arm, and between them they were to create havoc in the Mediterranean. In addition to the U-Boats which came by sea from Germany, ten smaller U-Boats were sent overland in parts to Pola (Pula), where they were assembled in the naval dockyard. Of these, one was lost with all hands in the summer of 1915 and five were sent to Constantinople to operate from there.

French and British problems in the Mediterranean were not eased by the oddity of the Italian entry into the war. She remained neutral until April 26, 1915 when she denounced her adherence to the prewar Triple Alliance of Germany, Austria, and herself, but without as yet declaring war on any of the Central Powers. This anomalous situation was eased when a declaration of war against Austria followed a month later. Turkey was included amongst her enemies on August 21, 1915, but war against Germany was not finally declared until August 1916. As the majority of the German U-Boats operating in the Mediterranean made their base in Austrian ports in the Adriatic, and as Italy was not officially at war with Germany during 1915, allied operations against them were thereby fraught with difficulties.

It was the influence of these German U-Boats and the realisation of the profound effect they could have on the Gallipoli campaign that determined the British Admiralty to order Admiral Pierse, whose command stretched from the East Indies to the Suez Canal and the coast of Syria, to neutralise the port of Smyrna (Izmir) in case it should be developed as a U-Boat base on the flank of the Gallipoli operations. With his flag in the *Euryalus,* and with the *Triumph* and *Swiftsure* temporarily borrowed from Admiral Carden's Dardanelles force, Admiral Pierse arrived off the port and proceeded to bombard the forts at the entrance.

For five days the three battleships poured shells into the Turkish forts and gun batteries while minesweepers cleared a channel up to the narrow entrance of the harbour, in which the Turks promptly sank two blockships. After the long bombardment, Admiral Pierse sent an ultimatum ashore demanding the unconditional surrender and destruction of all forts and batteries. The local governor refused the British demands. There was nothing left for Admiral Pierse but to withdraw, for a continuation of the bombardment without decisive result could only incur a loss of prestige and it would need an overwhelming force of battleships to make Smyrna surrender. On the eve of the Gallipoli landings, such battleships were just not available. Nor, in fact, was Smyrna ever developed as a U-Boat base.

French blockade Adriatic

It was, however, in the Adriatic that the main activity of the naval war in the Mediterranean, apart from the Dardanelles, was taking place during 1915. The problem there was the presence of the considerable Austrian fleet. The whole of the eastern coast of the Adriatic, with its magnificent deep-water harbours, was a part of the Austrian Empire, extending from Trieste in the north to as far south as Cattaro (Kotor). The main naval base was at Pola (Pula) while at Trieste and Fiume (Rijeka) were subsidiary bases with useful repair and docking facilities. Further to the south were fleet anchorages at Spalato (Split), Zara (Zadar), Sebenico (Sibenica), and Ragusa (Dubrovnik), while right in the south was the finest anchorage of them all at Cattaro (Kotor).

Naval Ministry, Rome

△ Italian Dreadnoughts (with a torpedo boat in the foreground) in the Adriatic. The Italian C-in-C, the Duke of the Abruzzi, commanded the Allied naval forces in this area when Italy entered the war.
▷ Part of the considerable Austrian fleet at sea in the Adriatic. The magnificent harbours of the eastern Adriatic belonged to Austria, while the Allies' nearest base, until Italy entered the war, was Malta

Until Italy entered the war, the nearest naval base available for the Allies was Malta, with Durazzo (Durrës) and Valona (Vlonë), on the Albanian coast and under Serbian control, useful as anchorages but with no base facilities. Italy's entry into the war provided the Allies with Brindisi and Taranto as main fleet bases, and with Venice in the far north as a subsidiary naval station but with limited maintenance facilities.

Because of the length and vulnerability of the supply routes through the Mediterranean, the first consideration for the Allies was to prevent units or squadrons of the Austrian fleet from emerging from the Adriatic. It was here that geography took a useful hand on the side of the Allies, for the Straits of Otranto, the only exit from the Adriatic into the Mediterranean, had a width of no more than 45 miles. With the British Mediterranean fleet so actively engaged in the Dardanelles operations, naval responsibility for the central and western Mediterranean fell upon the shoulders of the French Commander-in-Chief, Admiral Boué de Lapeyrère, and one of his first actions was the institution of a blockade of the Straits of Otranto.

The overwhelming superiority of the French naval force was sufficient to deter the Austrian surface ships from any offensive movements, but it was no deterrent to the activities of submarines. A foretaste of the trouble they were to cause came on the night of April 26/27 when the armoured cruiser *Leon Gambetta,* flagship of the 2nd Cruiser Division, was torpedoed by *U5,* commanded by Lieutenant Georg Ritter von Trapp, and sank with very heavy loss of life.

The loss of the *Leon Gambetta* underlined the fundamental weakness of the French blockade of the Otranto Straits, which was the lack of fast light cruisers. This lack was forcefully exposed on May 6 when the Austrian light cruiser *Admiral Spaun* made a rare sortie into the Mediterranean. She was sighted east of the toe of Italy by the armoured cruiser *Jules Ferry* and the destroyer *Bisson,* but had no difficulty in escaping from the slow French

ships. But by now Italy had denounced the Triple Alliance and was on the verge of signing a Naval Convention with Britain and France, in which the command in the Adriatic would devolve on the Italian Commander-in-Chief, Admiral H. R. H. Luigi di Savoia, Duke of the Abruzzi. Under the terms of the convention the Italian fleet in the Adriatic was to be reinforced by 12 French destroyers and as many French torpedo boats, submarines (minimum six), and minesweepers as the French could spare, six French seaplanes and a seaplane carrier. In addition, four British light cruisers and four British battleships, as soon as they could be relieved from the Dardanelles, were also to be placed under Italian command. This was to be known as the First Allied Fleet, based at Brindisi. A Second Allied Fleet was to be constituted from French, British, and Italian ships not included in the First Fleet, to be under the command of Admiral de Lapeyrère but to be available to the Duke of the Abruzzi on call for any major operations. The British contingent in the Adriatic, which was to consist of the battleships *Queen*, *Prince of Wales*, *London*, and *Implacable*, and the light cruisers *Dublin*, *Dartmouth*, *Sapphire*, and *Amethyst*, were under the command of Rear-Admiral Cecil Thursby, who took his orders from the Italian Commander-in-Chief.

With the coast on both sides of the Straits of Otranto now in Allied hands resulting from Italian ownership of Brindisi on the western side and the use of Valona on the eastern, the blockade was rendered easier. The Italian admiral set up three patrol areas which effectively covered the Straits, together with a covering force of destroyers. Three Italian light cruisers, with the four allocated from British sources, were not detailed for blockade duties but now were held available for additional support if required, for operations against the Austrian coast line, and for fleet scouting.

Austrians dominate Adriatic

The Austrians opened their naval war against Italy by bombarding the towns of Ancona, Rimini, and other small ports on the night of the declaration of war, catching Italian ships still unprepared for hostilities. Italian submarines at Ancona, instead of being at sea, were still in harbour. On the whole, not a great deal of damage was done, though the Italian destroyer *Turbine*, caught unsupported by a force of two Austrian light cruisers and three destroyers, was annihilated. Various small-scale operations against the Austrian coast were carried out in retaliation, though none of them really amounted to more than the destruction of a few lighthouses and signal stations.

This early phase of Adriatic operations came to an end on June 9 when the British light cruiser *Dublin* was torpedoed by an Austrian submarine and other losses were suffered by the Italians. On this same day the Italians suffered two losses. One was the submarine *Medusa*, returning on the surface to Venice from patrol, which was torpedoed by one of the small German U-Boats which had been brought overland in parts and assembled at Pola. The other was the rigid airship M2, which had been bombing the dockyard at Fiume (Rijeka) but had run out of fuel, coming down in the sea. She was burnt by the Austrians and her crew captured.

A series of minor coastal bombardments by the Austrians, including one at Bari, which was the home and the parliamentary constituency of the Italian Prime Minister, raised so much outcry that the Italian Admiralty decided to station a division of armoured cruisers at Venice. This, to say the least, was an odd decision as the armoured cruisers were fast enough neither to prevent Austrian ships bombarding Ancona nor to cut them off on their return home. This mistaken policy had its inevitable result on July 7 when the *Amalfi* was torpedoed and sunk, a painful demonstration of the danger to which heavy ships were exposed in those waters. Her loss resulted in the even odder decision not to withdraw the armoured cruisers from Venice, in spite of their obvious uselessness there, but to forbid them to go to sea. What purpose they were meant to serve was never made clear.

Another Italian cruiser, the *Guiseppe Garibaldi*, was lost on July 18. She, with others of her division based on Brindisi, had been sent out to destroy the railway bridge at Ragusa (Dubrovnik), which had been repaired after an earlier bombardment. The cruisers were sighted by an Austrian aircraft on their way across the Adriatic and a submarine from Cattaro was sent to cut them off. One torpedo hit the *Garibaldi* as she was returning from Ragusa and the ship capsized and sank shortly afterwards.

This last loss resulted in a yet further pulling in of Italian horns in the Adriatic. For some months now these waters had been considered too dangerous for battleships and for heavy cruisers, and the ridiculous situation had arisen in which the two major Mediterranean battlefleets, those of France and Italy, were being employed as no more than a distant covering force for the Dardanelles operations while a third and much smaller Mediterranean battlefleet (Austrian) dominated the Adriatic unchallenged. All British attempts to secure a more rational co-operation of the French and Italian forces under the command of one admiral, whether French or Italian, foundered against the rock of national pride. The results of the Adriatic campaign during the four months since Italy had entered the war had been profoundly discouraging. Italian losses had been two armoured cruisers, one destroyer, two torpedo boats, three submarines, and two rigid airships. In addition the *Dublin*, torpedoed in June, was still out of action and under repair at Malta. Against these, the Austrians had lost two submarines and three naval aircraft.

Public discontent was profound, and made yet more apprehensive by the frequency with which Austrian ships appeared off the Italian coast and bombarded towns and villages. On no occasion had the Italians succeeded in bringing the raiders to action. 'In four months,' wrote the British Naval Attaché in Rome,

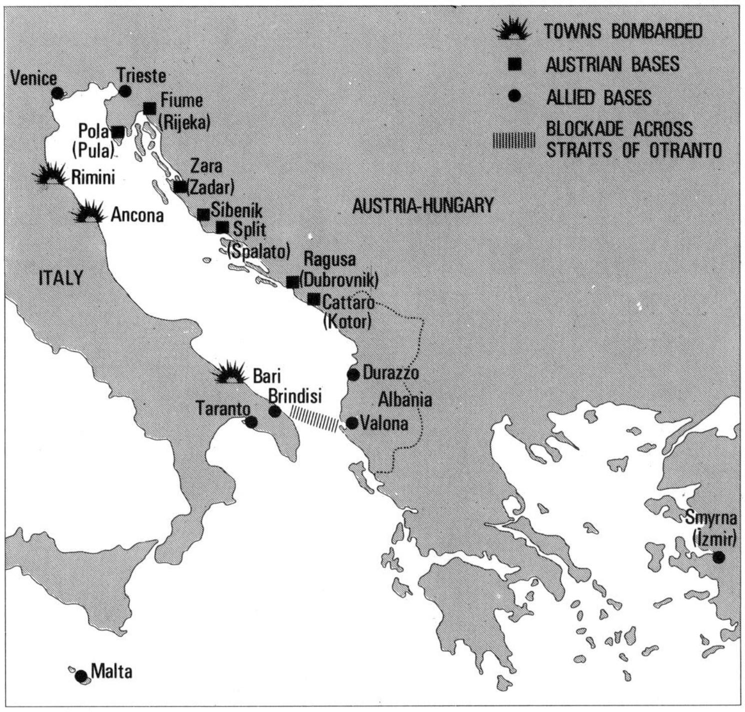
TOWNS BOMBARDED
AUSTRIAN BASES
ALLIED BASES
BLOCKADE ACROSS STRAITS OF OTRANTO
Venice
Trieste
Fiume (Rijeka)
Pola (Pula)
Rimini
Zara (Zadar)
Ancona
Sibenik
Split (Spalato)
AUSTRIA-HUNGARY
Ragusa (Dubrovnik)
ITALY
Cattaro (Kotor)
Bari
Durazzo
Brindisi
Albania
Taranto
Valona
Smyrna (Izmir)
Malta

The blockade of the Adriatic: it cleared the Mediterranean of Austrian warships, but could not prevent the Adriatic becoming an Austrian lake

'the Austrian fleet has established a moral ascendency in the Adriatic and has played the part of a weaker force with conspicuous success. Not only has it succeeded in weakening the Italian fleet, but it has immobilised a force very considerably superior to itself.'

The Italian Minister of Marine bowed to the public distrust and resigned on September 25. The serious deficiencies in light craft, and particularly in submarines, were laid at his door. In order to mitigate the shortage of submarines Britain offered to send six of her B-class boats to the northern Adriatic. Their small radius of action limited their use in the wide waters of the Mediterranean, but in the narrow waters of the Adriatic there were possibilities of a more advantageous employment. By the end of October five of them had reached Venice, the sixth was still in dockyard hands in Malta and could not be sent until she had completed her refit. Although the submarines had little actual operational success, their presence considerably restricted Austrian fleet movements, and the almost daily bombardment of towns on the Italian coast became a thing of the past.

Further Reading

Chatterton, E. Keble, *Seas of Adventure* (Hurst & Blackett, 1936)
Corbett, Sir Julian, *Naval Operations,* Vols. 2-4 (Longmans Green, 1921-1928)
Marder, A. J., *From the Dreadnought to Scapa Flow,* Vol. 2 (Oxford University Press 1965)
Naval Staff Monographs (Historical), Vol. 8, *The Mediterranean 1914-1915* (1923)

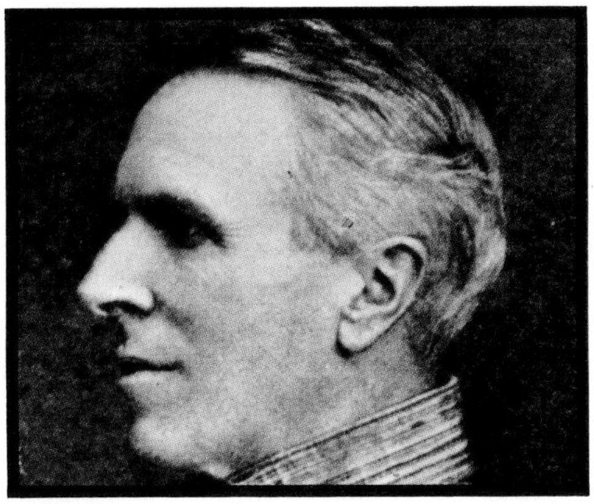

△ Admiral Sir Richard Pierse; he tried unsuccessfully to neutralise the port of Smyrna in case it should be used as a U-Boat base on the flank of the Gallipoli operations.
◁ The sinking of HMS *Triumph* off Gaba Tepe (Gallipoli), May 25, 1915. Small naval steamboats rush to aid the *Triumph* which had been torpedoed by the *U21.* The *Triumph* is a smudge on the horizon.
▷ The sailors of the rival Austrian and Italian navies. Here both the Austrian *(left)* and Italian *(right)* are shown wearing the dark-blue winter uniform.
▽ Admiral de Lapeyrère, commander of the Second Allied Fleet. British attempts to secure a rational co-operation between French and Italian naval forces foundered against the rock of national pride

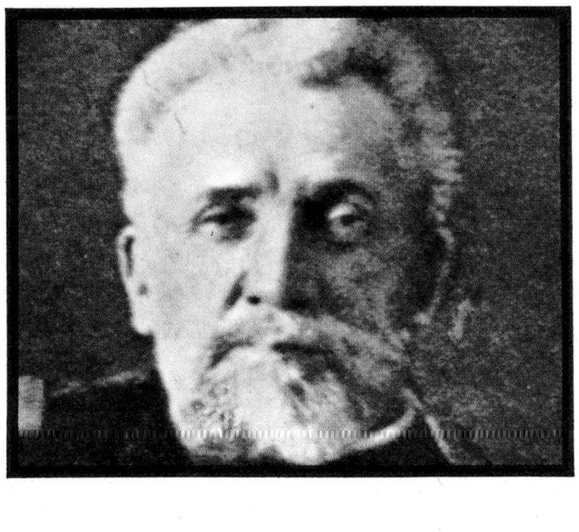

Australian War Memorial

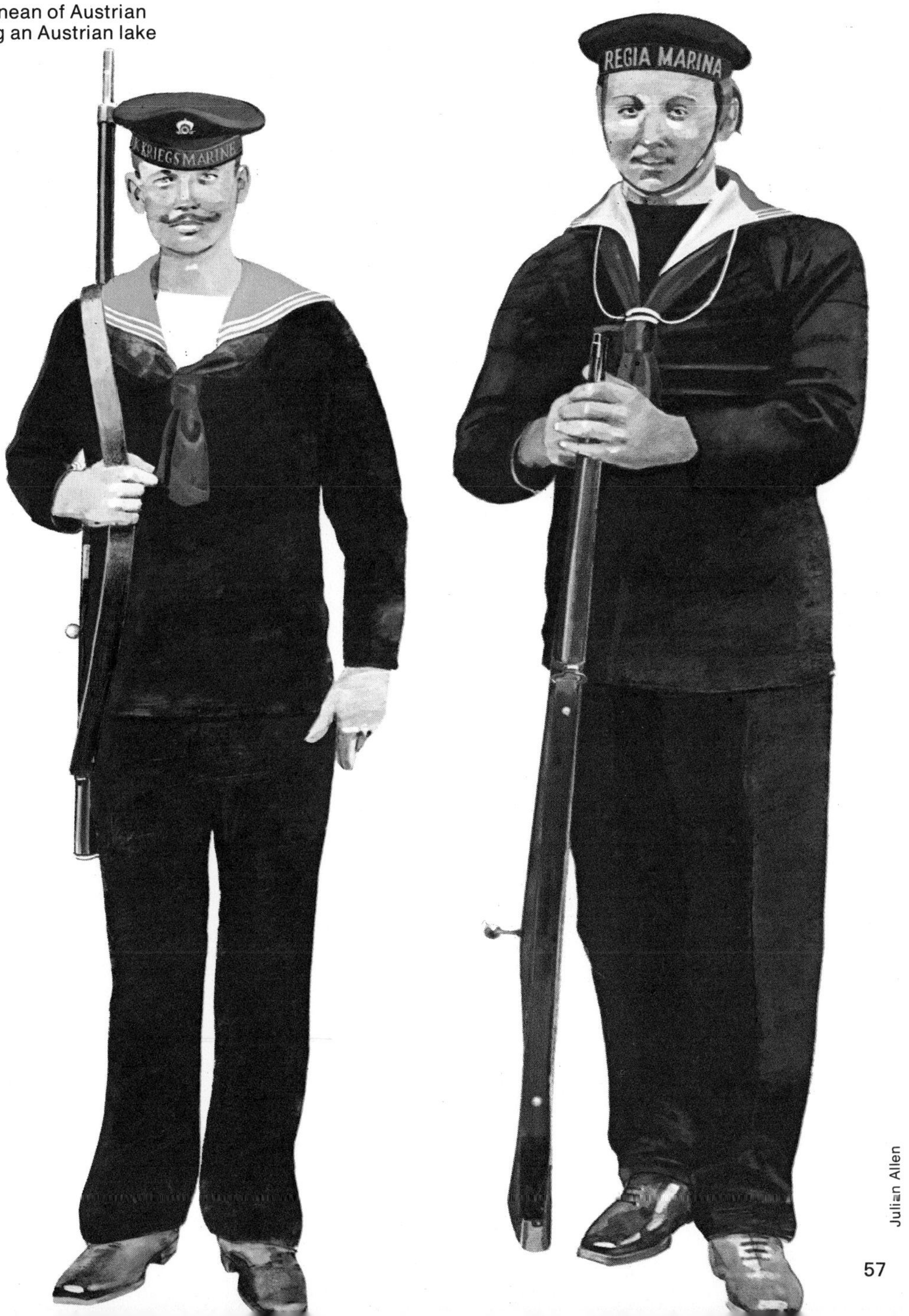
KRIEGSMARINE
REGIA MARINA

Julian Allen

Warships at the Dardanelles — the old and the new

Left: The old French battleship *Bouvet*, sunk at the Dardanelles

Right: HMS *Queen
Elizabeth,* sent to
calibrate her guns in
the Dardanelles

THE
UNDER
WATER
WAR

TECHNIQUES AND DEVELOPMENTS

After the protests of the United States had brought Germany's first U-Boat campaign to an end, Germany's political and military leaders plunged into endless rounds of talks about launching an all-out submarine offensive against Great Britain in an effort to drive her out of the war, despite the fact that this might force the United States' hand and bring her into the war on the side of the Entente. While these talks were going on, the U-Boat arm continued its limited offensive and applied the lessons and tactics learnt in the first campaign, as the British continued to try to find a counter to the submarine — in vain. *Bryan McClean Ranft.*
Above and left: The end of another Allied ship: the torpedo hits, the ship settles and then sinks

Weltkriegsbücherei. Stuttgart

Left: Contrary to the general belief engendered by Allied propaganda, German submarines did not invariably sink Allied merchantmen without warning and leave their crews to perish. If conditions allowed, and there was no danger from other Allied vessels, the U-Boat might well pick up the survivors, as in this painting by Hans Bohrdt of a U-Boat in heavy weather. *Above:* The control room of a U-Boat, a jungle of controls, wiring and pipes. It is unlikely that anyone in a submarine would have been as cleanly and tidily dressed as they are shown here

The first German submarine campaign against merchant shipping, launched in February 1915, had revealed all the factors involved in this new type of warfare. Attacking either on the surface with gun fire, or below the surface with torpedo, the U-Boat could sink Allied merchantmen faster than replacements could be built. This point was first reached in August 1915. If the trend were to continue, the Allies' ability to wage the war would gradually diminish because of shortage of vital sea transport. If the rate of sinkings could be increased they might have to seek a hasty peace. Naval countermeasures to the submarine had proved ineffective. Despite the deployment of many hundreds of patrol vessels, their lack of effective location apparatus and destructive weapons for dealing with submerged U-Boats made successful attacks very rare. A little more success had been achieved by the guns supplied to a small proportion of merchant ships and a few spectacular sinkings had been effected by the disguised Q-ships. During the whole of 1915, however, only 20 submarines were sunk as compared with the 61 new boats added to the German strength. The new year was to begin with an operational force of 58 boats available to attack merchant shipping. If these were to be ruthlessly used there seemed little that the Allied navies could do to prevent the year's losses soaring above the 855,000 tons lost by German action in 1915. But here was Germany's dilemma. If her submarines were to achieve a significant number of sinkings without exposing themselves to the attacks of Allied patrols or the guns of their destined victims, they had to attack without warning and thus without giving crews and passengers any chance of escape. Despite Germany's assertions that this departure from accepted international practice was justified by Britain's own breach of international law in the arrogant interference with neutral shipping involved in her strangling blockade of Germany's food and industrial supplies, neutrals had reacted violently to the sinking of their ships and the deaths of their citizens. So strong were the protests of the United States in particular that the unrestricted campaign in British home waters had been called off in September 1915 and was continued only in the Mediter-

Submarines: new menace at sea

AE2, the first British submarine to successfully run the gauntlet of the Narrows and emerge into the Marmara. She was an E-class boat of the EI type, built in 1913. *Displacement:* 660/800 tons. *Length over-all:* 181 feet. *Beam:* 22 feet and 6 inches. *Engines:* 1600/840 hp. *Screws:* 2. *Maximum speed:* 15.5 knots (10 knots submerged). *Crew:* 30. *Torpedo tubes:* 5 × 18-inch

The UB 14, one of the UB 9 German submarine class who made frequent raids on Allied shipping carrying supplies from the Italian Adriatic ports to Serbia via Albania. It was manned by a crew of 14 and had a maximum speed of 7.5 knots.

German UB II coastal submarine. *Displacement:* 263/292 tons. *Length:* 118½ feet. *Beam:* 14½ feet. *Power/speed:* 284/280 hp and 9/5¾ knots. *Armament:* Two 19.7-inch torpedo tubes and one 2-inch gun. *Crew:* 23.

engines became available, but they were limited in efficiency. They could only operate in good weather, several craft fitted with them were needed in order to get accurate cross bearings and the engines of all neighbouring craft had to be stopped while they were working. On the weapons side something effective had emerged, a powerful bomb released over a ship's stern and exploding at a pre-set depth. Two models of these depth-charges were decided upon by the end of 1915. The larger carried 300 pounds of high explosive and could be operated only by the larger and faster anti-submarine vessels. The smaller craft had to be content with one containing 120 pounds of high explosive. Both types were detonated by a hydrostatic pistol set to explode at either 40 or 80 feet. Although they had to burst within a few feet of a submarine to cause severe damage, and this was very difficult to achieve, they could also damage equipment and shake the morale of the crew by the noise and shock waves of their detonation. If only the location problem could be more frequently and accurately solved, they could be highly effective. Distribution to the anti-submarine forces began in January 1916, but for most of the year supplies were so short that only two could be allocated to each vessel. It was not until March when the Q-ship *Farnborough* sank the *U 68* that they scored their first success. Complementary to the depth-charge was the paravane which was in general service by the end of the year. This was a sweep carrying 400 pounds of high explosive which could be towed at high speed by destroyers and other fast craft to a depth of 200 feet. Its function was to search actively for submarines cruising underwater, whereas the depth-charge could only be used with any hope of success after a submarine had been detected and its location fixed.

Further attempts were made in 1916 to block the passage of submarines by minefields. In April and May a barrage of moored nets and mines, reinforced by deeply positioned mines, was laid off the Belgian coast between Nieuport and the Scheldt. It was designed to stop the exits from Ostend and Zeebrugge through which the smaller U-boats of the Flanders flotilla came to attack shipping in the Channel and its approaches. It may have added to the strain on their ships' companies but there is no evidence that it destroyed a single submarine.

The most encouraging results were obtained by the arming of merchant ships with guns capable of inflicting severe damage on the normal lightly-built submarine. In 1916 as in the previous year, the majority of attacks were made by surfaced submarines using their own guns. This enabled them to make use of their

ranean, where American ships were few. The central issue in the war against shipping in 1916 was to be the German government's vacillation between the increasing attractions of unlimited U-Boat warfare and the danger of antagonising neutral powers.

Although the Admiralty must have been aware of the gravity of a renewal of the submarine campaign, the losses of 1915 had not caused them to make any drastic reappraisal of the anti-submarine measures which had so demonstrably failed. There were some improvements in equipment and in the strength and organisation of the anti-submarine forces, but no systematic examination of the tactical problems involved in the location and destruction of underwater attackers. During the year hydrophones capable of locating a submarine by picking up the noise of its propellers or

superior surface speed and conserve the few highly expensive torpedoes which they carried. British policy was to arm all merchantmen but there was a chronic shortage of guns. Nevertheless, by December 1915 766 had been equipped, a number which increased to 1,100 by April 1916. In the 12 months from January 1916, of the 310 armed ships attacked, 236 escaped as compared with the 67 unarmed vessels which survived 301 attacks.

Despite all this, 1916 was to be a year of increasing merchant ship losses and of continuing failure to locate and destroy submarines. This was due entirely to the Admiralty's inability to grasp the true nature of the tactical problems to be solved. The root of this failure was the practice of using anti-submarine forces on the basis of two misleading conceptions. These were, that only 'offensive' measures would defeat the submarine and that the thing which needed protection was trade routes rather than ships. In combination these two concepts ensured that the hundreds of vessels employed on anti-submarine duties spent their time in fruitless offensive searches in areas where a submarine's presence was suspected or on equally fruitless patrols along the routes laid down for shipping to follow. The searches failed because of the inadequacy of locating equipment, the patrols because a lurking submarine would submerge until the patrolling craft passed by and then wait in safety until the next unprotected merchantmen came along the route. This pattern had become clear in 1915 when shipping had been diverted away from the normal routes, where U-Boat activity was expected. This must have increased the problems of the British. In the following year in order to concentrate the patrols, shipping was directed onto well-defined and obvious routes through the most dangerous waters near the British Isles. Although these were changed at intervals it was only a matter of time before intelligent submarine commanders located the new routes. Faced with increasing losses, the Admiralty could think of nothing but to demand more and better anti-submarine craft. A large destroyer building programme was launched and Jellicoe was under constant pressure to release some of his Grand Fleet flotillas for trade protection. In a letter to the First Lord, Balfour, in October 1916, the Commander-in-Chief put his finger on the problem but did not take his thought to its logical conclusion: 'The destroyer is, of course, very efficient defensively as a screen to individual ships or to a large number of ships, but, except in more or less confined waters, is not an efficient offensive weapon, because she must . . . actually get into contact with a submarine . . . which is a difficult matter if the submarine has plenty of sea room.'

Like almost all his British naval contemporaries Jellicoe failed to realise that the so-called 'defensive' screen of a convoy escort was in fact a most effective 'offensive' organisation because an attacking submarine had to come within the range of its locating and weapons systems if it were to launch a successful attack on the merchantmen being escorted. By the end of May 1916 the lesson was there to be read. Since the beginning of the war, despite all the 'offensive' strength of the anti-submarine patrols, only 32 German U-Boats had been lost. Of these casualties 12 could be attributed to mistakes or inexperience on the part of their crews. The remaining loss of less than one per month by Allied naval action was a clear demonstration of the failure of the methods being used.

The problems confronting Germany at the end of 1915 were of a quite different order. These were neither technological nor tactical but arose from the differences which arose between her naval and political leaders. The former argued that if they were allowed to reopen an unrestricted submarine campaign against merchant shipping, they could bring Britain to her knees within six months. The 1915 campaign had been devastating enough and now, with a far bigger submarine force available, and with the boats themselves having greater cruising range and underwater speed, a decisive result was possible. They admitted that the renewed onslaught would bring strong protests from the United States, but urged that Britain would be defeated long before America was likely to intervene. To the demands of the naval leaders were added the voices of the generals. They were now convinced that unless Britain's support of France were removed, victory on land was impossible, especially in view of the increasing effects of the blockade. If the navy, as it admitted, could not defeat the Grand Fleet, then a ruthless submarine campaign was the only way to drive Britain out of the war. The Chancellor and his political colleagues were unconvinced. They were doubtful of the navy's ability to defeat Britain in this way, perhaps through having too flattering a view of the Royal Navy's ability to find countermeasures to the submarine, and they were sure that the risk of quick American intervention was far greater than the admirals and generals admitted. The political leaders, up to November 1916, were successful in convincing the Emperor. Writing soon after the war, Admirals Tirpitz and Scheer both claimed that if they had had their way in 1916, the result would have been different. There can be no certainty in such arguments, but the assertion is far from being without foundation.

In September 1915, the German Naval High Command had de-

Another Allied ship lost, and with her the chance of many supply runs for the material-hungry war effort of the Entente Powers

cided that it was too dangerous for submarines to operate in British home waters if they were not allowed to attack without restriction. By November, attacks in the North Sea had also ceased and the only submarine activity to continue in this theatre was the minelaying of the smaller boats based on Flanders. This situation continued during the first two months of 1916. The mines, laid in small clusters along the crowded trade routes and frequently renewed, presented a continuous task to Britain's minesweeping forces. The Dover net-barrage was no obstacle to the U-Boats and ships were sunk by their mines as far west as the Needles. The heaviest losses came in the Dover Straits themselves and in the approaches to the Thames where the crowded shipping had to keep to a few well known channels. In January and February, 17 British and several neutrals were sunk in this way. As Germany introduced bigger boats, with a far longer range and a capacity of 18 mines instead of the 12 of the original craft, this was going to be an increasing threat. Even bigger submarines, carrying 36 mines, were being produced for more distant operations. All minelayers carried torpedoes and the majority of them a gun as well.

The lull in torpedo and gun attacks did not apply to the Mediterranean, where a force of less than six U-Boats based on Austrian ports did a significant amount of damage, chiefly by gunfire. They were soon operating in the western part of the sea, as well as the east and as near as 60 miles to Marseilles, such was their contempt for the Allied countermeasures. These countermeasures were nominally under the control of the French Commander-in-Chief but there was no effective co-ordination. Because of the narrowness of the sea, diversionary routing was virtually useless and patrols were as ineffective here as in British home waters. The only effective counter was the guns of armed merchantmen and ten attacks were repulsed in this way in January and February. During the same period 11 British ships were sunk. Although this was not a large number it was serious because most of them were large vessels employed on the long trip to the East or Australasia via the Suez Canal. Such was the Admiralty's inability to provide protection that in March they insisted that all such trade must go by the longer route via the Cape of Good Hope. This was the first instance in the war of submarine attack producing the abandonment of a major trade route. It also further strained Allied shipping resources by prolonging the voyage. The Mediterranean trade itself, much of it carrying vital grain and coal to Italy and the south of France, was faced with a perilous future if Germany could spare more or bigger U-boats.

No effective anti-submarine measures. Bigger and better German submarines, and more of them. At this stage an all-out submarine offensive could have been decisive

The knowledge that the U-Boats were being so effective in the Mediterranean gave additional strength to the advocates of the resumption of unrestricted attacks in British home waters and the North Sea. These had been reinforced by the appointment of Admiral Scheer to the command of the High Seas Fleet in January. Scheer was determined to end what he considered the unnecessarily defensive rôle of the German navy and saw the submarine as the main way of going over to the offensive. So he joined the Chief of the Naval Staff, Holtzendorff, in renewed pressure on the Emperor and his ministers. In this they were aided by the Chief of the General Staff, Falkenhayn, who wanted a weakening of the Allies' will to continue the war as an adjunct to the great offensive on land he was planning for the spring. At last the German leaders were beginning to see the advantages of the simultaneous use of land and sea power. While the military men were trying to overcome the objections of the hesitant Chancellor, Bethmann-Hollweg, the United States unintentionally aided them. In a diplomatic note on January 18, the US not only denounced the sinking of merchant ships by U-Boats, but also urged the Allies to disarm their merchantmen, as a step towards getting Germany's agreement to conducting attacks against them with humanity. This was interpreted in Germany as indicating that America was turning against the Allies and would not take any practical action against Germany if the U-Boat war was stepped up. The Chancellor's position was weakened and he agreed in principle to the resumption of the unrestricted campaign. On the plea that very promising negotiations were going on with the United States, he did secure a postponement of the opening of the campaign until April. In the interval, attacks on merchantmen were to be allowed 'according to the rules of prize law for the time being', as the decision was phrased. This meant that the submarine commanders were entitled to sink armed merchant ships and transports on sight but that on no account were ordinary passenger steamers to be attacked. The frustrations the restrictions imposed on aggressive submarine commanders are vividly expressed in an extract from the log of the captain of a U-Boat operating off the mouth of the Seine in the summer of 1916: *In all, 41 day-approaches (that is, approaches with torpedoes ready for discharge, but without actually discharging) were carried out, and none of the steamers showed the signs indicated as distinctive of transports . . . On the other hand in the early morning light, we saw in all six camouflaged steamers (three collier type and three cargo vessels). They were painted black with grey or brown upper works, and showed no flag . . . I was firmly convinced that they were transporting troops or important material, but as my view was not confirmed by the signs mentioned in the regulations (troops in large numbers, quantities of guns or waggons, men stationed on deck) I could not attack these either.*

Even with the restrictions, Allied losses began to mount and the greater range of the newer submarines was demonstrated by the frequency with which they began to operate in pairs off the west coast of the British Isles. The total losses for Britain were 90,000 tons in March, the bulk of them in the Channel and its approaches and the mouth of the Thames. Fortunately the pressure in the Mediterranean eased and only three ships were lost there during the month. But Germany was again doomed to frustration because of her continuing failure to understand American reactions. At a conference at Wilhelmshaven on March 6, the naval high command gained a relaxation of the restrictions. In future all ships in the war area, identified as British, except passenger vessels, could be sunk without warning. This, together with the finer weather and the new U-Boats operating far out into the Atlantic beyond the range of normal British patrols, soon increased the losses. In April, 37 ships were sunk by submarine attack and a further six by mines, making a total of more than 140,000 tons, approaching the peak of August 1915. This was checked not by any successful British countermeasures but, as in the 1915 campaign, by an extremely strong American protest over the loss of American lives in the sinking of the French cross-channel steamer *Sussex,* at the end of March. Faced with a threat by the United States to break off diplomatic relations, the German Chancellor was able to force a major retreat on the naval leaders. In future the submarine war against commerce was to be carried on in accordance with the strictest prize rules, ships being boarded and searched and their passengers and crew removed before they were sunk.

Admiral Scheer decided that it was too risky for submarines to operate in these conditions in British waters and the campaign was called off, although operations in the less dangerous Mediterranean were to continue. Even there the increased number of armed merchantmen kept the Allied losses in check. Of the 20 armed ships attacked in May and June only two were

sunk. So the fears of a huge increase in losses in the summer were not fulfilled. By June they had dwindled to 37,000 tons, the lowest figure since August 1915. In some ways this was a misfortune to the Allies, for even if it did not produce complacency, it certainly resulted in a lack of any sense of urgency to find more effective methods of dealing with the U-Boat should a major campaign again be launched. Furthermore, the long term attrition of Allied shipping deserved more consideration than the temporary decrease in monthly losses. Since January 1, 1916, nearly 500,000 tons of British shipping had been destroyed. This was two and a half times the output of the shipyards during the same period. This, added to the military demand on shipping space, was leading month by month to a diminution of the carrying capacity of the British mercantile marine. If imports of vital goods had not been proportionately reduced it was due to the continuing arrival of neutral ships. So far they had been ready to take the risks of submarine attack in return for the great profits to be made. Would this continue?

Neutrals were to be put to the test in the latter months of 1916. In October, recognising that the Battle of Jutland had ended any possibility of major action by the High Seas Fleet, Scheer ordered the reopening of submarine operations, under the prize regulations. The new campaign was particularly disturbing. There was an acceleration in sinking rates: in the first eight months of the year these had averaged 56,000 tons, while in the last four the figure was raised to 121,000 tons. Delivery rates of cargoes were being slowed down by delays in the ports and the effects of rerouting and zig-zagging. In the Mediterranean, where 40 ships were sunk in October, the number of attacks without warning went up each month. A new illustration of the increasing range of the submarines was given by the appearance of *U 53* off the American coast, where she sank five ships off Rhode Island in a single day. But it was in home waters and the North Sea that the losses were the greatest. The total losses for October were no less than 176,000 tons, more than 30,000 tons greater than the hitherto blackest month of August 1915. In addition to British tonnage, there were increasingly serious losses to the vital cross-channel French coal trade and to neutral shipping in the North Sea, chiefly Norwegian. 102,500 tons of neutral shipping were destroyed and there was a real danger that the Scandinavian shipping, which brought the Narvik iron ore essential for Britain's munitions industry, would be withdrawn. Prompt action by the British government in providing especially favourable insurance facilities, staved this off for the time being.

In the light of these mounting losses a greater awareness of the seriousness of the situation began to arise in the Royal Navy. Admiral Jellicoe, in particular, now realised that the defeat of the submarine rather than the destruction of the High Seas Fleet was to be the decisive factor in the war at sea. He was aware not only of the shipping losses but of the rapidly increasing number of U-Boats. At the end of 1916 there were to be 140 in service compared with 58 at the beginning of the year. Allied sinkings between June 1916 and the end of the year were to be only 15 as compared with 74 newly commissioned. Aware of this pattern, Jellicoe considered that there must be a complete reorganisation of the Admiralty directed towards producing effective offensive measures to defeat the U-Boat. If this were not done, he wrote to the First Lord, he foresaw the submarine campaign being able 'To force us into accepting peace terms which the military position on the Continent would not justify and which would fall far short of our desires'. In November a series of meetings of the War Committee of the Cabinet with Jellicoe present were held. As a result of these and of the government's growing dissatisfaction with the lack of drive in the Admiralty the decision was taken to make Jellicoe First Sea Lord with the specific task of defeating the German submarine campaign. Simultaneously in Germany, the advocates of unrestricted U-Boat warfare were gaining the ascendancy.

Further Reading
Campbell, Rear-Adm. Gordon, VC, *My Mystery Ships* (Hodder & Stoughton 1928)
Corbett, Sir Julian, *Naval Operations* Volume III (Longmans Green 1923)
Fayle, C. E., *Seaborne Trade,* Volume II (John Murray 1923)
Hezlet, Vice-Adm. Sir Arthur, *The Submarine and Sea Power* (Peter Davies 1967)
Marder, A. J., *From the Dreadnought to Scapa Flow* (OUP 1965-6)
Newbolt, Sir Henry, *Naval Operations,* Volume IV (Longmans Green 1928)
Scheer, Adm. R., *Germany's High Seas Fleet in the World War* (Cassell 1920)
Tirpitz, Grossadm. von, *Memoirs* (Hurst & Blackett 1919)

Out of date by contemporary standards, the *U 9* was nevertheless able to send three British warships to the bottom of the North Sea

Otto Weddigen, a daring commander after luck put prey in his way

John Batchelor

German submarine *U 9*

Displacement: 493/611 tons. *Length:* 188 feet. *Beam:* 19¾ feet. *Power/speed:* 1,050/1,160 hp and 14/8 knots. *Armament:* four 17.7-inch torpedo tubes and one 2-inch gun. *Crew:* 28

The southern patrol area of the Royal Navy in the North Sea. Here a series of coincidences, bad management and the weather brought together four old vessels and led to the loss of three British ships and 1,459 men

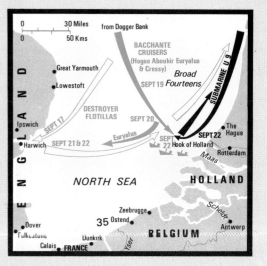

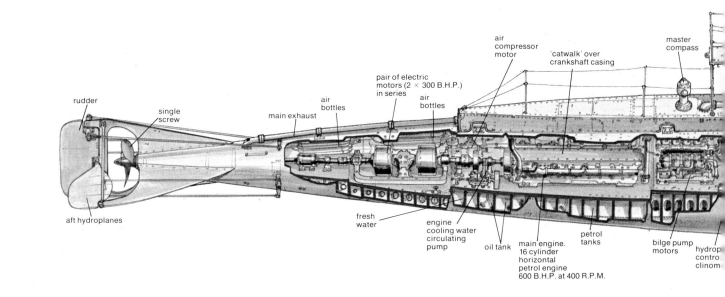

rudder
single screw
main exhaust
air bottles
pair of electric motors (2 × 300 B.H.P.) in series
air bottles
air compressor motor
'catwalk' over crankshaft casing
master compass

aft hydroplanes
fresh water
engine cooling water circulating pump
oil tank
main engine. 16 cylinder horizontal petrol engine 600 B.H.P. at 400 R.P.M.
petrol tanks
bilge pump motors
hydrop contro clinom

Submarines— the menace now beginning to make itself felt at sea

Above: The British submarine *B11*, which penetrated the Narrows at Gallipoli and sank the Turkish vessel *Messudieh*. *Displacement:* 280/313 tons. *Length:* 135 feet. *Beam:* 13½ feet. *Power/speed:* 600/190 hp and 12/7 knots. *Armament:* Two 18-inch torpedo tubes. *Crew:* 16. For the superb feat of torpedoing the *Messudieh,* the *B11's* commander, Lieutenant Holbrook, was awarded the VC, while all the other members of his crew were also decorated. During this trip, Holbrook showed that small submarines could penetrate heavily defended waters and cause considerable damage

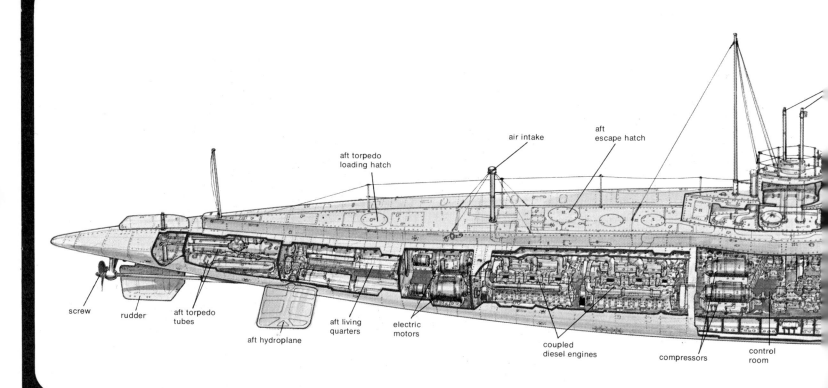

aft torpedo loading hatch
air intake
aft escape hatch

screw
rudder
aft torpedo tubes
aft hydroplane
aft living quarters
electric motors
coupled diesel engines
compressors
control room

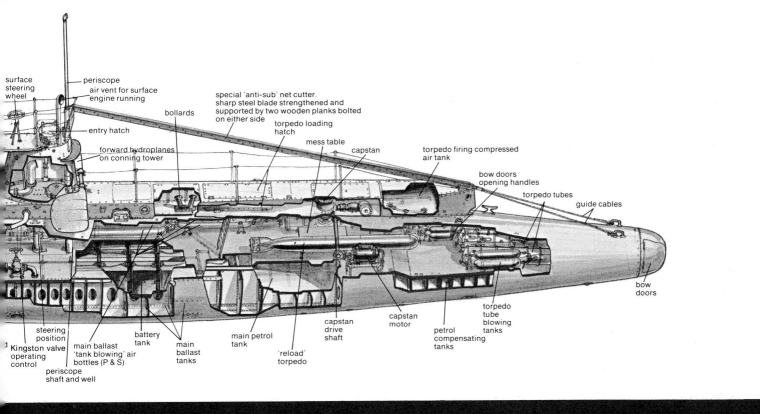

surface steering wheel

periscope

air vent for surface engine running

special 'anti-sub' net cutter. sharp steel blade strengthened and supported by two wooden planks bolted on either side

bollards

torpedo loading hatch

entry hatch

mess table

capstan

torpedo firing compressed air tank

forward hydroplanes on conning tower

bow doors opening handles

torpedo tubes

guide cables

bow doors

steering position

Kingston valve operating control

periscope shaft and well

main ballast 'tank blowing' air bottles (P & S)

battery tank

main ballast tanks

main petrol tank

capstan drive shaft

'reload' torpedo

capstan motor

petrol compensating tanks

torpedo tube blowing tanks

John Batchelor

Two old and small submarines – but powerful auguries for the future

Below: The German submarine *U-9,* which sank the three British armoured cruisers *Hogue, Aboukir* and *Cressy. Displacement:* 493/611 tons. *Length:* 188 feet. *Beam:* 19¾ feet. *Power/ speed:* 1,050/1,160 hp and 14/8 knots. *Armament:* Four 17.7-inch torpedo tubes and one 2-inch gun. For his feat in sinking the three British cruisers, the *U-9's* commander, Otto Weddigen, was awarded the Iron Cross (First Class) by the delighted Kaiser. The sinking proved that submarines operating on their own could successfully deal with much larger and more powerful ships in the open sea, even allowing for their tactical misuse

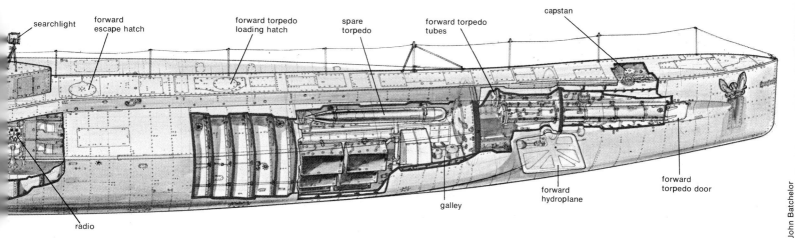

periscopes

searchlight

forward escape hatch

forward torpedo loading hatch

spare torpedo

forward torpedo tubes

capstan

radio

galley

forward hydroplane

forward torpedo door

John Batchelor

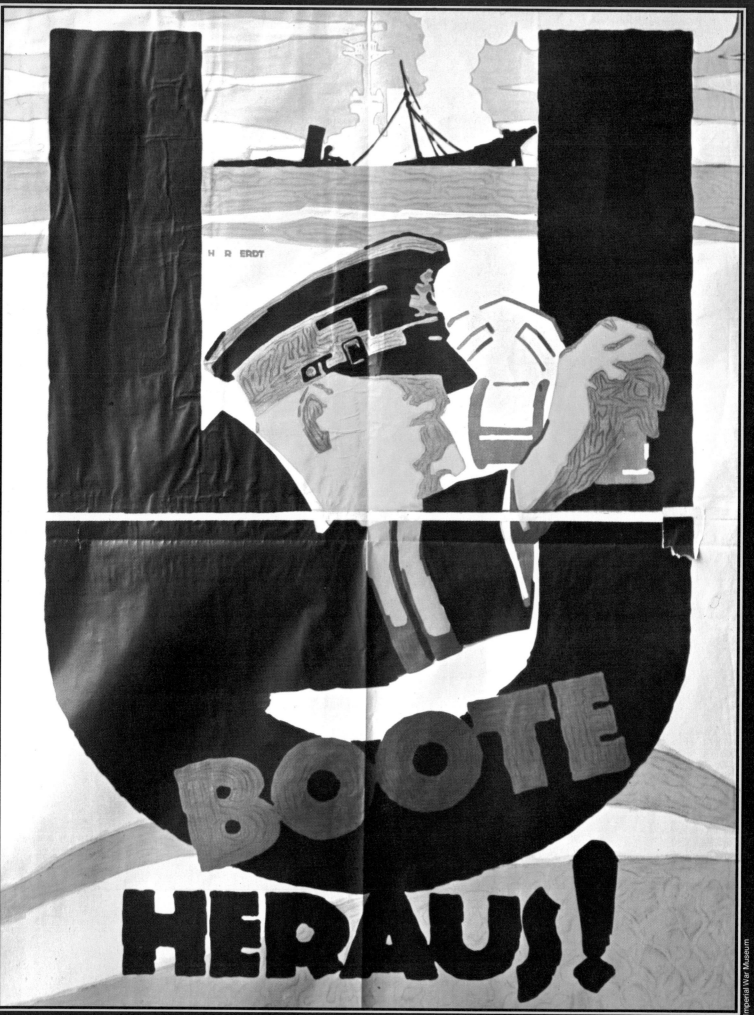

German approval for the new development —
'U-Boats Go Forth!'

PRELUDE TO JUTLAND

German victory in a fleet action between the navies of Britain and Germany could decide the war in a day. At the end of May 1916 chance and intent combined to bring both fleets to this momentous trial of strength. *Peter Kemp*

The long months of inactivity in the North Sea which followed the battle of the Dogger Bank (January 24, 1915) had its inevitable repercussions in the morale of the Grand Fleet, where boredom and frustration had wide reign among men thirsting for action, any action. 'I feel we are so impotent, so incapable of doing anything for lack of opportunity, almost that we are not doing our share and bearing our portion of the burden laid upon the nation,' wrote Vice-Admiral Beatty from Rosyth, and his sentiments were echoed in every heart in the Grand Fleet. The occasional sweeps in the northern half of the North Sea, tactical exercises, target practices and the continual need to coal ship so as to be ready when the great day dawned were not enough to satisfy even the least bellicose of the men immured in their ships in Scapa Flow, Cromarty and Rosyth.

All sorts of suggestions to stimulate some response from the German High Seas Fleet were put up both in the Admiralty and in the fleet, but in the end all were shattered against Jellicoe's rocklike refusal to be stampeded into any adventures that would threaten the British command of the North Sea. By 1916 it was clear that Britain was winning the war at sea, even though it was by default rather than action, and that the naval stranglehold on the German seaborne trade must, in the end, bring Germany down into defeat. This was Jellicoe's gospel, and though he was as ready and as eager for battle as any other officer in the fleet, every proposed operation, every suggestion to tempt the Germans out, had to be weighed against this overriding need to preserve the Grand Fleet's margin of supremacy over the German High Seas Fleet.

The Admiralty's dilemma was to some extent solved by a change of command in the German High Seas Fleet. Admiral Pohl, mortally ill with cancer, was in February 1916 replaced by *Vizeadmiral* (Vice-Admiral) Reinhard Scheer, a far more able officer with a determination to pursue a bolder line than Pohl had ever conceived. Moreover, with his appointment there came from the Kaiser an agreement which gave Scheer far more freedom of action than had ever been accorded his two predecessors. All this was known and appreciated in the British Admiralty, and hopes were high that Scheer's bolder tactics might bring about the long-hoped-for sea battle between the main fleets of the two nations.

Scheer, however, was no foolhardy adventurer. He knew, just as well as did his two predecessors, that the High Seas Fleet was no match in battle with the Grand Fleet, and it was no part of his plan to bring about any full encounter. His strategy was to try, through offensive movements and bombardments, to entice part of the Grand Fleet out to a position where it could be attacked piecemeal, and for the rest to concentrate on submarine attack and mine warfare to sting the British into a retaliation that might produce the same results, with the hope, through this attrition, of reaching the stage where a full scale encounter between the two opposing fleets would not be too hazardous an adventure.

Scheer's first two efforts to implement a more forward strategy were nothing if not timorous. On February 10 he made a destroyer sweep east of the Dogger Bank; three weeks later, in conjunction with a Zeppelin raid on England, he took the High Seas Fleet as far west as the Texel in the hope that the Zeppelins might tempt out the Harwich Force of light cruisers and destroyers. Neither sortie achieved anything, and although on both occasions the Grand Fleet, alerted by the Admiralty (which had decoded some of the German signals) put to sea, Scheer was back in his base long before the British, who were steaming from their Scottish bases, could reach the scene.

The British were the next to engage in this game of tip and run. The Harwich Force escorted the seaplane carrier HMS *Vindex* to a position west of the island of Sylt, and the seaplanes were launched in the early morning of March 25 to bomb what were thought to be Zeppelin sheds at Hoyer, on the mainland opposite Sylt. Beatty, with the Battle-Cruiser Fleet, was in position about 50 miles west of Horns Reef, with the main Battle Fleet further to the north. The Germans were very slow to respond. On the night of March 25/26 Hipper put to sea with the German battle-cruisers, with two squadrons of battleships in support, but turned for home after reaching Sylt. The official German report blamed the rough weather for Hipper's decision to return so soon. Beatty remained cruising in the vicinity of Horns Reef for over 24 hours, but at no time was Hipper nearer than 60 miles from him. The seaplane raid achieved nothing beyond proving that there were no Zeppelin sheds at Hoyer. (They were at Tondern, inland.)

Nevertheless the High Seas Fleet, or at least a major part of it, had put to sea as a result of this operation, and the British Admiralty was quick to suggest further similar raids to the Commander-in-Chief. But Jellicoe would have none of it. A main fleet action fought in the waters of the German Bight, so far from British bases, was just not in his book of possibilities. Such an action would raise acute problems of fuel for destroyers and light cruisers, quite apart from the risk of exposing the Grand Fleet dreadnoughts to submarines and mines. And Beatty was entirely of Jellicoe's opinion. If a main fleet action were to be fought, it would have to be in open waters where the dice would be less heavily loaded in the Germans' favour.

Scheer's next blow was the raid on Lowestoft and Yarmouth on April 25, an operation designed to coincide and support the Easter Sunday rising of Irish Nationalists, which was instigated and supported by Germany. Scheer put to sea with the High Seas Fleet at noon on April 24, but one of the bombarding battle-cruisers, SMS *Seydlitz*, struck a mine off the Norderney Gap and was forced to return. The British Admiralty, again as a result of decoded signals, was aware of this movement, though not yet of its destination, and ordered the Grand Fleet to raise steam and put to sea. Similar orders went to the Harwich Force. As the Grand Fleet steamed to the southward it ran into a strong head sea which was too much for the destroyers. They were forced to disperse, and Jellicoe continued without them.

Commodore Tyrwhitt and his Harwich Force sighted the German battle-cruisers at about 0700 hours while on their way to Lowestoft, and altered course to the south in an attempt to draw them away from their target. They refused to follow, but the *2nd Scouting Group* of four light cruisers, escorting the battle-cruisers, engaged the Harwich Force. Tyrwhitt, having failed to entice the Germans south, had altered round again to the northward, but now found himself faced with the German battle-cruisers ahead of him, and by now six light cruisers, with two flotillas of destroyers, on his starboard bow. He had no alternative but to turn again and retire at his best speed.

A plan misfires

Here, then, was just the situation towards which all Scheer's planning had been directed. A sizeable portion of the British fleet (three light cruisers and 18 destroyers) were out on a limb, unsupported by any other fleet formations. What did the German admirals do? *Konteradmiral* (Rear-Admiral) Bödicker, commanding the battle-cruisers in the absence of Hipper, who was ill, called off the pursuit and retired at full speed on the remainder of the High Seas Fleet which Scheer had brought to the west of Terschelling, about 70 miles east of Yarmouth. As soon as the battle-cruisers were within 50 miles of him, Scheer himself turned for home. As for Tyrwhitt, he altered course to the north-east as soon as the Germans retired, and shadowed them until the Admiralty ordered him home. The nearest that Beatty was able to get to the High Seas Fleet was 130 miles; Jellicoe was still 300 miles away when Scheer reversed course and made for the security of his base in the Jade river.

A British raid on the Zeppelin base at Tondern, on much the same lines as the Hoyer raid, was launched on May 4, again with the object of enticing the High Seas Fleet out. The Grand Fleet was off the entrance to the Skagerrak, but the seaplane attack provoked no immediate response. Jellicoe himself ordered the fleet to retire in the early afternoon, having waited for some seven hours in German waters for Scheer to make a move. In fact, Scheer did come out an hour after Jellicoe had left the field, but only proceeded as far as Sylt before returning to the Jade. Even had Jellicoe delayed his departure, it was unlikely that the two fleets could have made contact with each other.

All these pre-Jutland plans and operations, three German and two British, whetted the appetite in both fleets for further action. Early in May, Scheer reckoned he had found the ideal plan. Basically it was much in line with the previous operation at Lowestoft, where Bödicker had let slip the opportunity of annihilating the Harwich Force. Two things had gone wrong then: Hipper's illness, which had meant giving Bödicker the command, and the fact that Lowestoft was too far to the south for Beatty to get there in time. Hipper had now recovered from his illness, and Scheer had confidence that he would not repeat Bödicker's mistake if the opportunity offered. A raid by the German battle-cruisers on Sunderland, which was some 200 miles nearer to Rosyth than was Lowestoft, would draw Beatty out, and the High Seas Fleet, waiting conveniently out at sea, would overwhelm Beatty long before Jellicoe could get there from Scapa Flow.

Scheer had two additional refinements to add to this plan. He had recalled his U-Boats from commerce operations late in April following the unfavourable international outcry after the sinking of the hospital ship *Sussex,* and thus had them available to play a part in the forthcoming operation. They were to be sent out in advance of the fleet movement to lie off the main British naval bases, in particular Scapa Flow and Rosyth. There they had a dual purpose, to torpedo British warships as they put to sea and to report their movements to Scheer. To make more certain still, he also brought in his Zeppelins, which would carry out an extensive search of the northern North Sea to make quite certain that a report of Jellicoe's movements would be in Scheer's hands in plenty of time to avoid a meeting between the two main fleets. This was something that Scheer was determined to avoid.

The details of this plan were filled in during the first ten days of May. The early morning bombardment of Sunderland was to be carried out by the *1st Scouting Group*—five battle-cruisers under Hipper's command—with the *2nd Scouting Group* of four light cruisers under Bödicker in company and two destroyer flotillas to act as a screen. Scheer himself, with the High Seas Fleet, would be at sea in an area 50 miles east of Flamborough Head. The date was to be May 17. Soon this had to be postponed for six days, since the repairs to SMS *Seydlitz,* mined on the occasion of the Lowestoft raid, would not be completed until the 20th. Accordingly, the U-Boats sailed to take up their positions off the British bases by dawn of that day, and Scheer warned his Zeppelins to be ready to fly on the 23rd.

Meanwhile, Jellicoe had been preparing his plan, aimed at drawing the High Seas Fleet into waters much further north than it had yet reached. The plan entailed a sweep by two squadrons of light cruisers from the Skaw down into the Kattegat and as far south as the Sound and the Great Belt. There was to be a battle-squadron of the older battleships in the Skagerrak to act as direct support to the light cruiser squadrons, while to the north-west, off the south-western coast of Norway, the Grand Fleet, including the Battle-Cruiser Fleet, would be waiting, ready to move south at full speed if the Germans reacted in force.

Into this main plan Jellicoe built a subsidiary plan to damage the High Seas Fleet if it should not venture far enough north to give the Grand Fleet its chance. Three submarines were to be stationed to the south of Horns Reef and two more off the Dogger Bank, while the minelayer HMS *Abdiel* was to extend the minefield, already laid south of Horns Reef, to close the whole of the northern channel used by German ships when leaving the Bight. Also off Horns Reef was to be the seaplane carrier HMS *Engadine,* with an escort of light cruisers, to give warning of any movement by Zeppelins which might prejudice the execution of the plan.

Jellicoe's plan was due for execution on June 2, but it was Scheer who got in first. Towards the end of May there were indi-

cations in the British Admiralty of German preparations for an operation of some magnitude, and Jellicoe was warned accordingly. His plan was postponed indefinitely until the German movements were known in more detail.

Scheer, however, had been having his troubles. His U-Boats were already out, but the repairs to the *Seydlitz* had not been satisfactorily completed by the 23rd, and there was a further postponement for another six days, to the 29th. On that day, blustery winds from the north-east ruled out the Zeppelin reconnaissance. It was the same on the 30th, but by now Scheer had reached the end of his time allowance. His U-Boats had been in position since the 23rd, and would reach the end of their endurance on June 1. It was, therefore, now or never so far as his plan went. Yet without his Zeppelin reconnaissance, with its vital warning of Jellicoe's position and movements, he was not prepared to take the High Seas Fleet so close to the British coast.

Scheer substituted a second plan, not so daring as his first but designed to produce the same result. Instead of crossing the North Sea and bombarding Sunderland, the *1st* and *2nd Scouting Groups* were to show themselves off the Danish coast as though on the way to attack British shipping in the Skagerrak, with the remainder of the High Seas Fleet following in their wake some 60 miles astern. Scheer was pretty certain that this movement of the two *Scouting Groups* would be quickly reported in London and

achieve the result he wanted. The Grand Fleet, from Scapa Flow, Cromarty and Rosyth, would put to sea and thus give his waiting U-Boats their chance to use their torpedoes with effect. And there was still the chance that Beatty, eager to get at the reported German battle-cruisers, would come charging across the North Sea into his waiting arms. And if events did not work out as he expected, he would still be near enough to his own bases to get home in plenty of time. Lack of Zeppelins would not affect this operation, since his starboard flank was protected by the Danish coast, and his port flank could be efficiently guarded by light cruisers and destroyers. Scheer's mind was made up, and during the afternoon of May 30 he made the signal that the operation, as replanned, was to proceed. The battle-cruisers under Hipper were to sail at 0100 hours on the 31st, with their orders slightly amend-

Above left: Admiral Sir John Jellicoe, Commander-in-Chief of the Grand Fleet. *Above right: Vizeadmiral* Reinhard Scheer, Commander-in-Chief of the High Seas Fleet. *Right:* The prelude: British battle-cruisers lie at anchor in the Firth of Forth

ed at the last minute. Instead of showing themselves off the Danish coast, Scheer instructed Hipper to go as far north as Norway and make himself conspicuous there before dark on the 31st. If he made contact with any sizeable British force, he was to draw it southward until it came within range of Scheer's guns. Scheer himself sailed from the Jade at 0230 hours. Off the British bases the U-Boats were ready.

The British Admiralty was aware that something considerable was afoot as early as May 17. It was the departure from their German bases of the U-Boats which gave them the first indication. They knew, too, that the destination of all these submarines was the northern half of the North Sea, and the fact that no ships were attacked in that area during the succeeding few days made them doubly suspicious. Room 40, which was the centre inside the Admiralty which decoded intercepted German signals, came up during the morning of May 30 with a signal ordering the High Seas Fleet to prepare for sea and assemble in the Jade Roads by 1900 hours. Half an hour later Jellicoe was informed that the High Seas Fleet might be proceeding to sea the following day. During the afternoon another signal was intercepted (Scheer's orders that the operation was to proceed), and although it could not be decoded, it was obviously so important that the Admiralty ordered Jellicoe to sea, informing him that 'the Germans intend some operations commencing tomorrow'. A concen-

tration between Jellicoe and Beatty was to be effected eastward of the Long Forties, some 100 miles west of the entrance to the Skagerrak. Both the Grand Fleet and the Battle-Cruiser Fleet were at sea by 2300 hours, two hours before Hipper left the Jade.

These numbers, which show such an impressive superiority on the British side, do not tell the full story. The speed of the six German pre-dreadnought battleships, about 18 knots, reduced the speed of the German battle line to about two knots slower than Jellicoe's battle line of modern dreadnoughts. It is fair to say, however, that Jellicoe did not know that the pre-dreadnoughts were with Scheer, and so far as he knew both fleets were of roughly equal speed. In gun-power, the British superiority was overwhelming. And in torpedoes, the British also had a considerable superiority.

Of what was Jellicoe thinking as he stood upon the bridge of the *Iron Duke* as she forged ahead through the darkness? Perhaps his thoughts can best be summed up by a document which he had sent to the Admiralty seven weeks earlier, and had circulated to his Grand Fleet admirals:

The first axiom appears to me to be that it is the business of the Grand Fleet to nullify any hostile action on the part of the High Sea (sic) Fleet; secondly, to cover all surface vessels that are employed either in protecting our own trade or in stopping trade with the enemy; thirdly, to stop invasion, or landing raids, in so far as the strategical position of the Grand Fleet permits of this.

So long as the High Sea Fleet is confined to its harbour, the whole of these desiderata *are obtained, and although, of course, the total destruction of the High Sea Fleet gives a greater sense of security, it is not, in my opinion, wise to risk unduly the heavy ships of the Grand Fleet in an attempt to hasten the end of the High Sea Fleet, particularly, if the risks come, not from the High Sea Fleet itself, but from such attributes as mines and submarines.*

There is no doubt that, provided there is a chance of destroying some of the enemy's heavy ships, it is right and proper to run risks with our own heavy ships, but unless the chances are reasonably great, I do not think that such risks should be run, seeing that any real disaster to our heavy ships lays the country open to invasion, and also gives the enemy the opportunity of passing commerce destroyers out of the North Sea.

Beatty's thoughts ran in parallel with those of his chief. It is often considered that he chafed under Jellicoe's cautious attitude, that he was the sort of admiral who would have risked all on a single throw. This could not be further from the facts. In all his writings of this period there is clear evidence that he was as well aware as Jellicoe that the maintenance of the existing superiority in numbers of capital ships was the be-all and end-all of the naval war in the North Sea. And all his actions when, at the end of the year, he succeeded Jellicoe in command of the Grand Fleet are added evidence that he would never risk that superiority by action in unfavourable circumstances. He chafed, it is true, at the inactivity of the High Sea Fleet, but then, so too did Jellicoe and every other officer and man in the Grand Fleet.

And what of Scheer? He, too, was putting to sea with equally prudent thoughts. In no circumstances was he prepared to face an action with the Grand Fleet. His one hope was to isolate a portion of the Grand Fleet and bring it to action, and no more.

In accordance with the Admiralty instructions the British ships sailed late in the evening of May 30. From Scapa Flow the main body of the Grand Fleet under Admiral Sir John Jellicoe cleared the anchorage by 2215 hours; south of them a smaller detachment of eight dreadnoughts of the 2nd Battle Squadron, together with cruisers and destroyers, was steaming from the Moray Firth to join Jellicoe after noon on the following day, and to the south of them Vice-Admiral Sir David Beatty led his Battle-Cruiser Fleet down the Firth of Forth, which he cleared at 2300 hours.

Beatty's destination was a point 69½ miles south-south-east (159 degrees) of the Grand Fleet rendezvous. This separation was dictated by the need for Beatty's force to be sufficiently far south to cover any German tip-and-run raids on the East Coast, while the Grand Fleet had to be far enough north to cover the armed merchant cruisers on blockade duty to the north of Scotland. While perhaps not the best way to catch the German fleet with the maximum concentration of ships, it seemed a necessary split and there was little danger in it; Jellicoe's dreadnought force, even without Beatty, was stronger than the High Seas Fleet; Beatty's battle-cruisers were faster and could avoid any stronger German force. If Beatty had seen nothing by the time he arrived at his destination he was to turn northwards and join the Grand Fleet.

So they sailed through a clear night, the dreadnoughts in line ahead, each keeping station on the blue stern light of the one before, the cruisers spread in the van like a shield. With the dawn, reports of U-Boat sightings broke radio silence and the long columns split up into divisions and steered zigzag courses.

Meanwhile the German fleet was steaming northwards on a converging course through the divers minefields of the Heligoland the main battlefleet followed secretly. He had no intention of taking on the full strength of the Grand Fleet of course, and had no idea that Jellicoe was at sea in force; three separate reports from different U-Boats off the Forth and Invergordon that morning reported various units of the British fleet, but they were confused by the zig-zag courses being followed and Scheer discarded them as too vague and scattered to be meaningful. So he continued steaming northwards towards the British rendezvous.

Jellicoe and Beatty were equally unaware of the Germans' movements as they steamed east through the bright morning. This ignorance remained complete until shortly before 1300 hours. '1230 Admiralty to Commander-in-Chief Grand Fleet. No definite news of enemy. They made all preparations for sailing this morning. It was thought fleet had sailed but directional wireless places flagship in Jade at 11.10 GMT. Apparently they have been unable to carry out air reconnaissance which has delayed them.'

This ill-conceived message, which removed any sense of urgency from Jellicoe's progress towards the rendezvous, and which later caused him to distrust other Admiralty messages, was caused quite simply by lack of liaison between the Operations division at the Admiralty, who sent the message, and the Intelligence Department, who gave them the information. Operations asked Intelligence where directional wireless placed the German call-sign DK (call-sign of the flagship), and having been told 'in Wilhelmshaven', sent their message to Jellicoe. However, Operations were not aware that Intelligence knew that it was German custom to transfer this call-sign to Wilhelmshaven to confuse the British when the flagship put to sea, as no one had asked.

JUTLAND

The Battle-cruisers

In the afternoon of May 31 Beatty's and Hipper's battle-cruisers met, and the Battle of Jutland began. Seeking to lure Beatty on to the guns of Scheer's main fleet, Hipper led off to the south, but the rôles were reversed when Beatty sighted Scheer and decided in turn to entice him into Jellicoe's arms. *Peter Padfield. Right:* HMS *Indomitable* at 25 knots. The battle-cruisers' speed and firepower was thought to give them a decisive rôle in battle

Bight. In the van was the *1st Scouting Group,* or battle-cruiser squadron, under *Vizeadmiral* (Vice-Admiral) Franz Hipper, preceded by its light cruisers and destroyers; following some way astern and dropping behind all the time, the head of the battleship line was still visible in the clear morning light. First were the seven *Königs* of the *3rd Battle Squadron,* the most recent and powerful ships in the fleet, then the *1st Battle Squadron,* nine other dreadnoughts of the *Helgoland* and *Nassau* classes led by the fleet flagship, SMS *Friedrich der Grosse,* carrying the flag of *Vizeadmiral* Reinhard Scheer, and finally the six pre-dreadnought *Deutschland* class battleships of negative value, which made up the *2nd Battle Squadron*. These were the slowest units of the fleet and also the weakest, so they constituted a real danger to the rest.

Scheer's plan was a compromise, as we have seen. Frustrated in his original intention of an attack on Sunderland, he had ordered a sortie up the Jutland coast to the Skaggerak, and had instructed Hipper to show himself off the Norwegian coast while So on May 31 the two opposing forces, which comprised the major part of the first line dreadnoughts of both belligerents, steamed quite unwittingly towards their one great appointment with history. Those British officers and men not on watch basked in the early summer sun, far removed from thoughts of battle, the Germans, with their clocks two hours ahead of Greenwich, had finished their post-prandial stand-down and were at gun-cleaning stations, testing, adjusting, cleaning and oiling the whole elaborate apparatus of the great guns and fire control.

It is worth looking at this organisation in some detail now, for both sides had their points of advantage in the subsequent gun duel. By this date fire control from a central command position had replaced the initiative of the individual gunlayer in his turret. This was because effective gun range had lengthened rapidly since the beginning of the century and with it the time taken by a shell to reach its target. So when firing at a moving target it was no longer any use pointing the guns at the target at the instant of firing; a trigonometrical problem had to be worked to give the position of the target some 20 or more seconds after the gun was fired, when the shell was due to arrive. Both sides had therefore produced electro-mechanical machines to work out the answer from the known and estimated factors available. The known factors were one's own course and speed, enemy range and bearing, while the estimated factors were enemy course and speed. The answers required from the machines were the 'deflection' or 'aim-off' to the right or left of the target to compensate for its movement, the 'rate of change of bearing' and the 'rate of change of range'. These 'rates', when found, were set on 'clocks', so that if the initial range had been given correctly by the range-finders and the 'rate' had been given correctly by the computer, the 'clock' set to that 'rate' continued to show the correct range—until one or other of the ships altered course or speed. If the 'clock' range fell out of step with the rangefinder ranges as they came in or with the observed fall of shot, the 'clock' was 'tuned' until it kept to the correct 'rate'.

Of the systems in the opposing fleets, the British had by far the more elaborate. Each ship had a Fire Control Table situated in an armoured position, called the Transmitting Station, in the bowels of the vessel. Into this room came all the observed information about the enemy, and from it went the electrical leads which transmitted the required gun elevation and bearing to each turret. These 'elevation' and 'training' angles were not simply the result of the 'Table' answers, though; in between the plots and 'clocks' and the transmitters to the turrets were differential gearing systems which allowed the Gunnery Control Officer from a station aloft on the foremast to order any corrections which he considered desirable from his observation of the fall of shot

by a range 'clock' running at the 'rate of change of range'. This system, in its comparative simplicity, was probably as efficient as the more ambitious British fire control complex.

For sighting the guns the British had a complete director firing system; this meant that the guns of the main battery were sighted not by individual gunlayers and turret trainers in each turret, but from a master sight aloft in a revolving tower on the tripod foremast. As this master sight was rotated to follow the target so its angle of 'training' was passed automatically by leads down the tripod legs of the mast and through the ship to the Transmitting Station, where it was corrected by the Fire Control organisation previously described, then electrically transmitted to pointers on dials in each turret. The men who trained the turrets never saw the enemy; they simply followed these pointers with pointers which moved with their own turret. The Germans had a similar system except that their director sight was a periscope protruding through the deckhead of a heavily armoured position just abaft the conning position in the fore superstructure.

When it came to elevating the guns to give the projectile the correct trajectory for the range, the British system had a decisive advantage. British gunlayers followed a pointer moved from a Gun Range Counter in the Transmitting Station in exactly the same way as the turret trainers followed their training pointers. They also never saw the enemy. Further, they never had far to move their guns once they had been elevated from the loading position, as once all guns had been laid for range they were kept thus while the director layer up in his tower on the foremast waited for the order to shoot and then for the roll to bring his sight on target; as it came on, or fractionally before, he fired.

of the preceding salvo. The system, then, was not purely mechanical, but was a complex mix of trigonometry and observation.

However, it is possible that this Fire Control Table was ahead of its time; it relied on a multitude of flexible drives and bevelled gearing which must have produced small, but cumulative mechanical errors, and the instruments which fed it, particularly the rangefinders, were not sufficiently accurate in any case. It is probable therefore that observation or, as it was termed, 'spotting' was the more important component of fire control. Certainly the system had failed to hold the German range in the two high speed and long range dreadnought encounters which had taken place so far, at the Falkland Islands and the Dogger Bank.

The Germans had a simpler device, the *Entfernungs Unterschieds* indicator, which had no flexible drives to feed range and bearing plots onto a Fire Control Table, but was simply a machine for working a trigonometrical problem from the known and estimated factors fed in by the operators; gun 'deflection' could then be read straight off. The elevation for the gun sights was kept simply

The Germans on the other hand still employed a 'continuous aim' method in which each individual gunlayer had his own sight and kept it on target through every movement of his own ship. It was a strenuous system requiring months of training for a perfect union between hand and eye in every condition of weather, and in action it must have exhausted far more nervous energy than the British method. In addition it had the equally important disadvantage that the turret sights were much lower than the director sight aloft, and thus subject to continual fogging from spray, shell splashes, gun smoke and funnel smoke as well.

As if to compensate for what must have been a crippling disadvantage in rolling weather, the Germans had one brilliant point of advantage in their Zeiss rangefinders. Whereas the British Barr & Stroud rangefinders had a base length of only nine feet, except for those on the latest *Queen Elizabeth* battleships, the German ones had a much longer base length. As shooting to the correct range forms perhaps 90% of the art of naval gunnery, the longer German instruments gave them a great advantage.

Another point of advantage which has been claimed for the Germans was a faster rate of firing the opening salvoes in a 'ladder' spread 'up' or 'down' for range, without waiting to 'spot' the previous salvo. It seems from British reports that SMS *Lützow*, Hipper's flagship, used some such system at Jutland. This is curious, however, as other German gunnery logs prove that their system of finding the target was quite as slow and deliberate as the British, that is they fired a salvo, all right-hand or all left-hand guns, waited until the Control Officer had 'spotted' the fall of shot and had ordered a correction so many metres 'up' or 'down', 'right' or 'left', and only then fired the other salvo, again waiting to see the result from the shells before recorrecting and firing the reloaded first guns again. It was only when they had crossed or 'straddled' the target that they went into rapid fire. This was exactly the British system, bred on peace practice, which, of course, was all that most naval officers had to go on.

As for the opposing guns, shells and armour plate, British dreadnoughts invariably had larger calibre guns class for class than the Germans, and the Germans invariably had thicker armour. But, of course, they needed it; they were faced with heavier shells. So it is probable that until the British *Queen Elizabeth* 15-inch gun battleship tipped the scales decisively in favour of British offensive power the two sides were very evenly matched so far as power of resistance was concerned.

The quality of the steel in the shells and armour was slightly better on the British side, although unknown to the service the shells were liable to break up when they struck armour plate at an angle; for acceptance, they were tested at a 90 degree striking angle. The shells were also liable to explode on impact with thick armour instead of after piercing it as the bursting charge was unduly sensitive. However, it is doubtful if the German shells were any more efficient, at least on the first count. Finally, the German Krupp guns were more accurate than the British pieces, but the larger calibre of the British guns outweighed this advantage as their weightier shells had a flatter trajectory at any given range, and thus a better chance of hitting. They also had a greater maximum range and could keep the Germans under fire at distances at which they themselves could not be reached.

In balance, as the two opposing forces moved nearer together, all the decisive advantages in a gun duel, weight, range and director firing seemed to lie with the British; the Germans' sole point of real superiority lay in their rangefinders, and while this was likely to give them a good start it was scarcely decisive. But, of course, there were other factors, and as always the greatest of these was chance.

By 1400 hours on May 31, Hipper's advance force of five battle-cruisers in single line ahead with a semicircular screen of light cruisers ahead of it, had reached a position some 20 miles east of the position Beatty was making for. Hipper was therefore directly ahead of Beatty's line of advance, but going northwards at right angles to it.

Beatty did not know this. And estimating that he would reach his ordered position in 15 minutes time, he made a general signal for his force to turn northwards at 1415 hours in accordance with his instructions to close on Jellicoe. The British Battle-Cruiser Fleet was then sailing in three separate divisions of heavy ships. Beatty's flagship, HMS *Lion*, led the 1st Battle-Cruiser Squadron of the latest 13.5-inch gun ships, HMS *Princess Royal*, HMS *Queen Mary* and HMS *Tiger*; three miles east-north-east of them was the 2nd Battle-Cruiser Squadron, the 12-inch gun ships HMS *New Zealand* and HMS *Indefatigable,* and well astern, five miles north-north-west of Beatty, was the 5th Battle Squadron of four *Queen Elizabeth* class battleships. These were the latest, fastest, heaviest battleships in the Royal Navy, each mounting eight 15-inch guns with an effective range and battering power overwhelmingly greater than anything yet in the German service. The explanation for the distance between this powerful squadron and the battle-cruisers may be that they were being kept away from the probable direction of approach of any German force so that they would not be surprised by a stronger force, for although fast they were not as fast as the battle-cruisers; alternatively, Beatty might have been thinking of his junction with Jellicoe, and of fitting his force easily into the Grand Fleet formation.

Accidental meeting

On either side of the big ships were screens of destroyers, and eight miles ahead six pairs of cruisers six miles apart were spread on a 30-mile front on a north-east–south-west line, thus facing German waters. As 1415 hours approached, the time for the whole British force to turn northwards, the most easterly pair of cruisers, HMS *Galatea* and HMS *Phaeton,* were just 16 miles from the most westerly cruiser of Hipper's screen, which was therefore just below the curve of the horizon from them. At which point chance took a hand. Exactly splitting the distance between the opposing cruisers was a neutral merchantman, the Danish steamer *N.J. Fjord.* Both sides closed to investigate her. Thus ended the chain of events which was unwittingly to draw the fleets together into a copybook engagement between first, the light cruisers, then the battle-cruisers and finally the battle fleets themselves.

At 1420 hours, by which time the rest of Beatty's force had made the turn northwards, the *Galatea,* heading eastwards, hoisted the signal 'Enemy in sight', and at the same time sent a wireless message: 'Enemy in sight. Two cruisers probably hostile bearing ESE. Course unknown.' This was received by the Battle-Cruiser Fleet and the Grand Fleet 70 miles to the north with varying degrees of scepticism; there had been false alarms before. For Beatty, however, it was enough, and ordering his destroyers to take up a position for screening on a south-south-easterly course, he made a signal for a turn to south-south-east, leading ships together, the rest in succession, and immediately led around himself in the *Lion.* His course was designed to get between the Germans and their bases to the southward.

However, the signal was made by flags and these, together with the *Lion's* funnel smoke, were blown by the light westerly wind and by the speed of the *Lion's* progress in a general north-westerly direction so that the signal was not picked up by the 5th Battle Squadron. While the battle-cruisers turned south, the four *Queen Elizabeth* class battleships continued on their northerly course towards Jellicoe, and by the time that Rear-Admiral Hugh Evan-Thomas, commanding the 5th Battle Squadron, had received the signal by signalling lamp, his four ships were ten miles from Beatty.

Meanwhile, the opposing cruisers at the point of contact had opened fire on each other, and Hipper had turned his whole force south-west to investigate. At 1435 hours the *Galatea* saw his smoke and reported it on the eastern horizon as from a fleet. Way to the north, Jellicoe picked up the message; he had already ordered steam for full speed at the first contact report, and he now abandoned the leisurely zig-zag he was steering and made for the conflict at 17, rising to 18, knots.

At the point of conflict the main forces drew together with no clear idea of what they were up against. The *Galatea,* instead of pressing on to investigate the course and composition of the German fleet whose smoke she saw, made off in a north-westerly direction to entice them towards Beatty, reporting as she did so, 'They all appear to be following . . .', a message received with some amusement by the rest of the British fleet. The other cruisers bunched and followed, and the sound of the gunfire of this northward action gradually pulled both main forces after it. Hipper and Beatty, who had been converging southwards on the original point of contact, hauled up until they were converging northwards, Beatty steering north-east, Hipper north-west.

During this phase a seaplane launched from Beatty's seaplane carrier, HMS *Engadine* and piloted by Lieutenant F. J. Rutland, made history when it rose to seek out the Germans, the first aircraft ever to do so during a naval engagement. But he too steered north after the gunfire and made no useful scouting contribution before a burst petrol pipe forced him down. While Rutland was aloft, Evan-Thomas' powerful 5th Battle Squadron cut corners towards Beatty and made up some of the mileage lost by the earlier signalling misunderstandings, so that when the opposing battle-cruisers sighted each other he was only seven miles from Beatty towards the north-west.

It is probable that at this time the visibility from the eastwards was better than from the west, as Hipper made out the British battle-cruisers at about 1520 hours, some five minutes before the earliest British sighting of the German big ships. By 1530 hours, however, with the two main forces some 14 miles from each other and therefore hull down, both commanders were able to tell the approximate course of their opponents; Beatty, seeing Hipper's five big ships steering north, immediately altered course to the east to cross his wake and cut him off from his bases. Hipper was watching for the move and decided not to be cut off, but to fall back on Scheer some 50 miles to the south-east. He therefore reversed course to south-east, and in preparation for the gun duel which was bound to follow, arranged his battle-cruisers on a line of bearing in a west-north-west/east-south-east direction so that the funnel and gun smoke of his leading ships would be blown clear of his rear ships by the westerly wind.

So the forces closed. For the British these were intensely exciting minutes; they had been waiting over a year for this chance to settle the issue begun at the Dogger Bank, and their confidence in the outcome was as great as their unbounded confidence in the superiority of their own service. The last time they had met, Hipper had run and only fortune and British signalling misunderstandings had saved Hipper from annihilation, so they thought. This time they would have him. 'It looked like a sitter to me,' one officer from 'B' turret in the *Tiger,* confided to his diary afterwards. The only question was how long it would take to put all five German ships on the bottom.

Beatty has been criticised for his headlong charge at Hipper, and his impetuosity in not waiting to concentrate with Evan-Thomas' four great battleships trailing behind; no doubt these criticisms are valid in the cold light of hindsight and tactical law. But he was Beatty and his only experience had been German retreat, this was the Royal Navy and its only traditions were complete superiority and victory; it would have been unreasonable to expect anything but immediate chase designed to prevent any part of Hipper's force getting home. Besides, Beatty had six battle-cruisers to Hipper's five.

The Germans waited resolutely at their guns as the range closed. There had been a marked hush in the control positions at the news of the British battle-cruisers, but this had only lasted a minute or so according to Hase, Gunnery Control Officer of SMS *Derfflinger,* 'then humour broke out again, and everything went on in perfect order and calm.' Shortly afterwards Hase himself saw the British force through his gunnery periscope, 'six tall, broad-beamed giants steaming in two columns. They were still a long way off, but they showed up clearly on the horizon and even at this distance they looked powerful, massive . . .'

He watched fascinated as the British 2nd Battle-Cruiser Squadron joined Beatty's four ships: 'The six ships which had at first been proceeding in two columns, formed line ahead. Like a herd of prehistoric monsters they closed on one another with slow movements, spectre-like, irresistible. All was ready to open fire, the tension increased every second . . .'

Hipper expected the British guns to open outside his own effective range; the maximum range of the 13.5-inch guns of Beatty's leading four ships was 24,000 yards, the maximum range of his own guns was 19,700 yards, over 4,000 yards less. But unknown to him the short-base British rangefinders were over-estimating the range by as much as 2,000 yards, and as the two forces closed to within gun range, Beatty himself was not at his usual position on the *Lion's* compass platform, but was below on his bridge discussing a signal addressed to Jellicoe. His flag captain, Chatfield, waited impatiently above.

'I [Chatfield] wanted him [Beatty] to come on the compass platform and sent a message to Seymour, telling him to advise Beatty that the range was closing rapidly and that we ought almost at once to be opening fire . . . But I could get no reply . . . at 3.45 the range was 16,000 yards. I could wait no longer and told Long-hurst to open fire. At the same moment the enemy did so. Seymour hoisted the "5" flag [engage the enemy] and off went the double salvoes. Beatty came on the compass platform . . .'

As fire opened from both sides at 1547/1548 hours with some 15,500 yards separating the two forces, thus well inside German effective range, all the advantages lay with Hipper. First the visibility favoured him; the declining sun was brightening the western horizon and thus tending to silhouette the British ships. However, there is little in the eye-witness accounts to suggest that the British were seriously hampered by bad visibility at this stage, rather the reverse; an account from the conning tower of the *Tiger* states, 'The Germans were showing up splendidly . . .' The Gunnery Control Officer of the *Lion,* wrote, 'It is a perfect day, and all attention is concentrated on rangefinding . . . two ships of the same class are first and second in the enemy line and these two ships fill the field of view of the high power glasses . . .'

Undisturbed target practice

But it was not long before other factors intervened; first the funnel smoke from the leading British battle-cruisers was blown down the range by the westerly breeze to hamper the rear ships, despite Beatty's attempt to clear it by ordering his squadron on a line of bearing north-west, and secondly a part flotilla of destroyers which he had ordered into position ahead of the battle-cruisers strained up the *engaged* side further befouling the range with their multitude of funnels. Within 18 minutes of the opening salvoes the *Princess Royal* was manoeuvring independently out of the line to try to clear her range.

Hipper, as remarked, had formed his squadron on a line of bearing which, aided by the favourable breeze, successfully cleared his smoke from following ships. He was also in the classic position of crossing Beatty's 'T' as the British rushed in, and so he was able to maintain a steady course while Beatty had to alter course towards the south-east by degrees if he were to keep all his guns in bearing. Added to this, Beatty's standing orders for disposition of fire in action with a numerically inferior enemy were dis-

regarded by some of his ships, as was his signal to the same effect which was made by flags in the midst of a sudden rush of flag signals from the *Lion's* halyards. Consequently, while the two leading ships, the *Lion* and the *Princess Royal,* correctly concentrated their guns on the leading German ship, the SMS *Lützow,* the third ship in the British line took the third German ship, and the fourth took the fourth German. This left the second German ship, the *Derfflinger,* unengaged altogether, and she enjoyed the vital opening minutes at undisturbed target practice. Her Gunnery Control Officer, Hase, noticed this curious fact after a few minutes: 'I laughed grimly and now I began to engage our enemy with complete calm, as at gun practice, and with continually increasing accuracy. All thoughts of death or sinking vanished. The true sporting joy of battle woke in me and all my thoughts concentrated on one desire, to hit, to hit rapidly and true, to go on hitting.'

But probably the most important advantage that Hipper enjoyed was range-finding accuracy. While the opening British salvoes were falling as much as a mile over their targets many of the opening German salvoes were almost right on for range. The first salvo from SMS *Moltke,* for instance, landed just 200 yards short of the *Tiger* and the next straddled her. Before the rear two ships in the British line had even opened fire the *Lion* had been hit twice by the *Lützow* and shortly afterwards, at 1551 hours, the *Tiger* received her first two hits. Hipper's squadron was giving a superlative exhibition of shooting, its salvoes falling in tight bunches. The British fire control meanwhile was still generally overestimating the range and in some ships at least underestimating the rate of change of range. Indeed, the range was closing so fast in the opening minutes of Beatty's headlong charge, before his alterations brought him parallel to the German line, that the *Derfflinger,* having straddled the *Princess Royal,* was able to go into rapid fire including secondary armament so that a salvo left her guns every seven seconds. Meanwhile, the rear two ships in the British line watched for the splashes of their opening salvoes, guns silent, such was the advantage given to the Germans by Hipper's steady tactics and Zeiss's superb rangefinders.

'The German shooting at this time was very good,' wrote an officer from the conning tower of the *Tiger,* 'and we were repeatedly straddled, but funnily enough were not hit very often. I remember watching the shell coming at us. They appeared just like big bluebottles flying straight towards you, each time going to hit you in the eye; then they would fall, and the shell would either burst or else ricochet off the water and lollop away above and beyond you, turning over and over in the air.'

By 1600 hours the British ships had received between 12 and 15 hits while the Germans had received probably four; the range had by then closed to less than 14,000 yards and both commanders began drawing away, Hipper south-east, Beatty south, so that the range opened slowly. Then at 1603 hours the *Lützow* caught the *Lion* with a storm of accurate salvoes and Beatty turned another three points away to south-west by west.

Another landmark occurred one minute later at the rear of the line, when SMS *Von der Tann* landed three shells from a four-gun salvo on the upper deck of the *Indefatigable,* a remarkable feat. Smoke started billowing from the British ship's afterpart, and she failed to follow around on the alteration of course. From her next ahead, the *New Zealand,* the Torpedo Officer laid his glasses on her and saw the next German salvo straddle too, one shell hitting her forecastle, another the forward turret, both appearing to burst outside the armour. He continued to watch for some 30 seconds by his recollection, during which nothing happened, and then the ship quite suddenly blew up, commencing from forward. 'The main explosion started with sheets of flame, followed immediately afterwards by a dense, dark smoke, which obscured the ship from view. All sorts of stuff was blown high in the air, a fifty-foot steam picket boat for example, being blown up about 200 feet apparently intact, though upside down.'

It is usually considered that this explosion was caused by 'flash' from a shell burst inside a turret (whose armour was seven inches thick, and therefore penetrable by German shells) passing down the ammunition hoists, igniting unprotected charges on its way and so entering the magazine, the doors of which were at that time left open in action for rapid handling. Supporting evidence for this comes from the *Lion,* whose centre or 'Q' turret was pierced by a shell a few minutes before the loss of the *Indefatigable.* The shell struck at the joint between the front armour of the turret and the roof armour, folding this back 'like an opened sardine tin' and burst inside the turret, killing the guns' crews and starting fires which spread to cordite charges in the gun loading cages. The officer in charge of the turret, Major F. J. W. Harvey of the Royal Marines, who was in the silent chamber behind the gun breeches, was mortally wounded, but he had the presence of mind to order the magazine doors closed. This order, for which he was awarded a posthumous Victoria Cross, undoubtedly saved the *Lion* as flash from the cordite charges eventually passed down the hoists to the handing rooms outside the magazine, killing the men who were obeying the order to close the door; some were found as they died with their hands on the door clips. 'Q' turret and its crew was wiped out, but the magazine and the ship were saved.

It should not be thought that the 'flash' danger had been completely overlooked in the Royal Navy before Jutland; experiments had been conducted on it since the turn of the century, the conclusion of which was that if the lids of the metal boxes in which the cordite charges were stowed in the magazine were weakened so that they would blow off easily, and if there was an escape trunk for this blast to dissipate itself out of the magazine, an explosion in one case would not affect others. Further, it was doubted if 'flash' would pass down to the magazine with the current system of interrupted hoists at a 'working chamber' below the turrets. It is difficult to decide how seriously the 'flash' danger was taken before Jutland. All that can be said is that in the excitement of action all safety precautions built in to the turret/magazine system were nullified by the very understandable desire

on were the high white stern waves of the German ships and their clouds of smoke. Nevertheless they had several advantages; they had the great 15-inch calibre guns which had a flatter trajectory than lesser weapons at any given range, they had 15-foot base-length rangefinders, which while not as long as they might have been, were longer than any in the British battle-cruisers, they had the length of the enemy ships to fire at, thus giving a greater allowance for any ranging error than the width of the ships which was all the battle-cruiser men had, and finally they had recently been with Jellicoe's Grand Fleet in Scapa Flow and had worked up their gunnery in constant exercises; there was no such chance for the battle-cruiser men from their narrow base at Rosyth. All these advantages soon told; the squadron's fire became increasingly effective and spread further up Hipper's line. Within six minutes of opening fire the *Barham* scored a hit on the *Von der Tann*.

Hipper wrote of the 5th Battle Squadron's shooting: 'The fall of shot was practically on one spot as regards both range and deflection. The shooting demonstrated how carefully the British had eliminated all factors that increase the spread of guns firing as a battery, and how thoroughly their fire control installations are perfected [director with elevation control apparatus]. . .'

Beatty's flagship, HMS *Lion,* in action at Jutland after her 'Q' turret had been destroyed by cordite flash after a hit from a heavy shell

of the magazine hands to keep their turrets supplied as fast as they could. To this end it is probable that the lids of some of the cases containing the cordite charges inside the magazine were removed before the charges were needed, and certain that the magazine doors were left open to pass the charges out and that a stockpile of charges with no protection save their own silk cases was left just outside the magazine doors. There was consequently a perfect trail of almost bare cordite leading into the magazine.

To return to the battle, Beatty's turn away from the Germans increased the range to 21,000 yards by 1610 hours, and the battle-cruisers' guns fell silent. However, by this time a new force had entered. Evan-Thomas' 5th Battle Squadron, which had been straining to follow the dark smoke of Beatty's southerly chase, had at last caught up to within 19,000 yards of Hipper's rear, and at 1606 hours his flagship, HMS *Barham,* opened fire with deliberate ranging shots on the *Von der Tann.* This was a prodigious range, over ten miles, and all that the director layers had to sight

Beatty, no doubt heartened by this powerful reinforcement, altered back to a southerly, then a south-easterly course to close on Hipper, who had meanwhile also altered course to close on Beatty and come within gun range of at least one section of his opponents. So the two battle-cruiser forces soon opened fire on each other once more. For Hipper and his men, this stage of the action marks as heroic and successful a feat of arms as is to be found in modern naval history. While both Beatty and Evan-Thomas converged on him from positions just before and slightly abaft his beam, thus bringing an overwhelming weight of shells from nine heavy ships on his five more lightly armed vessels, he held on resolutely, zigzagging due south to bring his shorter range pieces into effective action. His boldness brought early rewards. As the *Lion,* leading the British line, came within range and hit his own flagship *Lützow*, so the *Lützow* replied with such devastating effect that the *Lion* disappeared temporarily beneath a cloud of smoke.

The second ship in the German line was the *Derfflinger*, and her gunnery officer, losing sight of the *Lion* altogether, aimed his broadside at the third British ship, the *Queen Mary*, thinking that she was second and therefore his opposite number. This unfortunate ship was also under fire from her rightful opposite number, SMS *Seydlitz*, and as the range closed quickly the action flared up to a crescendo; the *Queen Mary*, probably the best-shooting ship in the battle-cruiser force, fired full eight-gun salvoes with great precision and rapidity as she found the range. Another point of fierce concentration was at the tail of the German line where the *Von der Tann* found herself under fire from both Beatty's and Evan-Thomas' forces, sometimes as many as four ships concentrating on her, although without any 'concentration fire' systems such as were perfected after Jutland.

The *Derfflinger*/*Seydlitz*/*Queen Mary* duel developed in intensity. The British ship scored first with two shells which started fires in the *Derfflinger*, and followed this up with a succession of near misses which deluged the German decks with sea water and helped to extinguish the flames. At this time Hase was experiencing one of the drawbacks of the German periscope director

when one squeezes it. *There was another dull red glow somewhere forward, and the whole ship seemed to collapse inwards. The funnels and masts fell into the middle and the hull was blown outwards. The roofs of the turrets were blown 100 feet high, then everything was smoke . . .*

As with the *Indefatigable*, one of the *Queen Mary's* magazines had evidently exploded, either from a shell or shell fragment penetrating her armour or from flash passing down an ammunition hoist and entering through an open magazine door. Hase shifted his sights on to the *Princess Royal*.

Meanwhile the British destroyers which Beatty had ordered to attack earlier had reached a position ahead of the battle-cruisers and were steaming towards the German line at full speed. Hipper, who had been undeterred by all the great guns opposed to him, turned his battle-cruisers away together from the torpedo threat; it was the standard counter in both navies. As the little ships raced between the lines of armoured gladiators trading death by ballistic calculation, so the German destroyers came out from the disengaged side of their turning battle-cruisers to meet them, and there followed a fast, disorganised *mêlée*, quick-firing guns in rapid independent, maximum rate of fire, maximum deflection.

After the *mêlée* two German destroyers were seen to be sinking,

By courtesy of Earl Beatty

system; his lens was continually fogged by funnel and gun smoke. He had a midshipman wiping this away with a mop, but there were times when he was entirely dependant on his spotting officer in the fore top, who also had a periscope, the movements of which Hase could follow with his own temporarily blind instrument. However, after seven and a half minutes he straddled the British ship at a range of 14,200 yards and went into rapid fire, which meant a salvo leaving his main armament guns every 20 seconds. Each one of these straddled the British ship.

An officer in the conning tower of the *Tiger*, the *Queen Mary's* next astern, was watching her at the time. *I saw one salvo straddle her. Three shells out of four hit, and the impression one got of seeing the splinters fly and the dull red burst was as if no damage was being done, but that the armour was keeping the shell out. The next salvo I saw straddled her, and two more shells hit her. As they hit I saw a dull, red glow amidships and then the ship seemed to open out like a puffball or one of those toadstool things*

and a British one was stopped in the water; the rest of the British destroyers then chased after Hipper to try to regain position for another torpedo attack. It was while they were racing eastwards that there occurred in the main action one of those moments in which legends are born. A signal rating, looking astern from the *Lion's* bridge, saw a shell hit the *Princess Royal*, which immediately became wrapped in a dense cloud of smoke and disappeared completely, but fortunately not permanently from view. The rating, however, conditioned to sudden disaster, promptly reported the *Princess Royal* sunk. On hearing this Beatty turned to his flag captain, Chatfield, and said in a matter-of-fact tone, 'There seems to be something wrong with our bloody ships today,' after which he ordered an alteration of course two points towards the Germans. [This is not the generally accepted version of the story. As told by Chatfield himself, it was after the loss of the *Queen Mary* that Beatty made his famous remark. If this is so it could not have been followed by the equally famous order to turn toward the Germans; the *Lion* turned away shortly after the loss of the *Queen Mary*. It is, of course, possible that Chatfield and Chalmers (Beatty's biographer) misremembered the actual prelude to Beatty's remark in the stunning concussion of events. The author's version is more flattering to Beatty, and comes from another *Lion* eye-witness, but is given only as a possible alternative to the accepted story.] While this alteration of course was in part caused by the relief afforded by Hipper's turn-away from the threat posed by the destroyers, it was nevertheless a triumph of fighting spirit, and as Churchill has remarked, 'a moment on which British historians will be proud to dwell'. Then the smoke cleared and revealed the *Princess Royal,* the *Tiger* and the *New Zealand* following in perfect station, firing steadily.

Just before this, the light cruiser HMS *Southampton,* some two miles ahead of Beatty, sighted the masts and upperworks of the leading battleships of Scheer's High Seas Fleet advancing from the south-east, and immediately flashed a signal to Beatty. Five minutes later, at 1638 hours, she sent a more detailed report by wireless: 'Have sighted enemy battle-fleet bearing approximately south-east course of enemy north . . .'

'There seems to be something wrong with our bloody ships today . . .'

By this time the head of Scheer's line could be seen from the *Lion* herself. It was a momentous and thrilling sight, the first glimpse for the British officers in two long years of war of the main strength of the German naval challenge. More important, the whole complexion of the battle had altered suddenly and dramatically. At once the protagonists changed rôles. Beatty the hunter, who had been led by Hipper almost into Scheer's arms, turned into Beatty the hunted, whose task was to lead both Hipper and Scheer into Jellicoe's arms. He ordered an immediate alteration of 16 points (180 degrees) to starboard in succession (1640 hours) and led back north-west towards the Grand Fleet, which was by now steaming south-east at forced full speed, 20 knots.

Jellicoe made a signal to the Admiralty, 'Fleet action imminent'. And the signal halyards of the big ships jerked and twisted with a great and growing profusion of battle ensigns; white bunting crossed with red filled the air.

Round one to Hipper
It is interesting to compare the hitting rates of the forces up to the point when the battle took this reverse turn. In the opening 12 minutes between 1548 and 1600 hours the British battle-cruisers scored probably four hits against between 12 and 15 received; Hipper therefore achieved one hit per minute with five ships, Beatty one every three minutes with six. During the rest of the southerly action until the turn at 1640 hours, Beatty's remaining five ships scored probably nine hits against between 24 and 27 received; allowing for time outside effective range this gives very similar hitting rates to those of the previous period, one per $1\frac{1}{4}$ minutes by the Germans against one per $3\frac{1}{2}$ minutes by the British. Evan-Thomas' 5th Battle Squadron, coming into action at extreme range at 1606 hours meanwhile scored probably eight hits against none received before their turn northwards at 1650 hours, some ten minutes after Beatty. It is evident, therefore, that Hipper won the round in terms of hits as well as ships lost.

The reason for the 5th Battle Squadron's late turn north after Beatty was, once again, the fault of flag signalling. The battleship men scarcely saw the *Lion's* hoists before they were steaming

Pictures: Imperial War Museum

How disaster could overtake a great battle-cruiser. *Top:* First blows. HMS *Lion* takes some shells on her 'Q' turret. *Above:* The kill. HMS *Queen Mary* disappears in one huge explosion. *Below:* Aftermath. The pathetic remains of HMS *Indefatigable* sink. *Inset:* Beatty, after his promotion to full Admiral

past the battle-cruisers on a reciprocal course; Evan-Thomas then led round 16 points as ordered, but by that time he was within 21,000 yards of Scheer's van, which concentrated its gunfire on the turning point and hit the so far unscathed squadron nine times in as many minutes. The last ship in the line, HMS *Malaya*, seeing the small area of torn and convulsed sea into which she was heading, put her helm over before time to avoid the inferno.

Some two miles still nearer the High Seas Fleet, the *Southampton* and three other light cruisers of her squadron who had pressed in resolutely to investigate the exact composition of Scheer's fleet were also retiring, leading charmed lives among sprouting columns of water raised by the German shells. They were only saved by exploiting the accuracy of the German range corrections and the extremely close bunching of each salvo; by putting their helms over slightly towards the spot where the last salvo had fallen they were able to anticipate the German corrections and dodge successfully. The men on deck watched fascinated as the 'deadly and graceful splashes' rose mysteriously from the smooth sea around them.

Meanwhile, to the north and east of them, Hipper also had turned northwards to chase Beatty; as he did so the British destroyers pressed 'infernally near' and delivered a torpedo attack before being forced to retire. One torpedo from HMS *Petard* found a mark below the armour belt of the third German battle-cruiser, the *Seydlitz*, and tore a hole 39 feet long in her side with which she nevertheless managed to cope without leaving the line. One British destroyer paid the price of such close action and was brought to a standstill so that she and the destroyer previously stopped in the *mêlée* between the lines became impotent, sitting targets, sunk by Scheer's ships coming up behind Hipper.

So the chase proceeded north-west. In the lead, making something over 24 knots and drawing out of effective gun range, was Beatty with his four remaining battle-cruisers; following some six miles astern was Evan-Thomas with his four battleships going 24 knots and behind them the *Southampton*'s cruiser squadron. To the east Hipper and Scheer were doing their best to keep up, although Hipper was slowed to 22 knots by the torpedo damage to the *Seydlitz*.

'. . . And something wrong with our system.'

During the latter part of the southern chase and the turn, the visibility had greatly favoured the Germans. The sun had been obscured, leaving the western horizon bright, while the eastern horizon remained hazy, so that while the British ships had been silhouetted and still were, the Germans merged into the mist. But now the sun came out again, lighting the German ships, and the 5th Battle Squadron, still within effective range with its own great 15-inch pieces, resumed its former excellent practice on the German battle-cruisers from outside Hipper's own range. During the ten minutes between 1705 and 1715 hours they scored 11 hits against two received from the head of Scheer's line.

Hase's comments on this phase of the action provide the best testimonial to the British policy of heavier guns, offensive rather than defensive power; '. . . this part of the action, fought against a numerically inferior but more powerfully armed enemy who kept us under fire at ranges at which we were helpless was highly depressing, nerve-wracking and exasperating. Our only means of defence was to leave the line for a short time when we saw that the enemy had our range.'

A curious feature of this chase to the north is that Beatty, heading directly for a junction with Jellicoe's Grand Fleet, could not by any stretch of imagination have been making for any British base; all were westerly. It seems astonishing that neither Hipper nor Scheer apparently realised this, but in the heat of the chase followed him blindly into a trap.

As the British ships opened the range, the firing became intermittent; Beatty had lost contact with Hipper, and of the big ships, only Evan-Thomas' squadron was still exchanging shots with Scheer and potting at Hipper. Visibility still favoured the easterly German force greatly, but at extreme range hits were few.

However, by 1735 hours, with Jellicoe's fleet only some 16 miles away and the two forces closing at a combined speed of nearly 40 knots, Beatty altered from his north-north-west course to north-east for the double purpose of regaining contact with Hipper and crossing ahead of the Germans to prevent them seeing the Grand Fleet as it bore down on them. Hipper had meanwhile altered course to the north-west to regain contact with Beatty, and so it was soon after Beatty's alteration that the two battle-cruiser forces sighted each other again and opened fire. This time the advantages were with Beatty. He was now crossing Hipper's 'T', and the sun at last clear and low in the west both dazzled the German gunlayers and lit their ships for the British, who found spotting conditions better than ever before. About the same time the 5th Battle Squadron also opened fire on Hipper, and caught between these two at ranges between 15,000 and 16,000 yards the German battle-cruisers turned north-east and then east as Beatty closed and forced them round. It was a brilliant move; Jellicoe was little more than ten miles to the north-west of the Germans at this point, but Hipper caught no glimpse of him.

Meanwhile Beatty's 3rd Light Cruiser Squadron, ahead of the battle-cruisers, had sighted Jellicoe's cruiser HMS *Black Prince* at the extreme western end of the line of cruisers ahead of the Grand Fleet, and at 1740 hours, about the time Hipper was forced off to the north-east, the *Black Prince* herself made out Beatty's battle-cruisers through the murk of the northward action. Shortly afterwards two more of Jellicoe's cruisers were sighted by Beatty's force. It was a moment of intense relief and excitement.

'I can hardly even now describe the thrill we all felt — the Grand Fleet had arrived.'

For the Germans, though, it was the beginning of a period of infinite confusion, frustration and rapidly increasing danger. Even as Hipper turned east across the line of advance of the Grand Fleet he heard, incredibly, gunfire from right ahead in a position that no British ships from Beatty's force could possibly have reached. This was Rear-Admiral Hood's 3rd Battle-Cruiser Squadron and attached cruisers, which Jellicoe had previously ordered forward independently to support Beatty. Hood had steered east to cut the Germans off from their bases, and this, combined with natural errors in the estimated positions of the two British forces, had taken him down 15 miles east of Hipper. His ships soon disappeared in the patchy mist, but not before Scheer had received a report of enemy 'heavy ships' in the east.

PETER PADFIELD was trained for the sea aboard HMS *Worcester*, and subsequently served as an officer on the P & O Line. After leaving P & O in his late twenties for a job ashore in industry he began writing naval and merchant naval history, first attracting international notice with *The Titanic and the Californian* in 1965. He then turned to writing as a full-time occupation. His other books include *An Agony of Decisions* urging the need for reform in the collision regulations, *Aim Straight* and *Broke and the Shannon*, both biographies of great naval gunnery officers. He has just finished a history of naval gunnery, tracing the influence of the developing art of gunnery on naval tactics.

The Fleets

JUTLAND

Lured on by Beatty, Scheer suddenly found himself faced by the might of the Grand Fleet, perfectly deployed for action. Poor visibility and expert seamanship enabled Scheer to escape, but on turning for home waters he ran into Jellicoe again. In the action that followed, many ships were mauled and another British battle-cruiser lost before the Germans broke away once more
Vice-Admiral Friedrich Ruge

Collide

Below: Two years of waiting, and now the final clash: a dreadnought unleashes a salvo from her main armament at her opposite number

The situation when the main fleets met was influenced by several factors. The foremost was the difficulty faced by the commanders-in-chief in trying to get something like a clear picture of the disposition of their own forces and those of the enemy. And though wireless Intelligence had been greatly improved since its inception, much was still left to guesswork and intuition.

After contact between the two fleets had been made, visibility continued to play an important part in all decisions. Both fleets covered large areas, and during its pursuit of the British battle-cruisers, the German fleet stretched over 20 miles from the foremost scouts to the tail of the battle line. The fleet flagships were stationed in central positions, which made observation difficult, but smoke from hundreds of funnels, together with artificial smoke screens, soon aggravated the natural haze. It proved impossible for the commanders-in-chief to keep the whole of their own forces in sight, let alone those of the enemy. Binoculars were of great use and rangefinders helped, but as yet there was nothing like radar, and so the commanders had to rely to a great extent on the reports of their scouting forces, combined with their own intuition and judgement.

This became strikingly evident when Admiral Jellicoe had to decide which way to deploy his Battle Fleet. During the battle-cruiser action, the Battle Fleet had continued to steer south-east in six columns, with a screen of cruisers about five miles ahead. It was most trying for Jellicoe that he did not receive a single report on the position of the German heavy ships between 1700 and 1740 hours. HMS *Lion* did not pass any messages to HMS *Princess Royal* for onward transmission to Jellicoe (as was normal procedure), but the 3rd and particularly the 1st Light Cruiser Squadrons were all the time excellently placed to observe the German battle-cruisers and the van of the German battle fleet too. They relayed no information, however, although at 1713 hours Jellicoe gave his own position, course and speed as at 1700 hours to the Battle-Cruiser Fleet.

As a result of various errors, there was a discrepancy in the dead reckoning of the two British flagships, which placed them five and a half miles too far apart. In this way the Battle-Cruiser Fleet drew the Germans towards the British main fleet, but did not give Jellicoe the bearings he so desperately needed to deploy his battleships at the right moment and in the best tactical way.

As his fleet was much superior numerically as well as in the number and calibre of heavy guns, Jellicoe's plan was to form a single line ahead, if possible at right angles to the approaching German fleet, thus crossing its 'T', and so to bring an overwhelming weight of fire to bear on its van. To do so successfully, he needed accurate information of the position, course and speed of the German fleet. In exercises, Jellicoe had tried several methods of deployment and had gained much experience in handling his fleet. In addition to this, he possessed the equanimity and keenness indispensable in a man manoeuvring 150 fast-moving ships in quickly changing situations.

While Jellicoe waited for the information on which to base his decisive manoeuvre, quite a number of events happened at very short intervals. At 1735 hours Beatty altered course from north-north-west to north-north-east. It is not known whether he did so to steer clear of his own Battle Fleet or to get closer to his German opponents. The German battle-cruisers also altered to this new course because they came under heavy fire from the 5th Battle Squadron, of whom they could see nothing except gun flashes. SMS *Derfflinger*, for example, did not fire a single salvo from 1742 to 1816 hours, but was hit repeatedly.

As a consequence of Beatty's manoeuvre, the *1st Scouting Group* did not run straight into the arms of Jellicoe, which it would have done if it had continued on its original course. A minute later, the German *2nd Scouting Group*, which had kept its position about four miles north-east of SMS *Lützow,* sighted and attacked the British light cruiser HMS *Chester.* This ship was scouting on the starboard bow of the 3rd Battle-Cruiser Squadron, which was still steering south-south-east and which, in the decreasing visibility, might have passed the German van completely but for this encounter.

A posthumous VC

With her six 5.5-inch guns, the *Chester* was no match for the four German light cruisers, with 30 5.9-inch guns in all. Within a few minutes she received 17 hits, half her guns and all her fire control apparatus were out of action and she had had 30 of her crew killed and 46 wounded, almost one fifth of her ship's company. Fatally injured, Boy 1st Class John T. Cornwell (aged 16), remained at his post at one of the guns and was awarded a posthumous Victoria Cross. In spite of the heavy damage, the *Chester* succeeded in throwing the German fire out by zigzagging and by using her high speed, which she was able to keep up as her engines were unharmed.

When this fight began, Rear-Admiral Hood, commanding the 3rd Battle-Cruiser Squadron, changed course to starboard and steered north-west to intercept the pursuers of the *Chester.* At 1755 hours the Germans came in sight at a range of 11,000 yards at the most. They were taken completely by surprise, all the more so as two minutes earlier their attention had been drawn to the opposite flank by gunfire apparently directed at them but falling very short. Here freak visibility had enabled the armoured cruisers HMS *Defence* and HMS *Warrior,* stationed ahead of the main British fleet, to sight the *2nd Scouting Group* at a distance of about 20,000 yards, but this was out of range of their old guns. More effective, however, was the fire of the 12-inch guns of the three *Invincibles.* The German light cruiser SMS *Wiesbaden* soon lay stopped with both engines disabled, while SMS *Pillau* was reduced to 24 knots after a shell had put four boilers out of action. She found shelter, however, in a smoke screen, as did SMS *Frankfurt* and SMS *Elbing.*

What influenced the course of the battle more than the damage to the two light cruisers was the sudden appearance of British heavy ships east of the German battle-cruisers. They were taken for battleships with their tripod masts, and were reported as such. The three destroyer flotillas attached to the *Scouting Force* (the *2nd, 6th* and *9th*) and waiting on the disengaged side of the battle-cruisers now tried to attack the new adversary to the east. Some of them met with four destroyers of the British 4th Destroyer Flotilla, led by Commander Loftus Jones in HMS *Shark.* A sharp brush ensued, in which the *Shark* was hit and stopped, and HMS *Acasta* severely damaged. On the German side only the *B 98* was hit: her mast fell overboard and the twin torpedo tubes aft were put out of action. The German light cruisers and destroyers launched a number of torpedoes at the British ships but the *Shark* was their only victim.

That the 3rd Battle-Cruiser Squadron, reinforcing Beatty on Jellicoe's orders, was a number of miles east and ahead of the *Iron Duke* would not have been important but for the fact that it broke up the strong concentration of German destroyers just before the deployment of the British Battle Fleet. From their favourable position the three German flotillas could have launched a mass attack which might have brought considerable results.

Scheer, of course, was fully aware of the superiority of the Grand Fleet in numbers and gun calibre. His aim, therefore, was to surprise the British and to catch only part of their forces. In fact he had already done so, but from his point of view it was unfortunate that not a single British ship had been reduced in speed. Two had blown up, but the others had got away. Should he be confronted with the whole might of the Royal Navy he planned to avoid a gunnery duel at long range by very mobile tactics, by the use of smoke screens and by massed destroyer attacks.

The same visibility that had revealed the *2nd Scouting Group* to the *Defence* and the *Warrior* enabled Beatty's battle-cruisers to keep their opposite numbers under fire. When Hipper saw his ships being hit repeatedly without being able to answer, he ordered a turn together of 180 degrees (1759 hours). This brought him back to the German battle fleet. Eleven minutes later he swung round again to take up station ahead of SMS *König,* now less than a mile away.

During these events the British Battle Fleet steamed on at 20 knots, still in its compact cruising formation of six columns. At 1750 hours HMS *Southampton* correctly reported that the German battle fleet had changed course to the north, but put the German battle-cruisers to the south-west of their battleships, whereas they actually were to the north-north-east. Again, there was a discrepancy in the mutual positions. In the same minute, HMS *Calliope,* flagship of 4th Light Cruiser Squadron, stationed about three miles ahead of the Battle Fleet and in visual touch with Jellicoe, reported by searchlight that there were gunflashes at a bearing south-south-west. This was the *Lion,* but the ships themselves could not yet be made out. At the same time, Vice-Admiral Sir Cecil Burney in HMS *Marlborough,* leading the starboard wing column, reported 'gun flashes on the starboard bow'. Jellicoe asked him by searchlight for details at 1755 hours. Five minutes later the *Lion* could be made out from the bridge of the *Iron Duke.* At 1801 hours and again at 1810 hours Jellicoe asked Beatty by searchlight: 'Where is enemy battle fleet?' In between (at 1802 hours) he gave orders by flags to change course by columns to the south, evidently in preparation for deploying on the starboard (right) wing which would have corresponded to the tactics evolved in exercises. It would have put the Grand Fleet in a favourable position, because the Germans would have been compelled to fire against the sun, which was already rather low over the horizon. It would also have facilitated cutting off the German fleet from retreating towards Heligoland, a move which figured prominently in the British plans. However, only four minutes later (1806 hours) Jellicoe ordered his columns to turn back to the south-east, for he still had no information on the whereabouts of the German battle fleet. The moment for deployment to starboard was gone beyond recall. At 1814 hours Beatty reported 'Enemy battle fleet SSW', and immediately afterwards (1815 hours) Jellicoe made the signal for deployment to port on the course south-east by east (122 degrees). He had delayed as long as possible, and in consequence some of the British units had got into awkward situations, for the cruisers and part of the destroyer flotillas were still screening the Battle Fleet while some flotillas had just begun to move to their battle stations in compliance with a flag signal hoisted a few minutes before, and a simultaneous wireless message.

Action now was fast and furious in several places. The destroyer HMS *Onslow* (Lieutenant-Commander J. C. Tovey) had tenaciously kept on the engaged bow of the *Lion* all the time and now made for the disabled *Wiesbaden* to attack her with guns and torpedoes

Naval power incarnate: a line of British dreadnoughts steams on towards the great clash with the embodiment of Germany's dream of naval supremacy— the High Seas Fleet. Note how the signal flags flying from the yards are being blown out by the wind and partially obscured by funnel smoke, both factors which materially affected the outcome of the battle, particularly in the battle-cruiser action in the afternoon.

since the German ship was in a position to launch torpedoes at the British battle-cruisers. Rear-Admiral Sir Robert Arbuthnot in the *Defence,* in company with the *Warrior,* also set course for the *Wiesbaden,* bent on destroying her. He crossed the *Lion's* bows and compelled Beatty's flagship to make a sharp turn to port to avoid a collision. *Wiesbaden* still defended herself hotly and obtained several hits. At 1815 hours the two old British armoured cruisers suddenly came into full view of the van of the German battle fleet and at least six of the German ships opened a tremendous fire upon them, at a distance of no more than 7,500 yards. After five minutes, the *Defence* disintegrated in a terrific detonation which could be seen and felt by most ships on either side. Not a man survived.

The *Warrior* continued to fire at the *Wiesbaden,* but was compelled to turn away severely damaged. She was saved from annihilation then and there only by the fortuitous intervention of the *Warspite.* When the deployment of the Battle Fleet began, Rear-Admiral Evan-Thomas in HMS *Barham* had assumed that the *Marlborough* would lead and had manoeuvred to take up station ahead of her. To do so he altered course to the east, in the direction of the German battleships. When he saw that the fleet deployed to port it was clear to him that he could not reach the van without interfering seriously with the gunnery of many of his own ships. Therefore he decided to take station astern of the battle line and turned back. But he was soon compelled to slow down, for there was not yet room for his squadron. When the columns turned 90 degrees to port to form line ahead, some were too extended, those behind them had to decrease speed and the rear of the long line was badly bunched up. Moreover, the light cruisers and destroyers on their way to their battle stations at the head and the rear of the line crossed the course of the battle squadrons, which were exchanging a lively fire with the leading German battleships.

Ocean torn up by shells

An officer who witnessed this scene from a British light cruiser described his experiences as follows: *The point where all this turning took place has been called Windy Corner. It well earned its name. Apart from the risk and excitement of 15 or 20 large ships and 30 or 40 small ships all converging on to a point from every direction, the Germans were concentrating a heavy fire into the 'brown' or the turning point so that the whole ocean was torn up by shell splashes, and the noise was terrific. Every ship was steaming at high speed, and the majority of them were vigorously replying to the German fire by firing their own broadsides over the heads of any light craft that lay between them and the enemy . . . There was handling of ships in that ten minutes of crossing the battlefleet's front such as had never been dreamt of by seamen before.*

In this confused situation the steering engine of the *Warspite* jammed and put her helm at 20 degrees starboard. She barely missed the stern of HMS *Valiant* and continued to turn. Her captain decided to go on at full speed as long as the helm could not be moved. The *Warspite* completed two full circles, confusing the laying of the German fire but herself replying vigorously with all her guns. Nevertheless, she received at least 11 hits by heavy shells, but her stout construction saved her and bad visibility enabled her to get away after the helm had been repaired. By her spectacular stunt the *Warspite* saved the *Warrior,* which with the last revolutions of her engines succeeded in creeping past until she remained stopped just outside the sight of the German gun-layers. Two hours later she was taken in tow by the seaplane carrier HMS *Engadine* but had to be abandoned the next morning. She lost 71 killed and 36 injured of a total of 822.

In spite of the hammering the *Warspite* had received, her main fighting elements—guns, engines and conning tower—were almost unimpaired. A great part of the living quarters were wrecked. The Executive Officer described a hit thus: *A 12-inch shell came through side armour in boys' mess deck. Terrific sheet of golden*

Iron grey against a sea of grey and a sky of grey: Britain's survival resting in steel hulls stretching back to the horizon

flame, stink, impenetrable dust, everything seemed to fall everywhere with an appalling noise. And somewhat later: *Went aft again and found my cabin had been completely removed overboard. Lobby in an awful state, and hole about 12-feet diameter in the centre of the deck. Lot of burning debris in my cabin which we put out. In the middle of this heap was my wife's miniature, without its case, but otherwise perfect.*

Where shell hit the deck, planks and fastenings were removed as cleanly as if they had been shovelled away, in several places over an area of 10 or 12 square feet.

However, the *Warspite* had several large shell holes in the waterline. Through them much water entered the ship, where it exerted dangerous pressure on the engine room bulkheads when the battleship steamed at high speed. Therefore she was reduced to 16 knots at most but at 2050 hours she reported repairs complete and asked for the Germans' position. Admiral Evan-Thomas ordered her to return to Rosyth directly, however.

The concentration of ships at 'Windy Corner' gave Admiral Scheer the idea of 'doubling', attacking from two sides. To do so SMS *Friedrich der Grosse* would have turned to port and steered about north-west followed by the rest of the battle line. This would probably have meant the end of the *Warrior* and possibly of the *Warspite*, particularly as the visibility would have been better. The main difficulty faced by Scheer was in maintaining contact between the two parts of the battle fleet, however, and in bringing them together again at the right time. The manoeuvre had never been tried by a modern fleet although it was well known in the times of sail. There was no short signal for it, and after a brief discussion with his chief-of-staff, Admiral Scheer abandoned this promising plan.

While the *Defence* was being destroyed by German fire, the *Onslow* fired 58 rounds at the *Wiesbaden* and then advanced to attack the ships of the *1st Scouting Group* with torpedoes. After receiving two 6-inch shells in the forward boiler room she fell back and fired one torpedo at the *Wiesbaden*, and this detonated under her bridge. Then this tough destroyer launched her last two torpedoes at the approaching German battleships but scored no hits. She took three more shells but managed to get away, until she came to a dead stop near the circling *Warspite*. When the battle had moved away she was joined and taken in tow (1915 hours) by the destroyer HMS *Defender* whose foremost boiler room had been wrecked by a 12-inch shell which failed to explode but nevertheless reduced her speed to ten knots. Their homeward journey was described by Rudyard Kipling under the apt title *The Cripple and the Paralytic*.

And still more happened in those crowded minutes. While the British main fleet was forming line ahead with an angle of 60 degrees where one division after the other changed course from north-east to east-south-east, and Beatty's force still blanketed a good deal of its fire, quite a number of battleships made out the unfortunate *Wiesbaden*. Each fired a number of salvoes at her and claimed to have sunk her. However, she remained afloat. Scheer received several reports about her, and in an attempt to help her, he ordered a turn together of two points to port (at 1818

hours) but the German battleships were not able to keep this course for more than a few minutes because they, as well as the battle-cruisers, now came under tremendous fire on the new course. Evidently, they could be clearly seen by the British, whereas they had nothing but a seemingly endless line of rippling flashes before them. The *Derfflinger* retorted directly to Scheer: '*1st Scouting Group* turning away because observation against the sun impossible', not to mention the numerous hits which the leading ships had received. Scheer realised the situation clearly enough to permit all ships, by flag signal, 'to manoeuvre by independent turns' to throw the British range and aim out.

When, on the British side, Hood in the *Invincible* sighted the *Lion*, he reversed course by a turn to starboard in succession and now (1820 hours) led the British line. At a distance of 11,000 yards and less his three battle-cruisers opened a heavy fire and repeatedly hit the *Lützow*, *Derfflinger* and *König*. Hood told the gunnery officer of his flagship: 'Your firing is very good. Keep at it as quickly as you can. Every shot is telling.' But now visibility improved for the German battle-cruisers. Between large areas of artificial and funnel smoke, a wide lane to a clear horizon suddenly opened, with the *Invincible* in sharp outline in the middle, no more than 9,500 yards away. The *Derfflinger* and *Lützow* found the range at once, and their first salvoes straddled and hit the target. Then the *Invincible*'s 'Q' turret blew up, throwing its roof high into the air, the magazines exploded and the large ship literally broke in two. Both halves came to rest on the bottom of the sea in a depth of about 150 to 180 feet, in an upright position with stern and bows high above the surface (1833 hours).

Only six survivors

There were only six survivors out of a crew of more than 1,000 men. The gunnery officer had 'simply stepped from the falling foretop into the water' as he put it when rescued by the destroyer HMS *Badger*. He and three of his ratings had at once found a raft, from which they had already cheered the *Indomitable*, the next astern but one, when she passed them. The other survivors were a lieutenant who had been in the conning tower, and a marine from the after part of a turret. He simply did not know how he got into the water alive. The *Badger* had been sent to the rescue by Beatty, though her captain thought he had to deal with the wreck of a German ship, and had not only a doctor but also an armed guard ready to deal with the prisoners.

During these events the light cruiser HMS *Canterbury* kept to the east of the German fleet all by herself. Scouting ahead of the 3rd Battle-Cruiser Squadron on its run to the south-south-east she had joined action with some German destroyers and the *2nd Scouting Group,* and continued to shadow them on their southerly courses, exchanging a few salvoes. She was hit once only, by a dud. At 1820 hours she turned to the north and came into an excellent position to watch the next important event, the first German battle turn.

For Scheer it proved as difficult to get an exact picture of the tactical situation as it had been for Jellicoe. Only for rare moments could British ships be made out distinctly from the German flag-

ship. Heavy fire forced the *3rd Battle Squadron*, which was leading, to fall off more and more to starboard. The battle-cruisers were evidently under strong British pressure, too. An attack by the *3rd Torpedoboat Flotilla* on the British van, ordered by *Kommodore* Michelsen, the leader of the group of torpedoboats, might have brought relief but was called off by him just after it had started (1832 hours) because he wanted to conserve his destroyer strength for later emergencies. A few torpedoes were launched, however, and did reach the British battle-cruisers. But they were sighted in time and the British vessels avoided them.

On turning back, the German destroyers met the crippled *Shark*, which fought back furiously with her remaining 4-inch gun. She disabled the *V 48*, probably with a hit in an engine room (1840 hours). From then on, the *V 48* could move only very slowly at best. Attempts to help her failed, she was sighted and fired at by several British ships and finally sunk by ships of 2nd Light Cruiser Squadron (1850 hours). There were no survivors. The *Shark* herself could not be kept afloat. About 30 men took to two damaged rafts, though most of the survivors were compelled to hold to the life lines. At 1900 hours the *Shark* sank, and three hours later a Danish ship picked up the last six survivors. Lieutenant-Commander Loftus Jones, who had lost a leg during the last attack on his ship, was not among them. He was awarded a Victoria Cross.

To get the situation in hand again, Scheer ordered a battle turn together of 16 points to starboard as a manoeuvre quickly to reverse course with the whole battle fleet. The cruisers and destroyers had to turn as best they could on the edges of the main fleet. On the whole, the British and German admirals had much the same ideas on the problems of leading large numbers of warships of various types in battle, but, in this method of completely reversing the course the Germans were one step ahead. Under normal conditions an evolution is prepared by hoisting a flag signal on the flagship and executed simultaneously the moment this signal is hauled down. In battle this could lead to difficult situations and even collisions, because the formation might be in disorder and vision of the signal obscured. Therefore this kind of complete turn around was begun from the rear when the last ship had received the signal. This was very short, one flag only or two words by wireless; every effort was made to get it through the line rapidly. The signal was not only flown from the bridges fore and aft but also from a battle signal station amidships on the disengaged side. In addition, there was a special short-range wireless station for battle signals in the conning tower of each big ship. As soon as the last ship had received the signal she started turning to starboard with standard helm and showed this by flying green flags (for a battle turn to port red ones) from several battle stations. As soon as the next ship ahead saw these flags she put her helm over, and so on. With this method each ship turned away from the next one, and the danger of collisions was reduced as much as possible. This was one of a number of tactical moves in battle. The signals were short and terse, the entire system simple and therefore practicable even under great stress.

In training their fleet, the Germans had put great value on encouraging commanders and captains to take the initiative in accordance with the situation. Therefore Captain Redlich, the commanding officer of the *Westfalen*, the rearmost dreadnought of the *1st Battle Squadron*, started the battle turn on sighting battle Signal Green (1836 hours) and the pre-dreadnoughts of the *2nd Battle Squadron* followed his ship. However, the old pre-dreadnoughts had not been able to keep the speed of the newer ships and were about a mile behind, so there was no danger of collision. They conformed at once, turning more quickly than their larger brothers. The whole manoeuvre went without a hitch although the theoretically straight line from the *Lützow* to the *Westfalen*, eight miles long, was bent almost to a semicircle, and the van was under heavy fire. SMS *Markgraf* was hit while turning, and a shell descended on the conning tower of the *König*, glanced off and burst about 50 yards away, its splinters wounding several people, among then *Konteradmiral* Behncke (tall, gaunt and dark, with a short greying beard, called 'the Arab Sheik' because he looked exactly like one) who continued, however, to lead his *3rd Battle Squadron*.

The battle-cruisers followed the battleships with the exception of the *Lützow* which was damaged so severely and was so much down by the bows that she could not keep up speed and manoeuvre in company. Several destroyers hid her by laying smoke screens between her and the British line. This may have prevented the *Canterbury* from getting a picture of the situation although she must have seen part of the battle turn at least. In any case she joined the 3rd Battle-Cruiser Squadron again and stationed herself on its disengaged bow without making any special report. The *Lützow* was not fit to act as flagship any longer. From the translation of a book on the battle of Tsushima he had made some time ago *Korvettenkapitän* (Commander) (later *Grossadmiral)* Raeder recalled the unfortunate consequences of the Russian Admiral Rojestvensky clinging too long to his damaged flagship. In his capacity as 1st Operations Officer he persuaded Admiral Hipper, but only with difficulty, to change over to another battle-cruiser. The admiral and his staff went aboard the *G 39* which was called alongside. Hipper intended to go to his old flagship *Seydlitz*. He ordered Captain Hartog of the *Derfflinger* to lead the battle-cruisers until he could take over again. But the battle had now reached its climax and the *Seydlitz* was too much damaged already to act as flagship. It took them a long time to be transferred to the *Moltke*.

A single hit

By 1840 hours the battle turn had been completed, and Scheer gave west as the general course. On the British side the full extent of the German manoeuvre was not realised at the time. The Grand Fleet was now in perfect order after some bunching caused by a temporary reduction of speed. It now steamed at 17 knots, the battleships preceeded by the six battle-cruisers whose lead the *Lion* took again. Visibility was baffling, in some places hardly 2,000 yards, in others more than ten miles. Most ships had no targets, but the *Wiesbaden* and the *V 48* came under fire again, although neither was sunk. At around 1850 hours the rear divisions of the Grand Fleet sighted battleships far away to the southwest and a few ships took them under fire and obtained a single

HMS *Agincourt* (foreground) with HMS *Erin* beyond her. The *Agincourt* carried the largest number of heavy guns mounted on any one capital ship: 14 12-inch guns in seven centreline turrets. The *Erin* was armed with ten 13.5-inch guns in five turrets. Both ships were originally ordered by foreign buyers (the *Erin* by Turkey and the *Agincourt* by Brazil) but taken over by Britain at the beginning of the war

hit, on the *Markgraf,* at 20,000 yards. The van passed the wreck of the *Invincible,* while the destroyer *Acasta,* severely damaged by several shells, came to a stop and lay out of control a few hundred yards off the engaged side of the battle line. Its crew greeted each passing ship with loud cheers. Beatty turned first to south-south-east (1853 hours) and then to south, reducing speed to 18 knots in order to prevent his distance from the battleships becoming too great. At this moment *Lion* had a gyro failure and turned a whole circle, because in making an S turn to give the battle fleet time to catch up, Beatty forgot to reverse his helm. When this happened, the *Marlborough,* near the rear of the line, was hit by a torpedo (1854 hours) probably fired by the *Wiesbaden,* which punched a hole 70 feet long and 20 feet deep at the place of impact abreast of the starboard forward hydraulic engine room. She took a list to starboard but could keep up 17 knots, although water seeped into the forward boiler rooms and some bulkheads came under a considerable strain.

All this contributed in hiding the fundamental change in the situation from Jellicoe, although this state of affairs could not have lasted much longer in any case. Now Scheer took the initiative again by another battle turn. The High Seas Fleet reversed course to the east and again headed for the British battle line. Scheer did not know this for certain, for he had no accurate picture of the situation, but his intention was to come to grips with the British again. His main reason for this move was, as he put it, 'to surprise the enemy by a heavy blow against his battle line and to enforce a situation favourable for a mass attack by the destroyer flotillas'. If he continued to steer west he was sure that the British fleet would soon locate him and attack him in overwhelming strength. By taking the offensive himself he expected to bridge the interval of about an hour until it would be too dark for a general action between the battle fleets, but give the destroyer flotillas an opportunity for a night attack. He also hoped that it would be possible to aid the *Wiesbaden,* or at least to take her crew off.

On the British side, Jellicoe (at 1856 hours) ordered his fleet to change course by divisions to approximately south by east (167 degrees). At the same time he received several reports of submarine sightings (which actually were not there) and of the torpedo hit on the *Marlborough.* Commodore Goodenough gave a correct report (1900 hours) on the position and easterly course of the German fleet. Three minutes later the *Iron Duke* passed the wreck of a big ship and was informed by the destroyer *Badger* that it was the *Invincible.* Immediately afterwards, the British battleships again sighted German ships and began to fire on them. Jellicoe decided to speed up the approach and at 1905 hours ordered his battleships to turn together three points to starboard to about south-south-west (201 degrees). However, he held this course only for four minutes and then turned back to south by east (167 degrees) under the impression of what seemed to be a planned destroyer attack on the centre of the British line. Actually the *5th Half-Flotilla* was making an attempt to save the crew of the *Wiesbaden,* but came under such a heavy fire (mainly from the *Colossus* Division of the 1st Battle Squadron) that it was forced to turn away prematurely. In doing so, the *V 73* fired one torpedo,

the *G 88* three. Neither the British shells nor German torpedoes found targets. The torpedo tracks were sighted by HMS *Neptune* and the *Barham,* who had sufficient time to avoid the torpedoes.

Now most of the British battleships could make out their targets and began shooting in earnest, whereas the Germans rarely saw more than the flashes. Again they were heading into an arc of deadly fire. Soon Scheer realised that he would lead his fleet into annihilation if he kept on much longer, for the British gunnery was becoming increasingly effective. Visibility was still very patchy and each battleship had only a few German ships in sight at the same time. Ranges varied from 19,000 yards down finally to 8,000 yards.

In order to support the destroyer flotillas at the head of the line, Scheer at 1903 hours hoisted the battle signal '9 R', in German *'Panzerkreuzer ran!',* 'Battle-cruisers, go at them regardless of consequences.' This they did, battered, as they were. The *Derfflinger* (Captain Hartog) led the charge, for the *Lützow* now was entirely out of action after receiving 23 heavy shells, and was moving slowly to the south-west. A death-ride, and they knew it.

In the *Seydlitz,* the second ship, Captain von Egidy wanted to bring home to his men what was about to happen. Therefore he ordered the ratings manning the telephones in the conning tower to pass on the following message:

'From Captain to Ship: Signal from C-in-C Fleet: *Schlachtkreuzer ran!'*

As they had been trained, the men transmitted this message in measured and well-articulated tones to all battle-stations. The confirmations came from below in the same monotonous way. *Then,* as Captain von Egidy reported it later, *there followed a kind of awed hush for a second or two, the ship seemed to hold its breath. Then they had grasped the idea, and through voice pipes, ventilation shafts and armoured passages an echo came back to the commanding officer which literally caused his heart to beat faster. The whole ship was one great wave of enthusiasm, they cheered, some sang the national anthem, others the* Wacht am Rhein, *stokers hammered with their shovels at bulkheads, over and again they shouted* 'Drauf, Seydlitz!' *('Attack, Seydlitz!'), the battle cry of the Seydlitz cuirassiers of the Seven Years War, which we had adopted for our ship.* 'Drauf, Seydlitz!' *now was to lead us to the attack.*

Meanwhile (from 1915 hours onwards) the *3rd, 6th* and *9th Flotillas* overtook the battle-cruisers and went at full speed into the blazing crescent formed by 33 big British ships with their numerous cruisers and destroyers. Only 17 of the original 27 destroyers could take part, for three were out of action, while the others were on tasks such as assisting the *Lützow* or trying to help the *Wiesbaden.* Had the German battle-cruisers drawn the British fire in preparing the way for the mass attack, this would soon have brought relief to the hard pressed *1st Scouting Group.* The distance between the lines was so short that the destroyers were recognised and fired on as soon as they left the pall of smoke and fumes obscuring the German van. Soon several German boats were hit, but all kept on until they could fire their torpedoes, 33 in all, at distances between 8,000 and 6,000 yards. Turning away

Below left and right: Gunnery officers, German and British. For two years they had been able only to practise, but now the outcome of the war depended on their skills. Both were drawn from the Deck or Executive branch of their respective services. *Bottom left:* SMS *König* opens fire. Note her broad beam, making for a steady firing platform. *Bottom right:* The main action of Jutland. It is easy to see how the haze, smoke, shell explosions and cordite fumes soon fouled the range

they tried to throw out the British fire control by putting up smoke screens and making sharp changes of course. The *S 35*, however, received a heavy shell amidships, broke in two and sank with her entire crew and all the men she had rescued from the *V 29*.

Not a single one of so many torpedoes damaged a British ship, but nevertheless they had a considerable tactical impact. Both sides knew the dangers from mass attacks of this kind and had developed tactics to counter it. Exercises had shown that there existed a sizeable chance of several torpedoes hitting unless the targets turned away several points and then individually manoeuvred away from the torpedo tracks if these could be made out. In a comparatively smooth sea this was not difficult because the compressed air driving the engine of the torpedo drew a fast advancing line of bubbles on the surface. It had to be taken into account that the torpedo itself streaked along under water some dozens of yards ahead of that line.

Other measures were to turn into the tracks, a manoeuvre which gave less time for evasive action, however, or to intercept the attack in an early stage with light cruisers and destroyers. It was also possible to combine the two methods.

Jellicoe chose the surest way. When the attackers reached positions favourable for launching their torpedoes, he ordered the battleships to turn away two points (at 1922 hours) and when this appeared insufficient, two more points (1925 hours). The conditions of sea and light were good for track spotting, but even so a hectic few minutes ensued for some ships.

At least ten British battleships sighted tracks, and most of them were compelled to avoid them by the energetic use of helm and engines. Even so it was a question of luck. The *Marlborough*, already damaged, sighted three tracks on the starboard bow and turned into them. One passed ahead, the next one very close to the stern, which was swinging away from it, while the third broke surface abeam and then dived under again. Then its track hit the battleship amidships, but not the torpedo, which had probably dived too deep when it disappeared from the surface again.

The distance from bridge to bridge of the various vessels was about 550 yards, the ships themselves almost 200 yards long. When suddenly they had to turn with full helm and high speed, some awkward situations were bound to result. However, collisions were avoided by skilful ship-handling and by what Jellicoe called in his memoirs 'neighbourly conduct towards each other'. Yet rapid changes of course and speed were inconvenient for gunnery and so most ships lost sight of their targets, their fire slackened and eventually ceased altogether.

But avoiding torpedoes was not the only reason for the diminishing contact. When Scheer saw that at least two of his battle-cruisers were heavily damaged, and fire from three directions (to quote his war diary) forced the van to turn away more and more, he repeated his orders to the flotillas to attack and at the same time (1918 hours) hoisted the signal for another battle-turn to starboard to reverse course. This was more difficult than before because the battle line was curved, distances between ships very small in some places (nominally 500 metres or 550 yards) and the British fire so heavy that several ships temporarily left the line to avoid concentrated salvoes. Here, too, neighbourly behaviour pre-

Julian Allen

Bayr. Armée Museum

vented collisions, the fleet flagship setting an example when at Scheer's suggestion, the *Friedrich der Grosse* turned to port instead of starboard to make more room for the others. A few ships slowed down and changed positions but soon the battle-fleet was on a westerly course which Scheer in a short time changed to south-west (1928 hours).

Immediately before and during the third battle turn, a number of German ships were severely punished. The *Markgraf* received four heavy shells within two minutes of turning whereas SMS *Kronprinz Wilhelm*, the next astern, was shaken violently by near-misses but not struck once during the entire battle. Again the battle-cruisers suffered the gravest damage. In the *Derfflinger* all the 6-inch guns of the port battery were put out of action. Then the right gun of the fourth turret received a direct hit which slewed the whole turret round and ignited some cordite charges. With the exception of one rating, everybody inside was killed and the turret silenced. A few minutes later a similar fate overtook the third turret and its crew. In both cases the magazines could be flooded in time. Simultaneously the conning tower was struck by a 12-inch shell which, however, did not pierce the armour but shook the whole tower to its foundations. Several officers and men were injured by splinters and yellow gasses got in through the vision slits. Gas masks proved helpful until the air was pure again. The *Lützow* and the *Seydlitz* were also hit, although the latter retaliated by putting two shells into the battleship *Colossus*, which, however, caused little damage other than wounding five men. Around 1945 hours both sides ceased firing entirely.

Later on, the tactics of both commanders-in-chief in this part of the battle were criticised in some quarters, Jellicoe's as too cautious, Scheer's as too crude. The task of the British navy was not primarily to destroy the High Seas Fleet regardless of costs, but to ensure that Great Britain continued to have unimpeded use of the vital sea lanes on the one hand and to deny them to the Germans.

Jellicoe was much impressed by the dangers to his fleet during a general action from 'an intelligent use of submarines, mines, and torpedoes' as he put it himself. In a letter to the Admiralty dated October 30, 1914, he had outlined his overall plan to fight a general fleet action only in the northern North Sea, not near the German bases. In battle he was going to rely on his gunnery superiority and to avoid the threat from the German underwater weapons as much as possible. His turn away on recognising the mass attack of the German destroyers was fully in accordance with this plan, which the Admiralty had approved.

Neither commander-in-chief had anything like a comprehensive picture of the situation. The technical development of means of extensive reconnaissance had not kept up with that of weapons and engines. Therefore momentous decisions had to be based on personal impressions and limited knowledge. Admiral Scheer was greatly influenced by the fate of the *Wiesbaden* and tried to help her. In his very short war diary this is the only special point he mentions in connection with his second battle turn. But he told his staff on the bridge that he was resolved not to slink away but to deal an unexpected blow to his adversary in order to upset his plans for the rest of daylight, which Jellicoe might otherwise utilise to get to grips again under circumstances unfavourable to the High Seas Fleet.

It was a simple plan founded more on the intuition of a fighting man that on sober calculation utilising confirmed facts. When he saw his van again in a very dangerous position he acted with speed and energy. In this phase his ships suffered much more than their opponents, but he succeeded in delaying a new deployment of the Grand Fleet so long that serious contact was not re-established before darkness fell. He could not save the *Wiesbaden*, although several destroyers had tried to approach her and help as best they could. Contrary to the reports of several British ships, this tough cruiser was not sunk by their fire. Battered out of recognition she kept afloat till after midnight. A few survivors left her on a damaged raft but only one man was rescued, after three days, by a neutral steamer.

From the few belated reports which Scheer received, he got the impression that the British fleet had turned away in an easterly direction for good, whereas from 1945 hours on it steered south-west, in good order, with light cruisers scouting ahead, the battle-cruisers in single line, the battleships following at a distance of six miles. Beatty could make out some German battleships against the western sky and reported their bearing and approximate distance (10 to 11 miles) and then the bearing of the leading ship (1945 hours). Two minutes later he made the urgent suggestion that the British battleships should follow his battle-cruisers in order to cut off the whole of the German fleet.

Scheer evidently was more concerned with the possibilities of

the following morning because he expected to meet British reinforcements from the southern North Sea bases. Therefore his main endeavour was to get nearer to Heligoland. He ordered a course south (1945 hours) and repeated the order several times. He did not take any steps to get his fleet into the old order again. The *1st* and *3rd Battle Squadrons* steamed in inverse order with the fleet flagship in the middle of the line, the old pre-dreadnoughts of the *2nd Battle Squadron* proceeded on a parallel course a mile to the west, and on the other side the four battle-cruisers tried to reach the head of the line again.

The result was that the courses of the two fleets converged, and there followed a series of short contacts. At 2000 hours Beatty gave orders to the 3rd Light Cruiser Squadron 'to sweep to the westward and locate the head of the enemy's line before dark'. Soon they made out the old cruiser of the *4th Scouting Group* and opened fire (at 2017 hours), which was answered promptly, with some damage on both sides.

At that time (2014 hours) Jellicoe sent a wireless message to his leading battle squadron (the 2nd) to follow the battle-cruisers, but neither side found the energy to enforce a decisive action. Immediately afterwards Beatty sighted the German *2nd Battle Squadron* which had drawn slightly ahead, and took it under fire as well as firing on the *1st Scouting Group,* which showed clearly for a short time against the western sky where the sun had just set. After receiving some hits, both German groups turn to the west because they could see nothing of the British but their gun flashes. To avoid a collision the van of the dreadnoughts turned away, too. This again opened the range to the British Battle Fleet which had steered south-west and for a few minutes west-south-west from 2000 hours on. The light cruiser *Calliope*, scouting in the direction of the German fleet, was in full sight of the *Iron Duke* when she came under the fire of German battleships (2030 hours). She was hit five times but escaped by clever manoeuvring.

Meanwhile it drew darker, visual contact between the British battle-cruisers and battleships was lost and there were increasing doubts whether ships sighted in the dusk were friend or foe. The four German battle-cruisers were again sighted and fired on for a few minutes at around 2100 hours, but were soon lost from sight. Jellicoe now ordered a course south and somewhat later, the adoption of night cruising formation. The day battle was over.

Further Reading

Bacon, Adm. Sir Reginald, *The Life of John Rushworth, Earl Jellicoe* (London 1936)
Bacon, Adm. Sir Reginald, *The Jutland Scandal* (London 1925)
Bennet, G., *The Battle of Jutland* (Batsford 1964)
British Admiralty, *Narrative of the Battle of Jutland* (HMSO 1924)
Chalmers, Rear-Adm. W. S., *The Life and Letters of David, Earl Beatty* (London 1951)
Chatfield, Admiral of the Fleet Lord, *The Navy and Defence*
Churchill, W. S., *The World Crisis* (Mentor 1968)
Corbett, Sir Julian, *Naval Operations Volume III* (Longmans, Green 1923)
Dreyer, Adm. Sir Frederic, *The Sea Heritage* (Museum Press 1955)
Fawcett, H. W. and Hooper, G. W. W., *The Fighting at Jutland* (Maclure, Macdonald)
Gibson, L. and Harper, Vice-Adm. J. E. T., *The Riddle of Jutland* (London 1934)
Groos, Captain O., *Der Krieg zur See 1914-1918* (Berlin 1920-1937)
Hase, G. von, *Kiel und Jutland* (Skeffington)
James, Admiral Sir William, *Eyes of the Navy*
Jellicoe, Admiral Viscount, *The Grand Fleet 1914-1916* (Cassell 1919)
Harper, Rear-Adm. J., *The Truth about Jutland* (Murray)
Kahn, D., *The Code Breakers* (Weidenfeld & Nicolson 1968)
Macintyre, Captain D., *Jutland*
Marder, A. J., *From the Dreadnought to Scapa Flow Volume III* (OUP 1966)
Rawson, R., *Earl Beatty* (Jarrold)
Scheer, Adm. R., *Germany's High Seas Fleet in the World War* (London 1920)
Temple Patterson, A. (ed.), *The Jellicoe Papers* (London 1966)
Waldemeyer-Hartz, Captain H. von., *Admiral von Hipper* (Rich & Cowan)

VICE-ADMIRAL (aD) FRIEDRICH OSKAR RUGE was born in 1894 and joined the German navy in April 1914. During the war he served in the North Sea, the Baltic and the English Channel, and was awarded the Iron Cross, 1st Class. In November 1918 he was interned at Scapa Flow and took part in scuttling the German fleet in 1919. He was a prisoner of war until the beginning of 1920. After this he was taken into the *Reichsmarine*, where he became a specialist in the development of mines and minesweeping. He travelled abroad widely between the wars. During the Second World War he served in the North Sea, France, the Mediterranean and finally as Director of Warship Construction in Berlin. He was recalled to the German navy between 1956 and 1961, but is now a professor at Tübingen University. He is also the author of numerous books, articles and pamphlets.

NIGHT ACTION CONFUSION AND ESCAPE

As in the growing darkness the main fleets drew apart, Jellicoe was confident, with some justice, that victory would be his the following day. As far as he knew, his fleet was still mostly intact, and he was astride the Germans' only avenue of escape. He could therefore afford to avoid the risks of a major night action and then annihilate the trapped Germans in the morning. But even these best laid of plans went awry. The Germans, moving more slowly than Jellicoe had anticipated, cut across the rear of the Grand Fleet towards the Horns Reef and safety. The only opposition, the British light cruisers and destroyers, could not halt the Germans despite their courageous attacks, and also failed to keep Jellicoe informed, so that he might intervene. *Donald Macintyre. Above:* The death of the pre-dreadnought SMS *Pommern*

Through the long summer twilight of the evening of May 31, the interminable line of British battleships of the Grand Fleet had steered to the south-west, probing for renewed contact with the High Seas Fleet. The latter, after twice recoiling from the unexpected confrontation with the greatly superior British, deployed across its path, had been steering south.

Between the two battle lines, skirmishes in the dusk had taken place between the opposing light cruiser forces, and Commodore Le Mesurier's 4th Light Cruiser Squadron had made an ineffective torpedo attack on the rear German battle squadrons.

Then, at about 2025 hours, Beatty's battle-cruisers, a dozen miles to the south-west, and out of sight of Jellicoe's van, engaged and drove westwards first the battered German *Battle-Cruiser Force* and then the German pre-dreadnought *2nd Battle Squadron*, leading Scheer's battle line since his 'about-turn'. News of these encounters did not reach Jellicoe until 2100 hours.

Scheer's main body, his dreadnoughts led by SMS *Westfalen*, had continued south, however, and was thus converging with the British battle line.

It was 2045 hours and almost dark when from two British light cruisers, HMS *Caroline* and HMS *Royalist*, stationed on the starboard side of Vice-Admiral Sir Martyn Jerram's 2nd Battle Squadron, leading the British line, the black bulk of battleships was seen dimly looming to the westward.

It was the head of the German dreadnought squadrons. Flashing a warning to Admiral Jerram, the two light cruisers went into the attack, being received with a fierce storm of gunfire as they swung round to launch torpedoes, one of which would have hit SMS *Nassau* had it not run too deep and passed below her keel.

Only after Captain Crooke of the *Caroline* had assured him of the identity of his target had Jerram given permission for the attack. But Jerram himself remained unconvinced that the silhouettes dimly seen against the afterglow of the sunset were not Admiral Beatty's battle-cruisers, which he had been vainly seeking (since being ordered, about 45 minutes earlier, to follow them) as a result of Beatty's much criticised signal made at 1947 hours. At barely 10,000 yards, a range at which tremendous execution could have been done by the 13.5-inch guns of his squadron, Jerram hesitated, while the German ships, unaware of his presence, swerved away to starboard to avoid the light cruisers' torpedoes. At the same time, Jellicoe, unaware of the momentous encounter at the head of his long battle line, and finally convinced that all chance of a day encounter had gone, signalled for the Battle Fleet's course to be altered to south, the leading ships of divisions to turn simultaneously.

Imbued with the doctrine of unquestioning obedience to orders from the Commander-in-Chief which governed the Grand Fleet and discouraged initiative by subordinate commanders, Jerram mutely complied. The two columns turned silently away from one another and faded into the darkness. Soon afterwards, Admiral Jellicoe, following his long-decided intention to avoid a night action, with all its advantages for the smaller, more manoeuvrable German fleet and the dependence largely on blind luck for the battle's outcome, signalled for the fleet to assume its night cruising disposition, a compact formation with squadrons in line ahead disposed abeam.

Vizeadmiral Scheer, for his part, equally unaware of the near encounter at the head of his line, held to his southerly course and pondered his tactics for the night. His much-damaged battle-cruisers and the *2nd Battle Squadron* of pre-dreadnoughts were ordered to the rear. In the van were nine light cruisers of his *Scouting Groups*, while in the rear the torpedoboat flotillas were being organised by *Kommodore* Heinrich in SMS *Regensburg* for night attacks on the British Battle Fleet.

Steering a parallel course eight miles to the eastward and now slowly assuming their night disposition were the Grand Fleet's battle squadrons with the 4th Light Cruiser Squadron out ahead, as was the swarm of destroyers, organised in five flotillas. Astern of the Battle Fleet were the four light cruisers of the 2nd Light Cruiser Squadron under Commodore Goodenough in HMS *Southampton*.

Fifteen miles to the south-west of the Grand Fleet were Beatty's battle-cruisers with the 2nd Cruiser Squadron and the 1st and 3rd Light Cruiser Squadrons. Following Beatty's brief exchange of gunfire firstly with the German battle-cruisers and then with the *2nd Battle Squadron*, they had continued to probe south-westward for a while, seeking Scheer's main body.

So closely ahead of Scheer's light cruisers did they pass that the Germans were able to read light signals passing between HMS *Lion* and HMS *Princess Royal*. One of these gave the challenge and reply for the night, a piece of information of which they would make good use later. At 2130 hours, the battle-cruisers turned to a southerly course at 17 knots to conform to that of the Battle Fleet, and this they held for the rest of the night.

They played no further part in the battle; for at 2110 hours, Scheer decided that in the desperate situation he was in, with the Grand Fleet between him and his escape route, his only hope of avoiding a renewal of the unequal battle at daylight was to steer directly for the entrance to the swept channels through the minefields, in the vicinity of the Horns Reef Light Vessel, 90 miles away. If necessary, he would have to bludgeon his way through the British fleet, accepting the consequences. He signalled 'Battle Fleet's course SSE ¼ E. No deviations. Speed 16 knots.' When an hour later the leading dreadnought, the *Westfalen*, was forced to turn to starboard to avoid the pre-dreadnought squadron which had not yet dropped to the rear, Scheer repeated his order, with the course amended to make up the lost ground, to SSE ¾ E.

Once again the two fleets were on converging, but not now on collision, courses. For Jellicoe, having in mind the possibility of Scheer steering for the alternative escape route through the Ems Channel to the south of the British mine barrage, the entrance to which lay due south of his present position, had ordered a speed of 17 knots, a knot faster than Scheer's slowest battle squadron, which would keep the Grand Fleet across this route. In case Scheer should, instead, try to cut across his wake to make for the Horns Reef, Jellicoe now ordered his massed flotillas to the rear, confident that they would offer an impenetrable barrier. As a further precaution he detached the fast minelayer HMS *Abdiel* to lay mines in the Horns Reef channel.

The British flotillas, few of whom had as yet taken any part in the battle, reversed course, passing between the columns of the Battle Fleet to make for their new station in the rear. Operating independently, the flotillas' order from west to east was: the light cruiser HMS *Castor* (flagship of Commodore Hawksley) and 15 of the 11th Flotilla; the 4th Flotilla, 12 boats led by HMS *Tipperary* (Captain C. J. Wintour), and HMS *Broke* (Commander W. L. Allen); the 13th Flotilla of nine boats led by Commodore Farie in the light-cruiser HMS *Champion*; a small division composed of four boats of the 9th and one of the 10th Flotilla led by Commander Goldsmith in HMS *Lydiard* and the 12th Flotilla, 15 boats led by HMS *Faulknor* (Captain A. J. B. Stirling).

Meanwhile, the German battle fleet was turning on to the course and into the formation ordered. The *2nd Battle Squadron* was turning up into line astern of the dreadnoughts. The battle-cruisers had also reached their station in the rear where *Vizeadmiral* Hipper was at last able to transfer his flag from the torpedoboat *G 39* to SMS *Moltke*, the least-damaged of his ships. With a battle-cruiser's deck under his feet once more, the indomitable Hipper soon chafed at the uninspiring station allotted him. He led off for the van at 20 knots; only the doughty SMS *Seydlitz*, in spite of the 21 hits by heavy shells and the torpedo damage she had suffered, felt able to comply, though the resultant strain on her damaged hull was soon to slow her down and eventually to bring her near to foundering. At the same time the light cruisers and some of the flotillas moved out to port to probe for the British Battle Fleet.

To appreciate the events which were to follow during the night, the reader must put out of mind the present-day warship where, in darkness or fog, the multifarious electronic equipment is able to present a picture of the situation around to the command and staff in a sheltered bridge or operations room. All bridges were open platforms; in destroyers they were only a few yards above the level of the sea; their canvas sides gave a little shelter from the worst of the spray whipped back from the curling bow wave and no relief at all from the wind streaming across screwed-up eyes which, with the doubtful aid of simple day binoculars, were the only means of detection of another unit near by.

The British, unlike the Germans, had no star shells with which to illuminate a suspicious stranger; nor had they the advantage held by the Germans in their iris shutters, behind which searchlights could be switched on and trained on the target prior to making the challenge. If an unsatisfactory reply, or none, was received, the target could be instantly illuminated by opening the shutters and the guns could open fire simultaneously. Communication between ships was by flashing lights or primitive spark wireless telegraphy, which was still at an early stage of development. Flashless propellants for guns did not exist; each salvo temporarily blinded all near by.

In addition to these *matériel* shortcomings, many of which affected each side equally, the Royal Navy, highly trained for battle by day, had neglected to practise night-fighting. Not so the Germans who, as a result, had developed the essential iris shutters, already mentioned, good searchlight control, star shells and the technique for using them to the best advantage.

It was shortly before 2200 hours that the British flotillas, some 50 boats in all, began to turn up into station astern of the battle squadrons. The eyes of all, squinting into the dark, were fixed on the next ahead as the close-order manoeuvre was being executed, when the *Tipperary* and her half flotilla of five boats were sighted by a German flotilla which, until their challenge was not answered at a distance of a few hundred yards, did not identify them as British. Four of the German boats fired a torpedo each before they faded back into the darkness. Luckily the sharp turn being made by the British flotilla saved them, the torpedoes passing astern of the rear ship, HMS *Garland,* the only one to appreciate what was happening; she radioed an enemy report and raised the alarm with a gunshot in the Germans' direction.

At about the same time, the most westerly British flotilla, the 15 boats of the 11th, led by the *Castor,* was similarly about to turn up into station when, unseen by them, the light cruisers SMS *Frankfurt* and SMS *Pillau* passed on an opposite course as they moved out to feel for the British Battle Fleet. Without opening fire or exposing their searchlight-beams, the German cruisers also launched a torpedo each and turned stealthily away. All unaware of their danger, the *Castor* and her flotilla at this moment turned to take up station; the torpedoes sped harmlessly by.

Once the manoeuvre had been completed and attentions on the *Castor's* bridge were less distracted, the presence of further black shapes off the starboard bow was suddenly discovered. Guns were hastily trained in their direction; but then, from the unknown ships came a winking light flashing a group of four letters. The first two were those of the British challenge (fruit of the battle-cruisers' carelessness earlier); and though the next two were incorrect, Commodore Hawksley hesitated; as he did so, a searchlight beam glared in his eyes; shells burst against the upper-works, spewing vicious steel splinters to spread savage wounds among the gun crews at their open mountings. The *Castor's* 6-inch guns slammed back in reply; but the combined fire of two of the German cruisers, SMS *Hamburg* and SMS *Elbing,* was too overwhelming. After firing one torpedo, the *Castor* turned away, as did the Germans to avoid it. The firing died away and the wild night skirmish ended as suddenly as it had begun.

Of the destroyers following the *Castor,* only the first two, HMS *Marne* and HMS *Magic,* felt confident enough that it was a German in sight to fire torpedoes, one of which ran true for the *Elbing* but passed underneath her; the remainder did not fire.

That well-trained British ships could give a good account of themselves in night action in spite of *matériel* shortcomings was shown when the four ships of Commodore Goodenough's 2nd Light Cruiser Squadron, pushing out towards the sight and sound of the *Castor's* engagement, next came up against four ships of the *4th Scouting Group,* the light cruisers SMS *Stettin,* SMS *München,* SMS *Frauenlob* and SMS *Stuttgart.* This time there was no doubt or muddle; the German challenge was answered by British gunfire and torpedoes. At the point-blank range of 800 yards each side inflicted fearsome damage on their opponents before mutually sheering apart. As they did so, a brilliant flash and a concussion that sent a shudder through all the ships engaged marked the destruction of the *Frauenlob,* sunk with all hands by one of the *Southampton's* torpedoes bursting in her magazine.

Of these several encounters, astern of the British Battle Fleet, distant flashes from which were seen from Jellicoe's flagship, HMS *Iron Duke,* only the *Garland's* signal and a brief report from the *Castor* that she had been engaged with German cruisers had reached Jellicoe. He assumed that this signified the repulse of a German attempt to deliver a torpedoboat attack, supported by cruisers, on his rear. For the time being there seemed to him to be no reason for any change of plan as he continued on his southerly course. The position, course and speed of the German battlefleet still remained a matter for speculation, though in fact a signal from the Admiralty which, in retrospect, can be seen to clear up much of the doubt, was at that moment being decoded in the *Iron Duke.*

Scheer, on the other hand, knowing from intercepted radio messages that the British destroyers had been ordered to the rear, and that his own destroyers had encountered some of them, was able to compile a clearer picture, one which showed that the Grand Fleet had drawn ahead during the last few hours. A small alteration of course to port would take him across its wake; soon after 2230 hours he signalled for a course of SE $\frac{1}{2}$ E.

The next hour passed undisturbed by any further violent encounters, though, unknown to the British, two units of the German fleet actually came in sight of the black bulk of some of the battleships of Jellicoe's starboard column. The *Moltke* and the *Seydlitz,* stretching ahead of Scheer's battle line, had had to weave their way through the scatter of light cruisers; some hasty

manoeuvres to avoid collision had resulted, in the course of which the *Seydlitz* had lost touch with the *Moltke.* Each thereafter operated independently; each, feeling her way south-eastwards for the Horns Reef, found her way barred. The *Moltke* twice came up against Jerram's squadron, being actually sighted on the first occasion by HMS *Thunderer,* whose captain, Captain Fergusson, decided against opening fire 'as it was inadvisable to show up our battle fleet', and did not even report the encounter. Blocked a third time at 2320 hours, the German battle-cruiser stood away to the southward and finally worked her way across ahead of the Grand Fleet, her path to safety clear.

The *Seydlitz,* her speed steadily falling away, came up against Vice-Admiral Burney's 1st Battle Squadron, lagging behind the Battle Fleet as a result of HMS *Marlborough's* torpedo damage. She was sighted by the *Marlborough,* HMS *Revenge* and HMS *Agincourt,* as well as two light cruisers, but was allowed to disengage, unchallenged, finally to limp safely across the wake of the Grand Fleet to safety.

While these almost incredible 'non-events' were taking place, and while the *Westfalen* was leading Scheer's line on a course which would take it across Jellicoe's wake, Jellicoe was pondering the signal from the Admiralty, the decoded version of which reached him at 2330 hours when he was snatching some rest in his little shelter on the *Iron Duke's* bridge. Consisting of a summary of three intercepted German messages, it read: 'German battle fleet ordered home at 2114 hours. Battle-cruisers in rear. Course SSE $\frac{3}{4}$ E. Speed 16 knots.'

Accepted at its face value, this put Jellicoe in possession of most of the facts of the situation – that the two fleets had for the last two hours been converging, with the Grand Fleet steaming at a knot faster than the High Seas Fleet, and that consequently Scheer was making for the Horns Reef and must eventually cross his wake. Furthermore, looked at in the light of calm reflection after the event, the gunfire, searchlights and starshells which had been at intervals seen astern might have been expected to indicate that this was just what was beginning to take place. Jellicoe, however, had doubts of the reliability of the Admiralty's information because, in an earlier message, they had given him a position of the Germans which he knew to be wrong. Another factor influencing him was a signal received from his most reliable scout, Commodore Goodenough, following his night encounter, which indicated that Scheer's battle fleet had been still to the westward at 2215 hours. Confident that if Scheer should later attempt to cross astern of him, his massed destroyer flotillas were well placed to repulse him, Jellicoe made no alteration to his course and speed.

At 2106 hours Scheer had signalled for airship reconnaissance of the Horns Reef at dawn. An hour later he had ordered all his flotillas to assemble there. Both these signals and several later ones giving Scheer's position, course and speed were rapidly decoded in Room 40 and were passed to the Operations Room. There they were pigeon-holed by the Director who was unable to appreciate their vital significance.

Had Jellicoe received these signals, he was subsequently to say, he would certainly have altered the course of the Grand Fleet and made for the Horns Reef Light Vessel. As it was, the information available to him and the flare and flicker of distant gunfire astern seemed consonant with encounters between the opposing destroyer flotillas. It is impossible not to sympathise with Jellicoe when he later learned of the Admiralty's fatal lapse.

Nevertheless, it is equally difficult to understand how Jellicoe could ignore the evidence of the night skirmishes in his rear, evidence which was to be reinforced during the next two hours, that some of the Germans at least were drawing across the rear of the Grand Fleet. The German battle line had swerved temporarily away, in spite of Scheer's strict orders, as a result of Goodenough's engagement at about 2215 hours. A lull had thus set in which lasted until 2330 hours, when the 4th Flotilla, the most westerly of the British units, once again came into action.

Following Captain Wintour's *Tipperary,* in single line on a southerly course, were HMS *Spitfire, Sparrowhawk, Garland, Contest, Broke* (divisional leader), *Achates, Ambuscade, Ardent, Fortune, Porpoise* and *Unity.* The whereabouts of the Germans – or indeed of other British units – was unknown, though Wintour suspected that the *Castor* and the 11th Flotilla were somewhere to starboard. When at 2315 hours he began to make out the dark shape of ships looming in that direction, therefore, he felt he must challenge. In reply came the blinding glare of searchlights and a storm of gunfire in which the little destroyer was reduced in a brief moment to a blazing wreck with her bridge swept away and all on it killed.

The ship the *Tipperary* had challenged was the *Westfalen,* head of Scheer's battle line. Further back on the battleship's port side were steaming the light cruisers of the German *2nd Scouting Group*, the ships which, no doubt, the *Garland*, the first to spot them, had taken for destroyers. The first five ships astern of the *Tipperary* each fired two torpedoes before sheering away to port; the *Spitfire*, however, the sixth destroyer, circled back to starboard as her captain, Lieutenant-Commander Trelawney, took her back to the leader's rescue. Blinded by the gun flashes and searchlight beams, he could not see the towering mass of the leading German ships which had turned away to avoid the torpedoes.

Out of the smoke and glare on his starboard bow there suddenly appeared the lofty bow of the battleship *Nassau* on a course to ram him. Trelawny swung his wheel to starboard in a desperate attempt to avoid the collision. It was too late for that; but he escaped the murderous ram and the two ships met, port bow to port bow, with a shock that heeled even the dreadnought over as, with a screech of tortured steel, they ground past on opposite courses. The blast from the 11-inch guns of the *Nassau's* forward turret wrecked the destroyer's bridge, bringing down her mast and foremost funnel, killing three men and wounding many more.

With her hull torn open for a third of her length, the *Spitfire* staggered away, carrying with her 20 feet of the battleship's side plating, a trophy which she still had on board when she eventually reached port.

While this wild encounter was taking place, disaster had struck further along the German line. There the light cruisers had also sheered away to starboard to avoid the British torpedoes, and to do so had been forced to cut between the battleships. One of them, the *Elbing*, misjudging the manoeuvre, was rammed by the battleship SMS *Posen* and so badly damaged that she had eventually to be abandoned and scuttled by her crew.

As the opposing units recoiled from one another and darkness swallowed them once again, the battleships were sternly ordered back to a course for the Horns Reef. On the port beam of the *Westfalen*, the cruiser SMS *Rostock* had taken station. The surviving destroyers of the 4th Flotilla, formed up astern of the *Broke* were led by Commander W. L. Allen on a converging course to renew the attack. Sighting the cruiser, and bemused by the events of the recent blind *mêlée*, he would not engage without first making the challenge.

The vital advantage of the first shot thus sacrificed, the *Broke* was immediately overwhelmed as, with the same deadly efficiency, the German searchlights from the *Rostock* and the *Westfalen* unmasked their blinding glare and shells from point-blank range smashed into her, destroying the bridge and all stationed there; with the wheel jammed hard-a-port, the *Broke* careered away out of control to send her knife-edge stern slicing murderously into the starboard side of the *Sparrowhawk*, her next astern, as she, too, swung to port to fire torpedoes. And, as the two lay helplessly locked together, the *Contest*, next in line and unable to steer clear, carved off 30 feet of the *Sparrowhawk's* stern. The *Broke* and the *Contest* were able to limp away eventually out of action; their luckless victim was left to drift helplessly until abandoned and scuttled by her crew on the following day.

Once again the German ships had been forced to sheer temporarily away to starboard to avoid the British torpedoes. The manoeuvre did not avail the *Rostock,* however: a torpedo exploding alongside a boiler-room wreaked such damage that she, too, had to be abandoned and sunk.

At the cost of five of their number knocked out, the 4th Flotilla had caused the loss of two of the German cruisers; and now, under Commander Hutchinson of the *Achates*, the remainder formed up and resumed their southerly course, the *Ambuscade, Ardent, Fortune, Porpoise* and *Garland* following in that order.

No attempt to pass to Jellicoe the vital information in his possession that they had clashed with the head of the German battle line was made by Hutchinson. A similar lack of tactical sense was displayed by ships of the British 5th Battle Squadron in the rear of the Battle Fleet. This squadron had had a fair view of the two encounters. Rear-Admiral Evan-Thomas, leading in HMS *Barham*, had assessed the glare and thunder of guns first on his starboard quarter and then right astern as engagements only between the opposing light forces. But from his rear ship, HMS *Malaya,* in the flash from the torpedo which hit the *Rostock* at about 2340 hours, the leading German ship had been identified as a dreadnought. Yet no word was passed to Jellicoe.

By now it was midnight. Eight miles astern of the *Iron Duke*, the head of the German line was about to cross the wake of the Battle Fleet. At this moment, from the bridge of the *Achates*, the black outlines of battleships to starboard were again in sight. She was about to fire torpedoes when, between the *Achates* and the target, appeared the lower silhouettes of two cruisers. They

were, in fact, two of the German *4th Scouting Group* steering to cross ahead of the battleships; but that they could be British caused Hutchinson to hesitate; and while he did so the blazing inferno once again burst around the line of destroyers as the *Westfalen* took the *Fortune* for her target, being quickly joined by others of the battleship line. Within a few moments the *Fortune* was a burning wreck.

The *Porpoise,* hit by a heavy shell, staggered away out of action. The remainder, having fired torpedoes, became scattered and played no further part in the battle, except for the *Ardent*. She once again came up against the head of the German line at 0015 hours. Closing to launch her solitary remaining torpedo, she was met by a concentrated storm of fire and sent to the bottom.

The 4th Flotilla had finally shot its bolt. Though their torpedoes had failed to score during these last attacks, the little ships had managed to get some telling shots home with their comparatively puny gun armament before escaping into the darkness; the battleship SMS *Oldenburg,* in particular, suffered many casualties on the bridge and was only saved from collision with her neighbour by her wounded captain who took the wheel from the hands of the dying coxswain.

The German battle line, indeed, though it had as yet suffered no losses as a result of the attacks, was, not for the first time, thrown into considerable confusion. The *Nassau,* since her encounter with the *Spitfire,* had been trying unsuccessfully to get back into line and was finally to take up the rear station. Other ships had hauled out of line and circled before rejoining the line in stations other than their correct ones. Thus the German battle fleet's progress was delayed; but it was never halted or for long diverted from its stubborn drive through the opposition.

Night encounter had brought disaster in the meantime to another British unit. The armoured cruiser HMS *Black Prince* of the 1st Cruiser Squadron, which had suffered such rough handling earlier when the two fleets met, had been left behind when the Grand Fleet turned to the southward after deployment. Steering to rejoin, she had blundered into the middle of the German line to be battered to a wreck by the passing battleships and finally blown up and sunk with all hands.

Though Scheer's battle line was by now across the rear of the Grand Fleet, there still remained a bar to his further progress and a means of informing Jellicoe of the situation: the 13th Flotilla of nine boats led by Captain Farie in the light cruiser *Champion,* five boats of the 9th and 10th Flotillas led by Commander Goldsmith in the *Lydiard* and the 14 boats of the 12th Flotilla, led by Captain Stirling in the *Faulknor.*

Confusion had been caused among these by an unfortunate manoeuvre by Farie who, when shells passing over the 4th Flotilla during its first encounter landed near the *Champion,* imagined himself to be under fire and turned sharply away to port without signal. Only the first two of his flotilla, *Moresby* and *Obdurate,* saw the move and followed. The remaining seven continued on their southerly course and joined Goldsmith's division, thus, unknown to him, increasing his line from five boats to 12.

Continuing eastward, Farie next ran across the 12th Flotilla, forcing Captain Stirling also to bear away in that direction until, by reducing speed, the latter allowed Farie's group to draw ahead, leaving himself free to resume the southerly course. As he did so, the German light cruisers *Frankfurt* and *Pillau* blundered into the rear of his formation. A brief, wild *mêlée* ensued during which the *Menace* barely avoided being rammed, while the *Nonsuch,* turning eastward at full speed to escape, lost touch with her flotilla and was never able to rejoin.

Meanwhile, Goldsmith had been steering south-westward at high speed. It is an indication of how ignorant of the situation were the destroyers, where facilities for recording and plotting it were rudimentary, that Goldsmith had remained convinced that the violent clashes he had seen to the eastward during the previous hour and a half had been the result of mistaken identity and that British heavy ships, presumably the battle-cruisers to whom he was rightfully attached, had been firing at the 4th Flotilla. Now, therefore, he was steering to cross their bows and take up station on their starboard side.

His course was effective to take what he still thought was his line of only five boats safely across. Indeed, about half-an-hour after midnight, the first ten boats had safely crossed ahead, unseen by, and not seeing, the *Westfalen.* The eleventh boat, *Petard,* narrowly scraped across the battleship's bow and escaped under gunfire which caused a number of casualties.

Next in the line was the *Turbulent.* Her way barred, she could only turn parallel to the battleship at full speed in the hope of drawing sufficiently ahead to cross her bows. It was a forlorn hope: with a few savage salvoes from her secondary battery

The smaller ships that wove in and out of their mightier brethren in the dark

1. SMS *Rostock*, light cruiser, the leader of the German torpedoboat flotillas at the *'Seeschlacht am Skagerrak'*, as the Germans called the battle. During the 4th Flotilla's attack on SMS *Westfalen*, the *Rostock* contributed greatly to the repulse of the British boats, but then herself succumbed to a torpedo and had to be abandoned and sunk by her crew. **2.** SMS *Stettin*, in which *Kommodore* von Reuter led the *4th Scouting Group*. **3.** SMS *Frauenlob*, one of Germany's older cruisers, sunk with all hands by a torpedo from HMS *Southampton*, after a severe battering by gunfire. The loss of the *Frauenlob* occurred in the sort of situation which happened all too frequently in the night action: a ship would be sighted and a challenge issued, which if the recipient were hostile would bring down a storm of fire on the original challenger. **4.** Possibly the most unfortunate victim of the night action — the destroyer HMS *Sparrowhawk*, whose bows were severely damaged in a collision with one British destroyer and stern cut off by another. She had to be abandoned and sunk the next day. **5.** The light cruiser HMS *Castor*, leader of the 11th Flotilla. She also fell a victim to the greatest problem of fighting at night — identification. Waiting too long before opening fire on two suspicious vessels, she was severely damaged by the fire from what turned out to be two German light cruisers. **6.** Like the *Castor*, the divisional leader HMS *Broke* was devastated by German gunfire before she herself could open fire, went out of control after her bridge had been wrecked, swung round and rammed her next astern, the unfortunate *Sparrowhawk*

of 5.9-inch guns, the *Westfalen* blew the little ship to pieces.

The lack of comprehension of, or even interest in, the situation beyond the confines of their own ship by destroyer men under the conditions of that era is nowhere better illustrated than by the fact that Goldsmith remained ignorant of the origin or outcome of the brief but intense display of gunfire and searchlights astern of him. He made no enquiries of the ships in his wake; indeed he did not realise until daylight that others than his own flotilla had been following him as he steamed on to the south-west through the night. It did not occur to Thompson of the *Petard* that it was his duty to initiate a report for Jellicoe that he had been in contact with the German battle line.

Another of the forces on which Jellicoe was relying to deny the Germans passage across his wake had now been eliminated. And, indeed, it was the last from which a signalled enemy report could have arrived in time for him to alter course to intercept Scheer before he reached the Horns Reef. There still remained Captain Stirling's 12th Flotilla; but the unfortunate manoeuvre of the *Champion*, noted earlier, had forced them away to the eastward. Scheer's route to the Horns Reef was for the moment clear; and dawn, which would remove much of the threat from destroyer attack, was little more than an hour away. The sands were running out for Jellicoe, who still believed himself to be between Scheer and his base.

Contact at dawn

Captain Stirling in the *Faulknor* had, indeed, been steering a southerly course since 0020 hours, a course which must in time bring him across the German line of advance; but the first streaks of dawn were already lighting the horizon behind him when at 0143 hours he sighted a line of large ships in the gloom to starboard, ships soon identified as German battleships.

The 12th Flotilla was in three divisions; a division of four boats in line ahead was on either quarter of the *Faulknor*; astern of this formation came the flotilla leader HMS *Marksman* leading the remaining four. The nearest division to the Germans, the *Obedient*, *Mindful*, *Marvel* and *Onslaught*, on Stirling's starboard quarter, were ordered to attack.

The four destroyers turned together at full speed towards the Germans; but already the growing light and the white froth of their bow and stern waves had betrayed them and the battleships had turned away. The latter were no longer a suitable target and the *Obedient* led her division back to rejoin the leader.

Stirling now led his flotilla on a south-easterly course at 25 knots to gain a good attacking position. While doing so, he earned himself a portion of fame as the only one of the many destroyer men in action that night who realised the prime importance of reporting what they had seen. An emergency signal was radioed: 'Enemy's battle fleet is steering south-east, approximate bearing south-west. My position is ten miles astern of the 1st Battle Squadron.'

This would at last, though too late, have given Jellicoe the vital information he so sorely needed; but, though it was sent out twice on full power, it was jammed by the Germans and never taken in by the flagship where, as daylight slowly spread, Jellicoe was preparing to reverse course in the expectation of being able to renew the battle.

The German line came in sight once again on the *Faulknor's* starboard quarter at 0206 hours, and Stirling led round 180 degrees to starboard to attack on an opposite course from ahead. The *Mindful*, with a boiler disabled, had been unable to keep up, but the remainder of his division followed round.

With the darkness now being replaced by a misty twilight, their powerful searchlights no longer gave the Germans any advantage. Unable to identify the shadowy shapes streaking across the grey waters they hesitated and Stirling's four boats were racing by at full speed at less than 2,000 yards before the battleships opened fire and swung hurriedly away to avoid the torpedoes already on their way, two from the *Faulknor*, one from the *Obedient*, and four each from the *Marvel* and the *Onslaught*.

Their torpedoes launched, the destroyers turned away together, covering their retirement with black funnel smoke. All escaped unharmed through a storm of gunfire except the *Onslaught*, where a shell hit square on the bridge, killing her captain, Lieutenant-Commander Onslow, two other officers, the coxswain, both quartermasters and both signalmen.

They had done their work well, however, and though by frenzied manoeuvres most of the battleships avoided the racing torpedoes, one failed. The pre-dreadnought SMS *Pommern* was struck fair and square. A series of internal explosions followed, culminating in one tremendous concussion as she blew up, broke in two and sank taking her entire crew of 844 men down with her.

By the time the 2nd Division, HMS *Maenad, Narwhal, Nessus* and *Noble*. had followed the 1st Division round, the target was already turning away; though the *Maenad* and the *Narwhal* launched three torpedoes between them and the *Maenad* then turned in chase to fire two more, they had little chance of hitting. For the *Marksman's* division, the situation was even more hopeless and by the time the *Opal*, having lost touch with the leader, led the *Menace, Munster* and *Mary Rose* to the attack, the German line had vanished into the deeper gloom to the westward. The *Opal* then led away to the southward.

It was now 0215 hours. All the 12th Flotilla except the *Marksman* had by this time crossed ahead of the German line, which soon resumed its south-easterly course for the Horns Reef, now barely an hour's steaming away. Only the ineptly wandering *Champion* followed by the *Obdurate*, the *Moresby* and the solitary *Marksman* remained to the eastward. The two groups encountered one another at the moment that the rear ships of the German line were sighted crossing ahead at 0225 hours.

'What are ships bearing south?' signalled the *Marksman* to the *Champion*. 'German, I think,' came the reply; at which the *Champion* inexplicably led away to the east to play no further effective part in the action. The stigma of this final spiritless reaction to the sight of the Germans was happily offset by the action of the *Moresby* whose captain, Lieutenant-Commander R. V. Alison, 'considering action imperative', as he reported subsequently, broke away, circling to port to launch a torpedo from the only tube he had available. That this lone effort failed to obtain a hit on the battleship target is not surprising. It is possible that it was responsible for the sinking of the German destroyer *V 4*, which blew up for reasons unknown, though the time given in the official German record discounts this.

The last of the massed destroyer strength from which Jellicoe had expected so much had been brushed aside. The way to the Horns Reef lay open to the German fleet. Nevertheless, with nearly an hour's steaming still to go, daylight was now gaining fast. It was a moment that Scheer had been looking forward to with deep anxiety. His battle squadrons were in considerable confusion with dreadnoughts and pre-dreadnoughts mingled. What losses had resulted from the wild encounters in the night he did not know. He was in no shape to renew battle.

But then as the light spread to reveal his battle line almost intact and no sign of the British, surprise and relief flooded Scheer's mind. His bold tactics had succeeded beyond his wildest dreams. He had not merely succeeded in extricating himself from the nearly hopeless position in which he had found himself as darkness fell on the evening of May 31, with a vastly superior fleet between him and his base, but had also converted a strategic defeat, seemingly certain to result in his annihilation, into a situation in which he could plausibly claim a resounding victory. At 0324 hours he thankfully hoisted the signal to return to harbour.

On the bridge of the *Iron Duke*, meanwhile, early optimism had faded to be replaced by a steadily growing gloom as the facts of the situation became known. At 0239 hours the Battle Fleet had reversed course to the northward and taken up battle order as eager eyes peered ahead for the Germans. At 0320 hours, hope had flared up briefly at the sound of heavy guns in the southwest and the fleet had turned in that direction, only to resume its northerly course when it was learnt that the firing had been one of Beatty's battle-cruisers, out of sight in that direction, driving off a prowling Zeppelin.

Certainty that his great opportunity to inflict a decisive defeat on the High Seas Fleet had slipped through his fingers finally came to Jellicoe when, at about 0415 hours, he read a message from the Admiralty reporting that at 0230 hours Scheer had been 16 miles from Horns Reef, steering south-east by south at 16 knots. It was therefore already entering the swept channel between the minefields. Ordering the Grand Fleet to resume its cruising disposition, Jellicoe steered to sweep the battle area for ships known to have been disabled—SMS *Lützow* and the *Elbing*—and in the hope that others might have fallen astern during the night.

CAPTAIN DONALD MACINTYRE retired from the Royal Navy in 1955 after a career divided largely between service in destroyers and as a pilot in the Fleet Air Arm. During the Second World War he commanded convoy escort groups in the Battle of the Atlantic, where he was awarded the DSO and two bars and the DSC. On retirement he took up authorship. In addition to his *Jutland*, he has published the autobiographical *U-Boat Killer*, and historical works such as *Narvik, The Battle of the Atlantic, The Battle for the Mediterranean* and *Battle for the Pacific* together with biographies of Admirals Lord Rodney and Sir James Somerville.

A GERMAN VIEW

Although the Germans did not lose any of their battle-cruisers in explosions such as those which destroyed HMS *Invincible* and *Queen Mary*, they did nonetheless suffer terribly. One ship which took an enormous pounding was SMS *Seydlitz*: battered almost out of recognition and with her foredeck level with the water, she managed to limp back home. Here we reprint the *Seydlitz'* captain's account of the feat. *Below: The Seydlitz almost, but not quite, gone*

When our battle-cruisers put to sea on May 31, 1916, SMS *Seydlitz* was no longer in the van but sailed as 'Tactical Number Three', for *Vizeadmiral* von Hipper had hoisted his flag in the new SMS *Lützow*. As always at the beginning of an operation, all watertight doors were thoroughly examined, every piece of apparatus tested and spare parts broken out to be handy in emergencies. The watch kept a sharp lookout for submarines, while the men off watch dozed. When at 1400 hours the message 'Enemy in sight' came in, bugles and drums sounded the General March to call all hands to battle-stations. Within minutes every station reported to the bridge that it was ready for action.

Soon the British light cruisers came in view, and behind them dense clouds of smoke. Then tripod masts and huge hulls loomed over the horizon. There they were again, our friends from the Dogger Bank. At 1545 hours we opened fire. After a short time HMS *Indefatigable* blew up, followed after 20 minutes by HMS *Queen Mary,* our target as Tactical Number Three. The spectacle was overwhelming, there was a moment of complete silence, then the calm voice of a gunnery observer announced *'Queen Mary* blowing up', at once followed by the order 'Shift target to the right' given by the gunnery officer in the same matter-of-fact tone as at normal gunnery practice.

Now four fast British battleships came up and directed heavy fire against our rear ships. But our main fleet came up, too; the British battle-cruisers turned away to the north, and we took up station ahead of our own battleships. We had not gone unscathed. The first hit we received was a 12-inch shell that struck the Number Six 6-inch casemate on the starboard side, killing everybody except the Padre who, on the way to his battle-station down below, had wanted to take a look at the men and at the British, too. By an odd coincidence we had, at our first battle practice in 1913, assumed the same kind of hit and by the same adversary, the *Queen Mary*. Splinters perforated air leads in the bunker below and smoke and gas consequently entered the starboard main turbine compartment.

Somewhat later the gunnery central station deep down reported: 'No answer from "C" turret. Smoke and gas pouring out of the voice pipes from "C" turret.' That sounded like the time on the Dogger Bank. Then it had been 'C' and 'D' turrets. A shell had burst outside, making only a small hole, but a red-hot piece of steel had ignited a cartridge, the flash setting fire to 13,000 pounds of cordite. 190 men had been killed and two turrets put out of action. Afterwards, a thorough examination showed that everything had been done in accordance with regulations. I told the gunnery officer: 'If we lose 190 men and almost the whole ship in accordance with regulations then they are somehow wrong.' Therefore we made technical improvements and changed our methods of training as well as the regulations. This time only one cartridge caught fire, the flash did not reach the magazines, and so we lost only 20 dead or severely burned, and only one turret was put out of action.

When Beatty turned to the north, we had a wonderful view of the British destroyer flotillas going full speed into the attack. They were intercepted by two of our flotillas, but we did not have much time to watch the furious engagement between the lines. Our foretop reported first one, then more torpedo tracks. We tried to avoid them by sharp turns but finally one got us a bit forward of the bridge. The blow was much softer than gunnery hits or near misses, no loud report, but only a rattling noise in the rigging. It was almost the same spot near the forward torpedo flat where we had struck a mine five weeks before. For the damage control party it was a repeat performance, and although they grinned it was otherwise not much of a joke. The torpedo bulkhead held, but it was seriously strained, as were parts of the armoured deck. Where the rivets had gone completely, the holes could be stopped with wooden pegs. Where they only leaked, which they did in great numbers—more than enough for our needs—they became a distinct menace because there was no way to plug them effectively.

Intolerable heat

Both forward generators were casualties; one stopped entirely, while the other ran but failed to generate any current. Soon all this part of Compartment XIII was flooded, and with one third of our electric supply gone, all circuits had to be switched to the generators aft. There the air leads had been damaged by splinters, and in the dynamo room the temperature rose to 72°C (162°F). The men had to put on gas masks but some fainted and had to be carried out. Eventually, the room had to be evacuated, although a stoker returned from time to time to lubricate the bearings. The lights failed, but the petty officer at the electrical switchboard succeeded in reswitching all the circuits from memory. In view of the

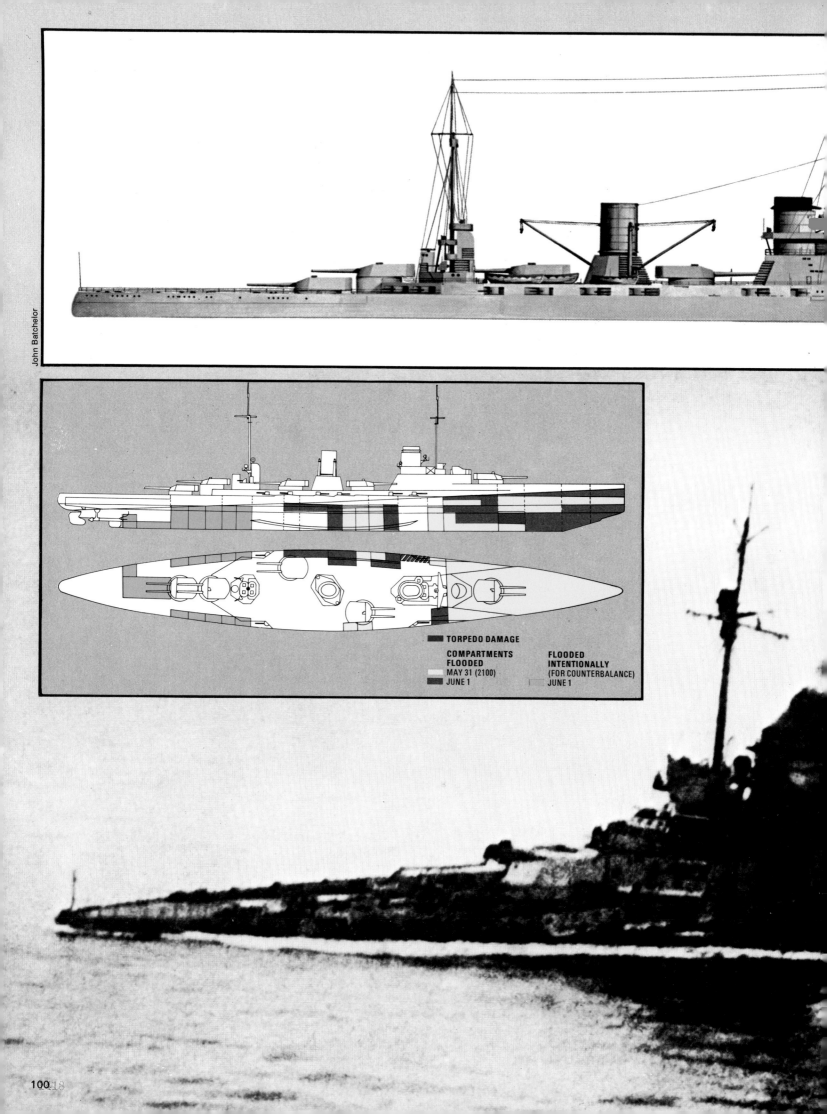

TORPEDO DAMAGE

**COMPARTMENTS
FLOODED**

MAY 31 (2100)

JUNE 1

**FLOODED
INTENTIONALLY
(FOR COUNTERBALANCE)**
JUNE 1

Left: SMS *Seydlitz. Displacement:* 24,610 tons. *Length:* 656 feet. *Beam:* 93⅓ feet. *Armament:* Ten 11-inch, 12 5.9-inch and 12 3.4-inch guns plus four 19.7-inch torpedo tubes. *Armour:* 11¾ inches and turrets 9¾ inches. *Power/speed:* 63,000-100,000 hp/27-30 knots. *Complement:* 1,068-1,143. *Below left:* The *Seydlitz* as she made her way home. Her bows torn open by a torpedo, she soon began to settle forward and to starboard. The only way to keep her afloat was to flood certain port and aft compartments, but even so her journey home was a chancy business. *Below:* The *Seydlitz* creeps back to Germany across the North Sea

intricate battle arrangements this was quite a feat. He could do it only because he simply lived for his work and among his work. Besides this, the turbo-fans, the strong lungs of the ship, repeatedly failed because their leads were damaged, casings bent and vents perforated. However, the repair parties took special note of them and got them working again every time.

In the conning tower we were kept busy, too. 'Steering failure' reported the helmsman and automatically shouted down the armoured shaft to the control room: 'Steer from control room.' At once the answer came: 'Steering failure in control room.' The order: 'Steer from tiller flat' was the last resort. We felt considerable relief when the red helm indicator followed orders. The ship handling officer drew a deep breath: 'Exactly as at the admiral's inspection.' 'No,' I said, 'then we used to get steering failure at the end, whereas now the fun has only just started.' Fortunately, we soon found that some springs holding down levers in the steering leads had not been strong enough for the concussions caused by the hits. Quite simple, but try finding that under heavy fire.

The helmsman was a splendid seaman but every six months or so he could not help hitting the bottle. Then he felt the urge to stand on his head in the market square of Wilhelmshaven. Each time this meant the loss of his Able Seaman's stripe. At Jutland he stood at the helm for 24 hours on end. He got his stripe back and was the only AB in the fleet to receive the Iron Cross 1st Class. The first casualty in the conning tower was a signal yeoman, who collapsed silently after a splinter had pierced his neck. A signalman took over his headphone in addition to his own. In our battle training we had overlooked this possibility.

Rippling salvoes

Meanwhile, visibility decreased and there seemed to be an endless line of ships ahead. But we saw only incessant flashes, mostly four discharges in the peculiar British 'rippling' salvoes. Our ship received hit after hit but our guns remained silent because we could not make out any targets. This put us under a heavy strain which was relieved, to some extent, by ship handling, changes of formation and zigzagging towards and away from previous salvoes. The port casemates suffered heavy damage, and chains had to be formed to get ammunition from the lee battery. In 'B' turret, there was a tremendous crash, smoke, dust and general confusion. At the order 'Clear the turret' the turret crew rushed out, using even the traps for the empty cartridges. Then they fell in behind the turret. Then compressed air from Number 3 boiler room cleared away the smoke and gas, and the turret commander went in again, followed by his men. A shell had hit the front plate and a splinter of armour had killed the right gunlayer. The turret missed no more than two or three salvoes.

In the port low-pressure turbine, steam leaked out and the men had to put on gas masks. The leak was repaired by a man creeping on his belly in the bilge directly under the turbine casing. Electric light and boiler room telegraphs also ceased to operate under the frequent concussions. Fortunately we had practised working in the dark. Our men called these exercises 'blind-man's-buff' because they were blindfolded to learn handling valves etc by touch. The stokers and coal trimmers deserved the highest praise, for they had to wield their shovels mostly in the dark, often up to their knees in water without knowing where it came from and how much it would rise. Unfortunately, we had very bad coal, which formed so much slag that fires had to be cleaned after half the usual time, and grates burnt through and fell into the ash-pits. The spare ones had to be altered in the thick of the battle because even the beams supporting the grates were bent by the heat.

Our repair parties were very efficient, the efforts of the electricians eclipsing all the others. They found solutions for the trickiest problems, invented new connections, created electric bypasses, kept all necessary circuits going and crowned their achievements by repairing the electric baking-oven so that on the morning we got pure wheat bread, a rare treat for us.

Our aerials were soon in pieces, rendering our ship deaf and dumb until a sub-lieutenant and some radio operators rigged new ones. The anti-torpedo net was torn and threatened to foul the propellers, but the boatswain and his party went over the side to lash it. They did it so well that later, in dock, it proved difficult to untie it again. According to regulations our paymasters were expected in a battle to take down and certify last wills, but we preferred them to prepare cold food forward and aft, and send their stewards round to battle-stations with masses of sandwiches.

Around 2000 hours we came under especially heavy fire, and then there followed a distinct lull, during which turrets could be opened and fresh air blown through the whole ship. When we left the conning tower we stood before a frightful scene. One of the last shells had passed through the admiral's charthouse and

burst in the lee of the conning tower, killing or mutilating my aide and his party of messengers and signal ratings there.

Now darkness fell, and we had to make preparations for the next morning – for we were sure to meet the British again. Searchlights were repaired, night recognition signals rigged and ammunition carried to the undamaged guns. At first we could continue to follow the battle-cruiser SMS *Moltke*, but soon we had to slow down, for water began to come over the forecastle as our bows settled. Steering was difficult, as was finding the right course, for the main gyro compartment was flooded and the after gyro unreliable. Its normal circuit had been destroyed and the new connection short-circuited off and on. The shocks had made the magnetic compass entirely undependable. Sounding had its problems, too. The sounding machines in the casemates were scrap, while the hand-leads fouled the torn nets and then parted. Our charts were covered with blood and the spare charts were inaccessible in a flooded compartment. Under these circumstances it was not at all easy to make the correct course for the Horns Reef lightship. Moreover, all coal near the boilers had been used up, and bringing up more supplies from the more distant bunkers became increasingly difficult as a result of damage and the amount of water in the ship. Fortunately, our boilers could also burn oil, and supplies of this continued to flow, although the oil-pipes needed constant attention to prevent them from clogging.

In this situation the aft look-out reported: 'Several large ships, darkened, approaching from astern.' Our night glasses showed four huge ships, British, no more than 2,000 yards away. Blast! They must have seen us and would therefore open fire at any moment. Should we try to ram? But their guns were still trained fore and aft! Our ship was too heavily damaged to attack, and I gave the orders: 'Hard-a-starboard, full speed ahead, engine room make as much smoke as possible – give British recognition signal.' A yeoman flashed the letter 'J', the leading ship promptly answered 'O'. That was the only light they showed for they had an excellently darkened ship. In a minute we got up so much smoke that they disappeared from view. [*Other accounts make it clear that there was no exchange of light signals, but* Thunderer *did not open fire as her captain thought* Seydlitz *was only a destroyer and to open fire would only give away the position of the British.*]

When we reported this encounter by W/T, bright sparks flashed all over our rigging because torn wires touched the improvised aerials when the ship heeled over. At dawn, neither the Horns Reef light vessel nor any other ship was in sight. Suddenly our stern wave rose high, a sign of shallow water. Before my order 'Full speed astern' could take effect our bows scraped over the sea bottom, but soon the water became deeper again. A buoy gave us our position, and at the light-ship we got in touch with the rest of our fleet, the light cruiser SMS *Pillau* being detached to pilot us to the Jade river. Now a dogged fight to save the vessel began. The entire forecastle was riddled like a sieve. Through rents, holes, leaky seams and rivets water entered one room after the other until only the forward torpedo flat could be held. This big 'swimming bladder' gave the forward part of the ship just enough buoyancy. But she was so much down by the bows that the sea started getting into the forward casemates. Their covers were destroyed or bent, and the wood for shoring up leaks was somewhere under the forecastle. We used everything we could lay our hands on, mess tables, benches, eventually even the empty shelves from the shell-rooms to the dismay of the head gunner.

Quite a number of compartments had to be kept clear by incessant bailing over a period of two days. Some bulkheads had to be watched carefully and shored up again from time to time. The whole ship's company was kept busy, and so sleep was possible only in snatches. Late on June 1, pump steamers arrived but so also did a stiff breeze from the north-west. We were off Heligoland then, with a list of eight degrees and very little stability, and could proceed at no more than three or four knots whether going ahead bows first or stern first, which we did part of the time. When seas started breaking over the waist, the *Pillau* made a lee on our starboard bow, and a tug laid an oil-slick. That helped until the wind abated. We could not have stood a heavy gale.

On June 2 we anchored near the Jade light vessel to wait for the tide, for we drew 47½ feet forward as against 30 feet amidships under normal conditions. But we made it and arrived in the early morning of June 3 off Wilhelmshaven locks, where we were welcomed by hurrahs from the crews of the battleships anchored there. The *Seydlitz* had been hit by 21 heavy shells and one torpedo, lost 98 men killed and 55 injured and had four heavy and two medium guns put out of action.

[*Reprinted from a talk by the captain of SMS* Seydlitz, *Kapitän zur See von Egidy.*]

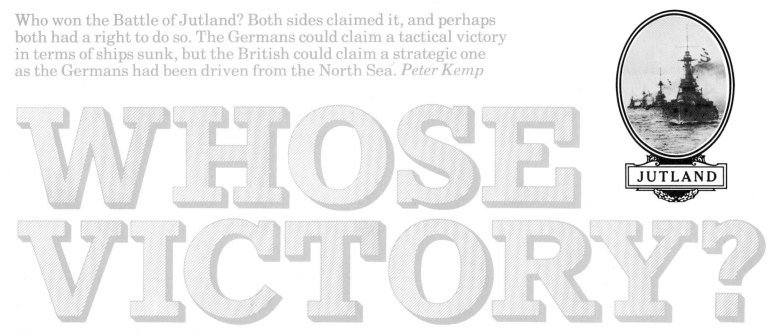

WHOSE VICTORY?

Who won the Battle of Jutland? Before this very vexed question can be decided – if ever it can be – there are a number of generalisations that need to be made. One of them is that battles are normally won by a superiority of tactics, but that wars are normally won by a superiority in strategy. And it follows from this that a basic principle of war must be (as it most certainly is) that tactics are governed by strategy; that any individual or particular battle must be subservient to the objective of the war as a whole.

Accepting this as a self-evident truth, one has therefore to take into account the higher strategic necessities which governed each commander-in-chief as he led his fleet into battle. Let us take Jellicoe first. He went into battle with the knowledge that, to quote Winston Churchill, he was 'the only man on either side throughout the war who could, by his actions, lose the war in an afternoon'. This is not hyperbole; it is fact. The whole basic British strategy, laid down and agreed before the war, was to subject Germany to a distant blockade based on the closing of the Dover Straits and the Orkney/Norway passage. This could only be achieved by British command of the sea; every other naval activity was subservient to this. It is pertinent in this connection to recall Jellicoe's memorandum to the British Admiralty of October 30, 1914, in which he stated unequivocally that there might, and probably would, be occasions in battle when he would have to refuse to comply with the enemy's tactics. For instance, if the enemy turned away, he would assume that it was their intention to lead the Grand Fleet over mines and would refuse to follow.

I desire particularly to draw the attention of their Lordships, he wrote, *to this point, since it may be deemed a refusal of battle, and indeed might possibly result in failure to bring the enemy to action as soon as is expected and hoped.*

Such a result would be absolutely repugnant to the feelings of all British naval officers and men, but with new and untried methods of warfare, new tactics must be devised to meet them. I feel that such tactics, if not understood, may bring odium upon me, but so long as I have the confidence of their Lordships, I intend to pursue what is, in my considered opinion, the proper course to defeat and annihilate the enemy's battle fleet, without regard to uninstructed opinion or criticism.

The Admiralty Board agreed with his thesis and expressed their full confidence in any action he might feel he had to take in the event of battle with the High Seas Fleet.

What would have been the effect of a defeat of the Grand Fleet? First, the essential command of the sea would have been lost, for it was upon the integrity of the Grand Fleet that it was solely based. Loss of British command of the sea would be followed inevitably by the breaking of the blockade of Germany, by German surface attack on British merchant shipping and transports, by the severance of sea communications between Britain and her armies overseas and by starvation of the home country.

One may, perhaps, quote here an Admiralty comment made shortly after the battle and recorded in a Naval Staff Monograph published in 1927. 'The British fleet is vital to the success of the Allied cause. The German fleet is of secondary importance; its loss would not vitally affect the cause of the Central Powers, and it can, therefore, be risked to a much greater extent than the British fleet.'

It can be appreciated from all this what exactly was Jellicoe's objective as he led the Grand Fleet to battle. His primary object was to retain command of the sea, his subsidiary object was to annihilate the High Seas Fleet. His primary object succeeded; his subsidiary object failed.

And what of Scheer? He had, as we know, put to sea to try to isolate a portion of the Grand Fleet and to bring it to action against superior force, but he was determined at all costs to avoid action with the fleet as a whole. In this intention he was out-manoeuvred, not once, but twice, and withdrew from the scene of action with precipitate haste. An all-out fight was the very last thing he wanted. And in his precipitate withdrawals he may well have raised in Jellicoe's mind the doubt which he (Jellicoe) had expressed to the Admiralty in 1914, that he would expect an enemy turn-away as a ruse to draw him over mines and submarines. Jellicoe, with the survival of Britain as a nation in his hands, was not going to be caught by tricks of that sort. We know now, of course, that at Jutland the Germans had no mines and no submarines, but Jellicoe did not know this. He had been informed (wrongly) by the Naval Intelligence Division in London that the German destroyers carried mines, and there had been reports of U-Boat sightings during the early stages of the action.

With two commanders-in-chief, each for different reasons refusing to take risks, it is not surprising that the periods of direct action between the battle fleets were of such short duration. Scheer turned away behind smoke as soon as he sighted the Grand Fleet; Jellicoe refused to risk possible decimation by mine and torpedo. Both, in their particular positions at that time, unquestionably made the correct decision.

Statistics inconclusive

If one judges the result of battles at sea by the number of hits made upon the other side, by the number of ships sunk, or by the number of men killed, then there is no doubt that the High Seas Fleet were the victors. Here, though, one may question some of the figures. Officially, the Germans fired 3,597 heavy shells and made 120 hits; the British fired 4,598 heavy shells and scored 100 hits. These are German figures. (There do not appear to be any official British figures of this nature.) But these figures do not give the true picture. As Professor Marder has pointed out (*From the Dreadnought to Scapa Flow*, Volume III), over a quarter of the German hits were made on the three armoured cruisers HMS *Warrior, Defence* and *Black Prince* at ranges from 7,000 to 1,000 yards. Nor do the German figures credit any British hits by heavy shells on the German cruiser SMS *Wiesbaden,* which was battered into a wreck and sunk.

So far as ship losses are concerned, the Grand Fleet lost 14 ships, totalling 111,000 tons; the High Seas Fleet 11 ships totalling 62,000 tons. The casualties amounted to 6,097 British officers and men killed, 510 wounded and 177 taken prisoner, against German losses of 2,551 dead and 507 wounded. Expressed as percentages of total strength, the British loss was 8.84% and the German 6.79%.

But here again, these figures tell only part of the story. In the Grand Fleet, after the day's fighting, Jellicoe had 24 undamaged dreadnoughts and battle-cruisers while Scheer had only ten. Eight British dreadnoughts and battle-cruisers had been damaged

S.M.S. THÜRINGEN
SKAGERRAK

	BRITISH		GERMAN	
	explodes	ENEMY SHELL	explodes	
	moves down	FLASH	moves down	
	lid off	SHELL BIN	lid on	
	single open	DOORS	double closed Interlocking	

GUN OPERATION
Shell from Magazine and Cordite from Handling Room move up Main Hoist to Working Chamber & up rails to Turret

Turret
Working chamber
Main Hoist
Handling Room
Magazine

Imperial War Museum

against ten German, and proportionally this was greatly in favour of the Grand Fleet. And but for the shortcomings of the British armour-piercing shell, which broke up on hitting instead of penetrating and bursting inside, Scheer would certainly have lost two more battle-cruisers (SMS *Seydlitz* and *Derfflinger)* and possibly one battleship (SMS *König)* as well. Finally, in trying to judge the results of the battle against these yardsticks, Jellicoe was able to signal the Admiralty at 2145 hours on June 2 that the Grand Fleet was at four hours' notice for steam and ready for action. Scheer, in his report to the Kaiser, gave the middle of August as the date when the High Seas Fleet would again be ready.

It must not be forgotten that when Jellicoe met Scheer at about 1800 hours on May 31, he had a vast superiority in ships of all types, even allowing for the loss of two of Beatty's battle-cruisers in the earlier action, about which he did not know until the following morning. His ascendancy in *matériel* was enhanced by his tactical skill in placing the whole Grand Fleet in line of battle between Scheer and his bases. It looked a certainty that the High Seas Fleet was doomed to extinction. Why was it not?

One obvious reason is that naval battles are not fought on paper but on the sea, and are therefore subject to conditions of wind, weather and, particularly, visibility. At 1800 hours, there were about three hours of daylight left, and the area was covered by a typical North Sea haze which gave a visibility of about five miles (10,000 yards) from HMS *Iron Duke's* bridge. The haze was made worse by the vast quantity of smoke poured into the sky from the funnels of the British battle-cruisers.

Previous page: SMS *Thuringen* engages a British cruiser during the night action. *Inset:* The dangers of 'flash' had already been shown during the Dogger Bank action. The German fleet had learnt that lesson from this, and a system of double doors and stringent security rules prevented the flash getting any further than the stricken turret. In British ships, however, there was still a 'chain' of explosive material going right down into the magazine

A second reason, mentioned above but equally relevant here, was the failure of British armour-piercing shell. Unlike the German, which were fitted with trotyl, the British shells were filled with lyddite. The combination of lyddite and a too sensitive fuse caused the shells to burst on oblique impact, so that the whole force of the explosion was outside the German protective armour and not inside. Lyddite, moreover, is in itself a very sensitive explosive, and liable to explode from the shock of impact alone, irrespective of the fuse setting. The German shells had a very efficient delay action fuse which, combined with trotyl, produced the burst inside the protective armour. In both short encounters between the battle fleets, where the British gunnery produced several hits, the German ships escaped destruction through the failure of the British shells. Admiral Dreyer, one of the greatest of the Royal Navy's gunnery experts and who was present at the battle, wrote that 'the hits that were made at Jutland as a result of tactical advantage and gunnery skill would, with efficient AP [armour-piercing] shell such as we had in 1918, have sunk six or more German capital ships.' Losses of this order at that stage of the battle would have inevitably led later to virtual annihilation.

A third reason for the escape from annihilation of the High Seas Fleet was the fact that almost throughout the battle (the exceptions were two periods of about 15 minutes each) Jellicoe never knew exactly where the Germans were. Jutland must surely rank as the classic example of how a lack of reports on the enemy's position during action can hamstring a commander-in-chief. Basically this was the duty of the light cruiser squadrons, of which there were four in the British fleet that day, but the importance of enemy reports being fed into the fleet flagship was stressed in the Grand Fleet Battle Orders, and every captain of every ship who had read these orders must have known how essential it was to keep the commander-in-chief in the picture. Only one light cruiser squadron (the 2nd, under Commodore Goodenough) took this duty seriously, and even Goodenough failed at one vital moment, just

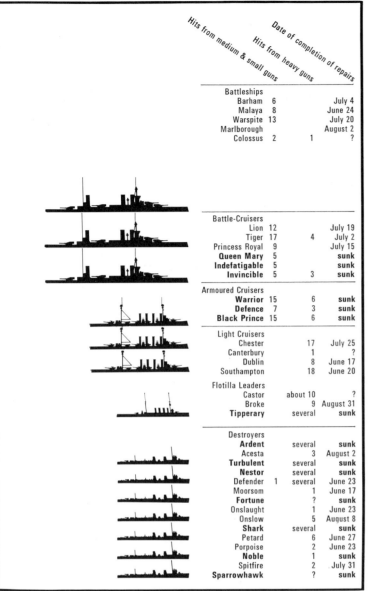

	Hits from medium & small guns	Hits from heavy guns	Date of completion of repairs
Battleships			
Barham	6		July 4
Malaya	8		June 24
Warspite	13		July 20
Marlborough			August 2
Colossus	2	1	?
Battle-Cruisers			
Lion	12		July 19
Tiger	17	4	July 2
Princess Royal	9		July 15
Queen Mary	5		sunk
Indefatigable	5		sunk
Invincible	5	3	sunk
Armoured Cruisers			
Warrior	15	6	sunk
Defence	7	3	sunk
Black Prince	15	6	sunk
Light Cruisers			
Chester		17	July 25
Canterbury		1	?
Dublin		8	June 17
Southampton		18	June 20
Flotilla Leaders			
Castor		about 10	?
Broke		9	August 31
Tipperary		several	sunk
Destroyers			
Ardent		several	sunk
Acasta		3	August 2
Turbulent		several	sunk
Nestor		several	sunk
Defender	1	several	June 23
Moorsom		1	June 17
Fortune		?	sunk
Onslaught		1	June 23
Onslow		5	August 8
Shark		several	sunk
Petard		6	June 27
Porpoise		2	June 23
Noble		1	sunk
Spitfire		2	July 31
Sparrowhawk		?	sunk

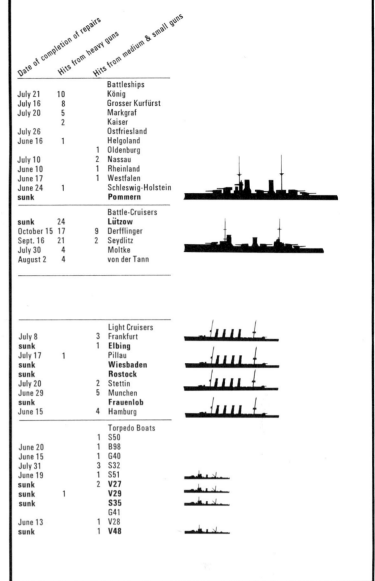

Date of completion of repairs	Hits from heavy guns	Hits from medium & small guns	
			Battleships
July 21	10		König
July 16	8		Grosser Kurfürst
July 20	5		Markgraf
	2		Kaiser
July 26			Ostfriesland
June 16	1		Helgoland
		1	Oldenburg
July 10		2	Nassau
June 10		1	Rheinland
June 17		1	Westfalen
June 24		1	Schleswig-Holstein
sunk			**Pommern**
			Battle-Cruisers
sunk	24		**Lützow**
October 15	17	9	Derfflinger
Sept. 16	21	2	Seydlitz
July 30	4		Moltke
August 2	4		von der Tann
			Light Cruisers
July 8		3	**Frankfurt**
sunk		1	**Elbing**
July 17	1		Pillau
sunk			**Wiesbaden**
sunk			**Rostock**
July 20		2	Stettin
June 29		5	Munchen
sunk			**Frauenlob**
June 15		4	Hamburg
			Torpedo Boats
		1	S50
June 20		1	B98
June 15		1	G40
July 31		3	S32
June 19		1	S51
sunk		2	**V27**
sunk	1		**V29**
sunk			**S35**
			G41
June 13		1	V28
sunk	1		**V48**

Above left: Battle damage—in this case one of the *Seydlitz'* lesser wounds, the damage to her deck caused by the fourth shell to hit her. The damage may appear superficial, but it is essential to remember that shells were designed to penetrate before exploding. *Above:* Comparative damage at Jutland. Although the British lost more ships, they were able to repair their damaged ones far more quickly

after Scheer's second turn-away at about 1915 hours, when he saw the movement and Jellicoe did not. At that moment Jellicoe was rendered blind by the Germans' smoke screen.

The number of enemy sightings by individual ships and squadrons which were not reported to Jellicoe was unbelievably high. Even Beatty, during the run to the north, failed to inform the Commander-in-Chief of the position, course and speed of Scheer's battle fleet, so that even at the moment of deployment Jellicoe had no sure knowledge of Scheer's position. Even the Admiralty, which had the priceless information of Scheer's route to his home base, failed to inform Jellicoe that Scheer was making for Horns Reef. There was plenty of time to get this information through to Jellicoe to ensure that the Grand Fleet would be there in time to bar the way on the morning of June 1. As for the number of individual ships which sighted the Germans, especially during the night actions, and kept silent, it is difficult sometimes to understand how mature and highly-trained naval officers could so lightly ignore their palpable duty in battle.

Here one can probably lay part of the blame on Jellicoe's method of command. He was a great 'centraliser' and fundamentally unable to delegate authority. One has only to look at the vast extent of the Grand Fleet Battle Orders, some 70 pages of small print, to appreciate the minute detail with which Jellicoe made known his orders and desires to the fleet. The effect of all this detail was to stifle initiative, to produce the feeling among subordinate admirals and captains that the Commander-in-Chief had his finger on every pulse, and was in full control of the battle throughout. Nevertheless, the rigidity of the Battle Orders cannot excuse the extraordinary lapse in passing information to the flagship. The GFBO's are quite specific on this point and were addressed to all cruisers, from battle-cruisers down to light cruisers. For the period of the approach, the Battle Orders lay down: 'It is of great importance that all cruisers should plot the position of the enemy's ships as they are sighted or reported'; 'After gaining touch with the enemy, the first essential is to maintain it'. And after battle is joined: 'Reports of movements, provided they are made in good time, may be of great value, *and any ship in a position to see clearly what is occurring, when it is probable that the Commander-in-Chief could not, should not fail to make a report*'. (Author's italics.) The instructions could hardly have been clearer.

The question of tactics during the battle is best left to last, for it is on this point that most of the controversy connected with Jutland has raged. Let us consider, first, the two battle-cruiser admirals in the handling of their forces before we turn to the two main protagonists. Within the general heading of tactics, one must include signals and fleet or squadron organisation. Let us deal first with Hipper. It is almost impossible to fault him throughout the battle. He did all that a battle-cruiser admiral could do, and he did it with precision, dash and the sure touch of the expert. All through, he kept the Commander-in-Chief fully informed of British movements with clarity and speed. And when called upon to launch their 'death ride' to extricate Scheer's battle fleet from disaster, his ships responded nobly and skilfully.

There are a number of criticisms which have been made against Beatty, some of them which do not bear serious investigation though others may well have some validity. One point of criticism has been in his stationing of the 5th Battle Squadron five miles to the north of the battle-cruisers during the period of reconnaissance instead of sailing as a concentrated force. Beatty himself always said that he wanted them there so that he could fall back on them at need. This would appear perfectly reasonable. Another criticism has been directed against Beatty for not concentrating

his force, which included the 5th Battle Squadron, when Hipper was first sighted and before trying to engage the German battle-cruisers. There was sufficient time for this, and it seems odd in the circumstances of the day that it was not done. Beatty's argument here was that, with his six battle-cruisers against the German five, he had a sufficient margin of superiority to dispense with the 5th Battle Squadron. This argues a faith in the gunnery excellence of his ships, which Beatty, knowing the facts as he must have done, should not really have held. The battle-cruisers' gunnery never approached the accuracy of that of the main Battle Fleet. It also seems a little unreasonable, when you have a weapon ready to hand, not to use it if time allows. This was a battle of the big ships, and in terms of fleet comparison, each German ship was worth one and three-fifths British ships. To try to make sure of two or three of them by using the whole weapon available was, in these terms, invaluable to the British cause.

The vast inefficiency of the *Lion's* signalling has been another point of criticism for which Beatty must surely bear the blame. To rely solely on flag signals on a day of limited visibility and much funnel smoke does not argue the meticulous attention to detail which an admiral must exercise in the control of his fleet or squadron. Some of the signals made by wireless were not as clear and as precise as they might have been. Two possible victories had already been missed by Beatty through the inefficiency of his flagship's signal department; this should surely have been enough to warn him that something was wrong and needed rectification. This failure in the *Lion* was not confined only to the battle-cruiser action; it occurred again later in the battle, with disastrous results during the night actions.

There was a failure, too, of correct concentration of the gunnery during the run south, which was responsible to some extent for the near loss of the *Lion*. Both the *Lion* and the *Princess Royal* concentrated, correctly, their fire on the leading German ship, the *Lützow,* leaving one British ship to engage one German all down the rest of the line. But the *Queen Mary,* third in the British line, engaged the third German ship, not the second. This left the *Derfflinger,* second in the German line, unengaged, and she was able to direct her fire untroubled by any return fire. The same error was repeated further down the line, where the *Tiger,* instead of engaging the third German ship, directed her fire at the fourth, throwing out both her own and the *New Zealand's* fire, since both were now shooting at the same ship unknown to each other and unable to differentiate in the fall of shot for the correction of range and deflection.

This had happened before at the Dogger Bank, when it was the *Tiger* which was the offender. This had been thrashed out at the time, and the captain of the *Tiger* was left in no doubt of his admiral's displeasure. It should not have happened again, and that it did once again argues a lack of attention to those organisational details which make a squadron or fleet efficient.

Beatty's tactics correct

Apart from the lack of preliminary concentration of force, which may or may not be a valid criticism, Beatty did all that was required of him on the purely tactical side. He made the initial contact, identified Scheer's ships when they came into sight, and led them back to the British battle fleet. Because of excusable errors in navigation, Beatty was seven miles to the westward of his estimated position, which meant that he appeared 65 degrees on the starboard bow of the *Iron Duke* instead of directly ahead, as Jellicoe had expected. Jellicoe himself had come down rather faster than he thought after taking in HMS *Galatea's* sighting signal and was $4\frac{1}{2}$ miles ahead of where he expected to be. The effect of Beatty being to the westward of his estimated position was that, when Jellicoe had to deploy, his squadrons were not square to the supposed line of the Germans' advance, so that his deployment would take longer, and take him further away from the Germans at the outset.

Of Scheer's tactics, the less said the better. He was supposed to be the great tactical genius of German naval warfare, but he showed no sign of this at Jutland. Twice he blundered into the whole British Battle Fleet, each time entirely by accident; and there was an element of panic in his withdrawals, as witness his 'Battle-cruisers, at the enemy. Give it everything' signal. To order a 'charge' against battleships in line by battle-cruisers argues a measure of desperation. In his own book, written later,

One problem of naval warfare often not fully appreciated is that of the difficulty faced by the commander-in-chief when trying to manoeuvre a fleet made up of several hundred ships of widely differing capabilities. This aerial photograph of two German battle-cruisers on exercises shows clearly the small margin of error needed to produce a collision

Scheer suggests that his second occasion of blundering into the Grand Fleet was a deliberate move 'to deal the enemy a second blow . . . to have the effect of surprising the enemy, upsetting his plans for the rest of the day.' This is nonsense. If this were the case, the last thing any admiral would do would be to station his battle-cruisers in the van of the attack. He did not surprise Jellicoe or upset his plans; any surprise there may have been was entirely Scheer's.

And finally Jellicoe. He has been criticised, first, for deploying on the port column of the Grand Fleet and not the starboard. Had he selected the starboard column on which to deploy, he would certainly have got into action ten minutes earlier, and at 4,000 yards closer range, but against this is the fact that the line of battle would have been led by the 1st Battle Squadron, which was the weakest of the three making up the Battle Fleet. In Jellicoe's opinion, it would also have opened the head of the line, at the point of deployment, to massed torpedo attack from the German destroyer flotillas. Finally, by deploying on the starboard column, the German battle fleet would have had a small but significant overlap over the British line of battle, and the only force left with which to try to stop Scheer reaching his base would be Hood's three battle-cruisers.

Deployment on the port column, however, gave a very considerable overlap on the German line of battle and gave Jellicoe the priceless advantage of placing his fleet squarely across Scheer's only escape route. It also brought the considerable advantage of crossing Scheer's 'T', whereby the British battleships could fire their broadsides while the Germans could only reply with their forward turrets. Also, most importantly, deployment on the port column gave Jellicoe the advantage of the light, making his own ships almost invisible to the Germans while the German ships were silhouetted against the light in the west.

Some critics have suggested that Jellicoe should have deployed on his centre column, which would have overcome the disadvantages of deployment on the starboard column and yet brought the Grand Fleet into action earlier and at a shorter range. There were two considerable disadvantages. One was that such a deployment required far more signalling and had not been practised by the Grand Fleet. The middle of a battle was no time to introduce a new manoeuvre. The second disadvantage was that deployment on the centre would have left Jellicoe leading the van of the Grand Fleet instead of being in the centre of the line. With the line of battle extending over six miles, it was obviously easier to control its movements from the centre than from the van.

If one looks dispassionately at this question of deployment, there can be nothing but praise for Jellicoe's decision to deploy on the port column. He had very little time in which to make the decision, which had been rendered harder for him by Beatty appearing so wide on the starboard bow instead of directly ahead. The first result of his deploying as he did placed the Grand Fleet in a position of great tactical superiority which would not have been gained with any other deployment, and after all, that must surely be the ultimate test on which to try to form a judgement.

The second great point of controversy in Jellicoe's tactics is the turn away by divisions at 1922 hours, in face of the German torpedo attack. It is difficult to understand the reasoning of this criticism provided that one approaches the problem with the knowledge that Jellicoe actually had at the time, and not with the knowledge that has subsequently been gained.

Anti-torpedo tactics
First, the turn-away as a countermove to a massed torpedo attack was incorporated in the Grand Fleet Battle Orders. All knew that this was the recognised defence, and no one had ever questioned it. Exercises carried out in Scapa Flow had shown that torpedoes fired at a line of ships in a massed attack would produce as many as 30% of hits, even with the ships manoeurving to avoid them. Moreover, Jellicoe had been informed by the Naval Intelligence Division (again wrongly as it turned out) that the Germans had developed a torpedo that left no track in the water, and so could not be seen approaching and thus give a ship a chance of dodging it.

By turning away, and thus lengthening the range, the German torpedoes were running very slowly as they reached the British line. Twenty-one torpedoes reached the British line, and even though their speed was by then very low, several ships (HMS Marlborough, Hercules, Agincourt, Revenge, Thunderer and Colossus among others) had to alter course violently to avoid them. Had the Grand Fleet not turned away, and thus presented a narrower target, there could well have been several hits, if only because the range would have been less and the speed greater.

One alternative was to turn towards the attack, and present

the smaller target bows on instead of stern on. This had never been practised by the fleet. If it had been tried, and had proved successful, Scheer's 'battle-turn' away might not have succeeded in breaking off the action. But it would at the same time have given an opportunity for the German 2nd, 5th and 7th Torpedo-boat Flotillas, which had been unable to get into a firing position because of Jellicoe's turn away, to launch their torpedo attacks.

One argument often advanced by the critics is that there was no need to turn the whole fleet away, as only the rear was threatened. This argument seems to ignore the torpedo which passed between the Thunderer and the Iron Duke. To turn only one division away, however, was to divide the fleet, and without exact knowledge of the Germans' position, divided tactics were unquestionably a risk. It must be remembered here that Jellicoe had no knowledge at this time of Scheer's battle-turn away. His view was blanketed by the German smoke screen. Other ships saw the turn (the 5th and 1st Battle Squadrons) but none of them reported the movement to the Commander-in-Chief. Goodenough, in the 2nd Light Cruiser Squadron, saw the German fleet on its new course after Scheer's turn-away, but, for the only time during the battle, failed to realise the importance of what he had seen and did not signal the information to Jellicoe.

Evasion tactics correct
Thus there is no real reason to condemn Jellicoe for turning the fleet away. It was the normal procedure on both sides. The Germans had already done so during the action; Beatty did so at the Dogger Bank battle. To continue on the existing course, or to turn towards, in the light of the knowledge then existing on the bridge of the flagship, was to risk the loss of or severe damage to about six ships at the minimum.

There is one other point here which is often forgotten when criticism is directed at Jellicoe for his turn-away. Even if he had been able to see the High Seas Fleet make their 'battle-turn' behind the smoke, had assumed that he could dodge all the torpedoes, had turned straight for the Germans and made a signal for a general chase, the Grand Fleet could not have caught up with the fleeing Germans before dark. Only the 5th Battle Squadron was faster than the König class battleships, and to allow one squadron of four battleships to forge ahead on its own would have been asking for its annihilation.

Finally, there has been much criticism of Jellicoe for not seeking a night action. This does not stand up to serious examination. One could, perhaps, blame Jellicoe for not having trained the fleet for night action in the two years before 1916, but this is as far as it can go. If we try to envisage the state of the battle as known on the flagship's bridge as darkness fell, we get the following picture. Jellicoe knew for certain that he was between Scheer and his base. He knew that night action was always a risky affair because of the difficulties of distinguishing between friend and foe. He knew that if he were reasonably served throughout the night with signals reporting the Germans' movements, a general action was certain on the morning of June 1. And so, reasonably and rightly, he settled down in night cruising formation to maintain his position between Scheer and his route home. If he had been served with the information which was actually gained during the night, from the British Admiralty, from the destroyers and from his own battleships, the battle would unquestionably have been renewed on the following morning. That he was not so served should not reflect either on his skill or his judgement.

Jutland, as fascinating a battle to study as any that has ever been fought at sea, has been many times described as a battle of missed opportunities. This is certainly the case; the opportunities which presented themselves and were not taken were there in full measure. Both sides made mistakes, but it is difficult to think that any single individual on either side made fewer mistakes than Jellicoe, except perhaps Hipper, in his junior command. True, Jellicoe was a great 'centraliser' and the rigidity of his Grand Fleet Battle Orders could, perhaps, be said to have stifled individual initiative in his divisional and squadronal leaders. But he had the right to expect (and the GFBO's gave him good reason for this expectation) that his admirals and captains would be aware of their responsibilities in this connection. Alas, they were not, and as a result Jellicoe had to fight his battle in the dark.

In recent years the most intense and analytical study of Jutland has been made by Professor Arthur Marder (From the Dreadnought to Scapa Flow, Volume III). It is difficult to disagree with him when he writes: 'Jellicoe has been most unfairly blamed for not doing miracles at Jutland. He was as brave and enterprising as the best of them, and he did the best that was possible.'

The defeat of the
submarine, rather
than the destruction
of the High Seas
Fleet, was to be the
decisive factor
at sea

THE CHANNEL WAR

Left: HM Monitor *Marshal Soult*
Displacement: 6,670 tons. *Length:* 355¼ feet.
Beam: 90¼ feet. *Armament:* Two 15-inch, eight
4-inch, two 3-inch and two 12-pounder guns.
Armour: Deck 1 to 3 inches, and bulges on the
waterline. *Power/speed:* 1,500 hp/5-7 knots.
Crew: 228. Monitors were nothing more than
floating artillery, so speed and protection
were minimal, sea keeping qualities were poor
but the beam to length ratio was smaller than
in ordinary warships to give the gun platform
greater stability in coastal waters

Above: HMS *Riviera*, seaplane carrier
Displacement: 1,675 tons. *Length:* 311 feet.
Beam: 40 feet. *Armament:* Two 4-inch and one
6-pounder gun. *Speed:* About 23 knots. *Crew:*
About 250. This was one of six vessels
converted into seaplane carriers from cross-
Channel ferries, the *Riviera* previously
belonging to the South Eastern and Chatham
Railway. The seaplanes were housed in the
specially built hangar on the stern and hoisted
out onto the water, from which they took off
and landed, to be hoisted in again

Top: HMS *Mohawk*, 'Tribal' class destroyer
Displacement: 890 tons. *Length:* 270 feet.
Beam: 25 feet. *Armament:* Five 12-pounders and
two 18-inch torpedo tubes. *Power/speed:* 14,000
hp/36 knots. *Crew:* 60. The 'Tribal' class was the
result of Lord Fisher's demand for ocean-going
destroyers. The orders were placed in 1905, and
the builders were given great latitude to design
ships within the given parameters, to try to
find the best design, later to be adopted as
standard. *Mohawk* was built by J. Samuel
White's yard and finished in 1907

With the conquest of Belgium, the German navy
acquired the important and strategically sited
bases of Ostend and Zeebrugge. From here the
Germans could send out their destroyers to
harry British coastal trade and, more important,
transports carrying supplies and reinforcements
to the BEF in France. To guard against this threat,
the British had to keep many cruisers and
destroyers in the area, but it was a hopeless
task to try to halt every lightning hit and
run raid. All they could expect to do was
inflict sufficient damage on the German
destroyers to deter them from pressing their
luck too often. *Paul Kennedy* and *Oskar Eckert*

At the beginning of the war, the kernel of the Channel Fleet consisted of 19 of the older battleships, based upon Portland, whose function was to prevent a German exit to the south or a powerful attack by the High Seas Fleet upon Britain's sea communications with France. But the importance and strength of this force declined with the realisation that such an attack was unlikely to occur: the German battlefleet had nowhere to go should it burst through the Channel, while a raid upon the Dover area would probably bring the Grand Fleet down from Scapa to block its return journey to Wilhelmshaven. Consequently, by 1916 it was only the cruiser, destroyer and lighter forces in the Channel which really mattered, and which could be expected to be called upon for action. The Harwich vessels, under Commodore Tyrwhitt, consisted of the 5th Light Cruiser Squadron (five ships) and the 9th and 10th Destroyer Flotillas, which usually totalled around 36 destroyers with four flotilla leaders or light cruisers at their head. However, Tyrwhitt's force had many duties in the North Sea and he was usually only able to detach part of one flotilla to the Straits of Dover when the prospect of action arose there. The main burden for the maintenance of the control of the Channel therefore lay upon Vice-Admiral Bacon, commanding the Dover Patrol, which normally comprised two light cruisers or flotilla leaders, 24 destroyers, eight patrol or 'P' boats and 14 monitors. Destroyers and monitors from these two commands were detached to make up a smaller force, which operated from Dunkirk and patrolled the eastern side of the Channel. In addition, a miscellaneous group of drifters, trawlers and yachts undertook the arduous and unrewarding task of patrolling the Straits.

The heterogeneous nature of these British Channel forces was amply reflected by the miscellaneous nature of their operations in 1916. Tyrwhitt's flotillas were constantly being detached to cover the transportation of the troops across the Straits, while on January 18 they formed the escort for the seaplane carrier HMS *Vindex*, which was to bomb the German bases at Hage on the Schleswig coast. Dense fog prevented this operation even before the Ems estuary had been reached, however, and the force withdrew. On January 29 a fresh attempt was made, but a submarine attack upon Tyrwhitt's flagship, HMS *Arethusa*, whose stern was grazed by a torpedo, forced him to order a further withdrawal. His vessels were again at sea during the action around the Dogger Bank on February 9/10. The sole result for the Commodore was the sinking of the *Arethusa* by a mine on his return to Harwich, which forced him to transfer his flag to the leader HMS *Lightfoot*.

The Dover Patrol forces were equally busy in the early months of 1916 and the mines laid by German submarines created much trouble for them, one liner being struck just outside Dover harbour while attempting to rescue another which had been similarly disabled. Moreover, aircraft from Flanders carried out bombing raids upon the English coast and on February 1 succeeded in sinking their first ship—a small coaster. Bacon was also engaged in offering support to Foch's troops along the Belgian coast and on January 6 he took command of a force of five heavy monitors, which pounded the Villa Scolaire batteries without provoking any reply. A few days later, these same vessels were engaged upon a quite different task, patrolling off the mouth of the Thames to protect London against expected Zeppelin raids. Although this work proved fruitless, it illustrates the multifarious nature of the Dover Patrol's duties. In March its destroyers were again diverted from their normal patrols to search for the steamer *Sussex* which had been torpedoed, an act of greater importance for German-American relations than for the Channel forces.

Combined operations

Later that month an extensive mining operation, aimed at closing the mid-sea approaches to the Thames and the Dover Straits, was carried out by four minelayers from Sheerness escorted by two divisions of Harwich destroyers. On the same day, March 20, an air raid by 50 Allied bombers and 15 fighters took place upon Houtlave aerodrome, near Zeebrugge, while the seaplane carriers HMS *Riviera* and *Vindex* launched attacks upon the German seaplane base on the Zeebrugge Mole. This ambitious plan achieved a fair amount of damage around Zeebrugge, while the only incident that occurred at sea was a short-lived attack by three German destroyers upon a division of the 9th Destroyer Flotilla, which was covering both the seaplane carriers and the minelayers. Although the destroyer HMS *Lance* suffered in this conflict, the German force was beaten off and the minelaying operation was carried out without further trouble.

Vice-Admiral Bacon, however, had even larger schemes to deny the Channel to the Germans, and particularly to their minelaying submarines. The Admiralty now allowed him to carry out his plan to close the passage between the Thornton Ridge shoal and the

Right: Commodore Reginald Tyrwhitt, commander of the Harwich Force throughout the war. *Below:* The after part of HMS *Nubian* (right) being towed home after her bows had been blown off. She was beached, and later joined to the forepart of HMS *Zulu*

The opposition: part of a German destroyer flotilla getting up steam in harbour

Belgian coast by a double line of mines across the entrance to Zeebrugge and by a parallel line of mine nets. In the early morning of April 24, six divisions of net drifters, six -mine-laying trawlers and four large minelayers were hard at work, covered by two monitors, the Flanders coast patrol from Dunkirk and three divisions of destroyers from Harwich. In less than four hours the mines and nets, in lines approximately 15 miles long, were in place and the minelayers were returning to port. The drifters with their escort remained to watch the nets and were thus subjected to bombing raids from German seaplanes and, later, to an attack by three destroyers. This force was so hotly pursued by the four 'M' class destroyers escorting the drifters that the chase was not broken off until the German shore batteries had scored hits on every ship in the division, bringing HMS *Melpomene* to a halt with a shell in her engine-room. As she was being towed to shelter, the German destroyers resumed their attacks and were not finally driven off until two monitors joined in the battle. After that, the drifters were left in peace to claim, by wishful thinking, the destruction of two German submarines in the nets and a possible further two in the minefield.

During the first half of 1916, the Harwich Force had been particularly busy, not only in carrying out its tasks in the Channel and Thames estuary waters, but also in operating in conjunction with the Grand Fleet in the North Sea upon a number of occasions, although, on Admiralty orders, Tyrwhitt's vessels had been held back from the Jutland action in case the Germans attempted the blocking of the Channel ports with their older battleships. It was possibly because of these larger-scale operations on both sides that little of note occurred in the Channel area in the months following the minelaying expedition of April. After Jutland, however, things began to warm up: raids upon the Dover Patrol's communications, together with submarine warfare, became the only methods by which the German navy could act offensively and maintain its crews' morale and the people's confidence. The German destroyer force at Zeebrugge was again built up when, in early June, a second German destroyer flotilla was despatched to Zeebrugge, a development which increased the British concern for their communications with France, Belgium and Holland.

On June 8 the British fears were confirmed by the appearance of 12 German destroyers near Dunkirk. This force turned back before the monitor HMS *Lord Clive* and the 'Tribal' class destroyers on patrol could engage it, but the Admiralty was not slow to get the message and ordered Tyrwhitt to detach some vessels from Harwich as a permanent reinforcement for the Dover Patrol. The British warships operating from Harwich, Dover and Dunkirk were, technically speaking, still far superior to the German light forces in the Channel and consisted of eight light cruisers, three flotilla leaders, 68 destroyers, eight 'P' boats and 14 monitors. But a large proportion of this total was often engaged upon other tasks and the German destroyers, which the Admiralty estimated as being as many as 22 in July 1916, enjoyed the incalculable advantage of being able to choose where and when to strike. The trade route to Holland remained particularly vulnerable to sorties from Zeebrugge, and Tyrwhitt was forced to allocate a permanent patrol of two light cruisers and from five to ten destroyers for use.

The events of July 22/23 soon proved this to be a wise disposition, for the German destroyer flotilla in Flanders had decided to interrupt the merchant vessels sailing to and from the Hook of Holland on· that night. On the evening of the 22nd, Tyrwhitt himself was at sea with the light cruiser HMS *Carysfort* flying his flag and leading four 'M' class destroyers, while a second division, of similar strength and led by HMS *Canterbury,* accompanied them from Harwich until the two groups separated along the patrol lines. At 0130 hours on the 23rd, Tyrwhitt's division spotted three German destroyers to the north and set off after them. This latter group, aware of the unfavourable odds, retreated eastwards and eluded the Commodore's ships during a sudden squall.

This manoeuvre, however, brought the German destroyers closer to the *Canterbury's* division, which had been patrolling some distance to the east. This division, commanded by Captain Royds, had turned south-eastwards under Tyrwhitt's order towards the Schouwen Bank and, at 0145 hours spotted six German destroyers steaming swiftly towards Zeebrugge. Drawing to within 5,000 yards, Royds' division opened fire and was at once replied to. At this point the destroyer HMS *Matchless,* newly emerged from the dockyard, was unable to keep up the pace and fell back, being joined by her somewhat anxious consort, HMS *Milne.* The other two destroyers pressed ahead, followed at some distance by the *Canterbury,* and pursued the German vessels until they approached the minefield off Zeebrugge. Here they were recalled. This short engagement revealed the alertness of the British forces guarding the Dutch route, but also showed that the German warships, in

the words of the British Official History, 'Had none the less a great capacity for mischief', particularly as their sorties could not be detected in advance, as could those of the High Seas Fleet.

It was this latter force which, by coming out on August 19, drew the Harwich vessels away from the Channel area once again, to resume their second function of assisting the operations of the Grand Fleet in the North Sea. Since June, Scheer had been preoccupied in attempting to evolve an operational plan whereby he could 'show the world the unbroken strength of the German Fleet' (German Official History) but avoid running into the Grand Fleet without warning as had happened at Jutland. Yet the only solution appeared to be a morale-boosting bombardment of the east coast of England, together with a larger concentration of airships and submarines, patrolling in regions through· which the British fleet would probably pass. It was, in fact, the original Jutland plan. Consequently, when the High Seas Fleet set forth with the object of bombarding Sunderland in the early morning of the 19th, Scheer had disposed two lines of submarines near the English East Coast and a further two lines north-north-west of Terschelling. In addition, four Zeppelins patrolled the area between Scotland and Norway, while a further six were stationed roughly parallel to the east coast. There was little chance this time of meeting up unawares with a superior force.

These patrols, he reasoned, should not only be able to give him sufficient warning of an approach by the Grand Fleet, but successful torpedo attacks by the submarines might well be able to swing the ratio of capital ships strength more into Germany's favour. As the obsolete *2nd Battle Squadron* had been discarded and three of the battle-cruisers were still under repair after Jutland, the High Seas Fleet totalled only 19 battleships and two battle-cruisers, together with the appropriate light forces. Yet although numbers dictated an avoidance of any full-scale conflict with Jellicoe's squadrons, Scheer still clung to his hope of being able to encounter and destroy a part of the British battlefleet—the only way by which he could even up the two opposing forces and thus be in a position to challenge the Royal Navy for the command of the seas.

The British forewarned

The various fleet preparations for this operation had not escaped the attention of the British Admiralty, who ordered the Grand Fleet to sea also. Thanks to the wireless-detection work of Room 40, it was speeding into the North Sea from Scapa Flow a few hours before Scheer's force left harbour. Twenty-nine dreadnoughts with accompanying escorts steamed steadily southwards early that morning to rendezvous first with their Commander-in-Chief (a rather tired Jellicoe had been recuperating at Dundee and rejoined his flagship by means of a fast cruiser), and then with the six battle-cruisers under Beatty, which had sailed from Rosyth and were cruising about 120 miles east of that point. In addition, 25 British submarines were sent out to patrol along the east coast of England and near the German and Dutch coasts. The Harwich Force (consisting of five light cruisers, a flotilla leader and 19 destroyers) steamed towards an assembly point near Brown Ridge, about 50 miles east of Yarmouth. Since the British had moved so swiftly in this matter and had reached their rendezvous positions while the High Seas Fleet was only approaching the Dogger Bank, the chances of an interception seemed bright.

Tyrwhitt's force was intended primarily to pick off damaged German dreadnoughts as they limped home, but it would also be in a position to join in a major battle should events demand it. However, the chief threat to Scheer was clearly Jellicoe's squadrons, steaming parallel to the east coast at 18 knots and preceded, 30 miles ahead, by Beatty's battle-cruisers. Ahead of these, in turn, were three squadrons of light cruisers. Dawn brought with it a great deal of haze and it was in these conditions that the light cruiser HMS *Nottingham* was suddenly torpedoed by the *U 52* at 0557 hours, while zig-zagging about the latitude of the Farne Islands. Unprotected by destroyers, the stricken vessel was struck by a further torpedo from the same *U 52*, half an hour later. At 0710 hours, shrouded by fog and with her crew in small boats, the *Nottingham* sank.

The news of this attack (reported as caused by a mine, with the possibility of a torpedo thrown in as an afterthought) did not reach Jellicoe until 0650 hours, only ten minutes before he received an Admiralty signal that the High Seas Fleet was still 170 miles east of the Flamborough Head. These two messages persuaded the Commander-in-Chief to order an abrupt about-turn by the Grand Fleet and for almost 120 minutes they steamed in a northward direction. It was a decision which was later much criticised, but the Admiral had his reasons. He was at this time developing a great unease, almost a fixation, about the menace posed by German submarines to his battleships. HMS *Iron Duke,* indeed, had been narrowly missed by a torpedo earlier that morning as she steamed ahead of the fleet to pick up Jellicoe. Then came the news of the attack upon the *Nottingham,* and a further report of a submarine sighting, raising the fear that the Grand Fleet was perhaps steaming into a trap laid by Scheer. Finally the message that the German battlefleet was still far from the English coast convinced Jellicoe that he could afford to give away time while getting well clear of submarine-infested waters.

The Admiralty's information about the position of the High Seas Fleet was based upon a radio message picked up from that point around 0600 hours: but, in fact, that particular call had been sent by the German battleship SMS *Westfalen,* which had been hit by a torpedo from the British submarine, the *E 23,* an hour earlier, and Scheer himself was many miles nearer the English coast when Jellicoe first received news of the damaged dreadnought's signal. Incidentally, the commander of the *E 23* persisted for several hours more in his attempts to sink the *Westfalen,* but he was successfully kept at bay by her escorts, who got the battleship safely back to Wilhelmshaven.

Scheer, too, was misled by reports of his opponent's whereabouts. The Grand Fleet, as he was aware, was at sea; but a report received at 0950 hours from the Zeppelin *L 31* indicated that it was steering north-eastwards—which was in fact true at the time of the sighting (0850 hours). A few hours earlier, the Zeppelin *L 13* had discovered the Harwich Force near Brown Ridge, reporting that it was heading to the south-west—which was also true, since Tyrwhitt was now patrolling in the vicinity of his rendezvous. Scheer was totally mystified at the news that the British forces were steering away from him and away from each other, and pressed on towards Sunderland. Although the same Zeppelin, *L 13,* later (0845 hours) reported that the Harwich Force had turned to the north-east, the presence of these light cruisers and destroyers did not bother the German admiral.

What really excited Scheer was a series of messages from the Zeppelin around noon, assuring him that a British force, which also included some battleships, was steering north-eastwards about 60 miles from Cromer. In fact, this group was none other than Tyrwhitt's vessels again, by then steaming quickly northwards to intercept the High Seas Fleet, believing Scheer to be much further to the east than he actually was. For the *E 23,* defeated in her attempts to finish off the *Westfalen,* had wirelessed that the German battlefleet was only 70 miles north-west of the Ems at 0919 hours—actually it was 120 miles from Sunderland by that time. But if Tyrwhitt and Jellicoe (to whom Tyrwhitt passed on the *E 23's* message) were misled, Scheer was even more so. The repeated assurances of the *L 13,* whose pilot was incidentally a reservist and not well trained in reconnaissance work, that a small battleship group lay to the south-east, completely changed the picture. In the words of the British Official History 'It seemed as though there were, within closing distance of him, a force so weak that it would stand no chance if he could meet it, and yet so important that its destruction would be a resounding victory.' Promptly forgetting about the bombardment of Sunderland, he swung his force to the south-east at 1300 hours.

A cruel blow

It was possibly the luckiest move Scheer ever made—and one of the cruellest strokes ever delivered to Jellicoe. For the Grand Fleet had been steaming steadily southwards since shortly after 0900 hours, making sure that it passed about 25 miles to the eastward of where the *Nottingham* had been torpedoed. Even so, the reports of submarine sightings further ahead were discomforting and Jellicoe had elected that his force would proceed southeastwards through the mine-free 'M' channel and not the 'L' channel, as originally intended. (These channels were swept areas pointing south-eastwards from the Forth approaches into the middle of the North Sea, like two fingers, 'M' 'finger' being nearer the English coast than the 'L' 'finger'.) Admiralty reports convinced him that the two battlefleets would cross each other at right-angles some time that afternoon and at 1415 hours he signalled to the Grand Fleet 'High Sea Fleet may be sighted at any moment. I look with entire confidence on the result.' In fact, Scheer was so far ahead of where the British reports placed him that, had he persisted in his course towards Sunderland, he would have been cut off from his base by the Grand Fleet in the late afternoon. Alas for British hopes, Scheer had turned away from their battlefleet and had been steering south-eastwards for over an hour when Jellicoe made his Nelson-like signal.

It was soon the turn of the Germans to be disappointed. The Harwich force had been unable to find the High Seas Fleet and, concluding that the *E 23's* sighting was perhaps false, had also turned southwards, at 1245 hours. Consequently, after steaming south-eastwards for almost two hours, Scheer could still see no sign of the small group of British battleships reported by the *L 13* and the High Seas Fleet was fast approaching the Humber minefields. Moreover, he had received an alarming report from the

submarine *U 53* at 1415 hours that the Grand Fleet was only 65 miles to the north. Shortly after this, therefore, he ordered a return to base.

Only gradually did Jellicoe learn, from Admiralty reports, that the Germans had once more eluded his grasp. Shortly before 1600 hours, he reluctantly ordered his battleship squadrons to reverse course, being then midway down 'M' channel and about the latitude of Whitby.

That afternoon and evening, the Grand Fleet underwent a most harrowing time in passing through the German U-Boat lines positioned near the English coast. The light cruiser HMS *Falmouth* was torpedoed at 1652 hours by the *U 66,* which attempted for a further two hours to finish off the damaged warship and was only forced away with great difficulty by light cruisers and destroyers. However, the *Falmouth* was later sighted and sunk by another submarine, the *U 63,* as she was being towed towards the Humber. Meanwhile the Grand Fleet was steaming hurriedly northwards in tightly packed order, unable to zig-zag in the narrow channel and experiencing repeated alarms as submarines were sighted. It was with great relief that Jellicoe and his force emerged into clear waters again, about 2030 hours. Most of these meetings with the U-Boats might have been avoided had the 'L' Channel been used, although Jellicoe was not to know that; but it is less easy to state with any certainty today, as several critics did at the time, that the use of 'L' Channel on the downward route would have ensured an interception of the High Seas Fleet.

While this was going on, Tyrwhitt's vessels had turned northwards again in the hope of attacking the German battlefleet on its return to Wilhelmshaven. After searching throughout the late afternoon, contact was made just before 1800 hours and soon, through the dusk, the Harwich Force could pick out Scheer's battleships, steering eastwards and flanked by a strong force of destroyers to ward off any night assaults. Even though warned by Jellicoe that no support could be given by the Grand Fleet, Tyrwhitt attempted to get ahead of the High Seas Fleet and then to rush down upon it at high opposing speeds: for to attack a fast-moving battlefleet from the rear was a hazardous tactic, which would have exposed the light cruisers and destroyers to lengthy bombardment from the capital ships they were gradually overtaking. Yet so fast was Scheer's force steaming that it soon became apparent to Tyrwhitt that he could not get in front of the High Seas Fleet before the expected fine moonlight illuminated the whole area. Reluctantly, therefore, the attack was abandoned.

If Scheer was afterwards satisfied at the clear run he had made and at the losses inflicted by his U-Boats (he erroneously believed that the battle-cruiser HMS *Inflexible* had been damaged by a torpedo), Jellicoe was bitterly disappointed—and very alarmed. Once again the High Seas Fleet had eluded his grasp. Moreover, not only had his force been dogged by Zeppelins for much of the day while his information of the Germans' whereabouts had remained scanty, but the Grand Fleet had repeatedly sighted and been attacked by German submarines, against which, for the light cruisers at least, there was inadequate destroyer protection. Scheer had obviously attempted to lead the British battleships into a mine and U-Boat trap, he concluded. Backed up by Beatty, Jellicoe insisted that the Grand Fleet avoid going further south than Latitude 55° 30' North (the Farne Islands) and further than 4° East unless it had sufficient destroyers: only if 'the need were very pressing' should this rule be broken.

In effect, Jellicoe was proposing to abandon most of the North Sea to the German forces, should they wish to occupy it. He also insisted that the Grand Fleet could not guarantee the east coast harbours against Scheer's 'tip-and-run' raids, a decision which, if known, would have greatly alarmed the British people. Unable to meet the Commander-in-Chief's demands for destroyers, the Admiralty accepted this policy on September 13. This revolutionary decision was also justified by the argument that 'it is impossible for our capital ships from the Northern bases to bring the enemy to action for some 16 to 30 hours after his ships have been reported off our coast', but this point cannot carry too much weight. Wireless indiscipline aboard the German warships in harbour usually gave the Admiralty a fair degree of notice of an impending sortie. After all, Jellicoe was much nearer to Sunderland than Scheer at 0700 hours on the morning of August 19, having set out before the High Seas Fleet sailed! It was the torpedoing of the *Nottingham* (due to the lack of destroyer escorts for the cruisers) which forced Jellicoe to lose four hour's valuable time by reversing course. This, and the harrowing return voyage up 'M' channel that same evening, were the deciding factors—not the inability to discover when the Germans would come out.

On October 18, this calculated British policy of abstention was carried into effect. Despite the news that Scheer was about to make a further sortie that evening, only such local forces as the British submarine flotillas and Tyrwhitt's vessels were sent out: the Grand Fleet remained at Scapa under short notice for steam. As it was, Scheer's operation soon fizzled out and the High Seas

German torpedoboats at sea. Once Michelsen's flotilla had arrived from Wilhelmshaven, the Imperial German navy was in a strong position to wreak considerable havoc on cross-Channel traffic

Above: A U-Boat takes on torpedoes at Zeebrugge, thorn in the Allies' side throughout the war. *Below:* The German destroyers SMS *S 49*. *Displacement:* 1,074 tons. *Length:* 261 feet. *Beam:* 27½ feet. *Armament:* three 3.5-inch, plus six 19.7-inch torpedo tubes and 24 mines. *Power/speed:* 23,500 hp/33 knots. *Crew:* 85/100. *Bottom:* A British motor launch. *Displacement:* 37 tons. *Length:* 80 feet. *Beam:* 12 feet. *Armament:* one 6-pounder. *Power/speed:* 440 hp/19 knots. *Crew:* nine.

Fleet turned for home before it reached the Dogger Bank. Rough seas, knowledge that the British were aware of the sortie, and the lack of U-Boats were probably the chief reasons for this about-turn. Moreover, the British submarine *E 38* had dampened the German enthusiasm somewhat by torpedoing the light cruiser SMS *München*. Although the stricken vessel was towed safely home, this short cruise was not without significance. For, while Jellicoe chose not to move the Grand Fleet into the North Sea without sufficient destroyers, Scheer, for his part, felt that the High Seas Fleet dare not venture forth without sufficient submarines, which served the vital dual purpose of spotting and crippling the superior battlefleet of his opponent. Indeed, in the August 19 operation, they had performed much better than the Zeppelins in their reconnaissance rôle. Now he was robbed of the use of this vital arm by the recent decision to employ the submarine force once again for the blockade of Britain's commerce; and, without the submarines, Scheer refused to move. The naval war in the North Sea, as far as the battlefleets were concerned, came to a standstill in the autumn of 1916. Seen in this light, the operation of August 19 could be rated as one of the most decisive in the history of the entire war.

Given this stalemate in the North Sea with regard to the battlefleets, the focus of attention swiftly swung to the Channel once again, especially as more German destroyers were available for that region now that they were not required in attendance upon the High Seas Fleet. Besides, Scheer did not want fleet morale and public confidence in the German navy to sink, nor to leave the monopoly of action to the U-Boat branch. On the evening of October 23, the commodore of the High Seas Fleet flotillas, Captain Michelsen, left Wilhemshaven for Zeebrugge with a force of no less than 24 destroyers. Getting wind of the move, the Admiralty ordered Jellicoe to place the Grand Fleet under short notice for steam lest this be a harbinger to a venture by Scheer into the Dover Straits or Thames Estuary. In this case, not only would the need be 'pressing', but there would be a fair chance of cutting off the High Seas Fleet on its return to base: thus the ruling of September 15 did not apply. The Harwich Force was also sent out, to the North Hinder lightship, but all these moves were in vain. Hugging the Dutch coast, Michelsen's destroyers reached Zeebrugge without incident.

Nevertheless, the Admiralty was greatly alarmed at this large reinforcement and the threat it posed, not only to the cross-Channel troop transports and the sea-lines to Holland, but also to the mass of coastal shipping which collected every night in the Downs anchorage before steaming to the port of London. Bacon was warned of the possible dangers, and one cruiser and four destroyers were sent from the Harwich Force to join the Dover Patrol. Nevertheless, given the large numbers of tempting targets, the strategic advantage clearly lay with the Germans and they were not slow to seize their opportunity. In the pitch darkness of the night of October 26/27, Michelsen's two flotillas set out from Zeebrugge, one (the *3rd*) to operate against the drifters watching the net barrage which stretched between the Goodwin Sands and Outer Ruytingen banks, the other (the *9th*) to interrupt British traffic encountered between Dover and Calais.

Believing the Belgian coast and the Downs to be the points most threatened by the German destroyer move to Zeebrugge, Bacon stationed eight of his destroyers in the former area and four in the latter. Six 'Tribal' class destroyers were kept ready at Dover, and another four formed a general reserve: two more, with two 'P' boats, patrolled near the barrage and Straits traffic. But, with no foreknowledge that a German raid was coming that evening, all these forces and the shipping they protected were very vulnerable to a sudden attack. Slipping unseen past one patrol and bluffing their way past a second, the German *9th Flotilla* steamed quickly into the Straits. Meanwhile, a division of the barrage drifters was set upon by the *3rd Flotilla,* which quickly sank three and set another on fire, and then sank the destroyer HMS *Flirt* when she came along to investigate the firing.

As soon as the news of these actions reached Bacon, he despatched the 'Tribals' from Dover and also ordered HMS *Laforey's* division out from Dunkirk. By that time, the German *9th Flotilla* was scouring the Straits route but all there was to be found was the empty transport, the *Queen,* which was sunk after the crew had been allowed into their small boats. Meanwhile, the *3rd Flotilla* was causing further havoc among the drifter divisions, sinking another four before they returned to Zeebrugge. Moreover, misunderstandings upon the British side had caused the 'Tribals' to get separated while HMS *Lawford's* division left the Downs traffic undefended. Fortunately, that area was not disturbed and the British destroyers, although scattered, were all in the central part of the Straits, towards which the *9th Flotilla* was

steering on its return up the Channel. At 1240 hours they rushed past HMS *Nubian,* setting her on fire and blowing off her entire forepart, hit HMS *Amazon* and *Mohawk* (though less severely), damaged a trawler and then raced clear to the Belgian coast.

Michelsen's flotillas, possessing all the advantages of the attacker, had blown a large hole in Bacon's Channel defences, although the latter could well be forgiven for telling the Admiralty that 'It is as easy to stop a raid of express engines with all lights out at night, at Clapham Junction, as to stop a raid of 33-knot destroyers on a night as black as Erebus, in waters as wide as the Channel.' Perhaps the only consolation on the British side was the rescue of the latter half of the *Nubian.* Joined together later with the forepart of the destroyer HMS *Zulu,* which lost her stern by hitting a mine, this unique hybrid was commissioned and given the name of HMS *Zubian.*

The German destroyer raid led to some hostile criticism of the navy leadership, and the Admiralty's bland assurances did not ease the matter when Balfour was later forced to admit that the loss of the drifters had been omitted in the first *communiqué.* Moreover, the First Lord's promise that a repeat of such raids would be severely dealt with was a large pledge to give, in view of the professional opinion that it was extremely difficult to check the sudden intrusions of the German destroyer force. Neither the withdrawal of the third German flotilla from Zeebrugge, nor the decision to reinforce the Dover Patrol by three patrols from Harwich (that force receiving destroyers from Scapa) eased the strategic disadvantages of Bacon's command, although they obviously gave the British a better chance of success if a large scale destroyer conflict did develop.

On the evening of November 23, 13 German destroyers set out from Zeebrugge towards the Downs in an attempt to emulate their previous feat. But this raid was much more timidly carried out and they headed for home as soon as they were challenged by the patrols: only one drifter was damaged. Nevertheless, the British Press gave it their full attention and reminded Balfour of his rash promise. Although small in itself, this second Channel raid played an important part in adding to the country's feeling that an offensive spirit was lacking in the navy's upper reaches.

One further incident took place in the North Sea in the last two months of 1916. On November 3 two German submarines, *U 20* and *U 30,* were stranded in the fog off the west coast of Jutland, and Scheer sent out a half-flotilla of destroyers, covered by four dreadnoughts and the battle-cruisers SMS *Moltke* to rescue them. The *U 30* alone was saved and, on the way back, the British submarine *J 1* succeeded in torpedoing the battleships SMS *Kronprinz Wilhelm* and SMS *Grosser Kurfürst.* Both dreadnoughts reached harbour safely but were in dockyard hands for a considerable time, and Scheer was personally rebuked by the Kaiser for risking a division of battleships to save two U-Boats.

The incident tended to confirm the Germans in the view that the battlefleet should be kept at home, because of the insecurity of the North Sea waters; and that the naval struggle against Great Britain should be waged, in the main, by the U-Boat arm. Scheer himself felt that 'during the further progress of the submarine war (upon which, in my view, our whole naval policy will sooner or later be compelled to concentrate) the fleet will have to devote itself to the single task of bringing the submarines safely in and out of harbour.' It was a remarkable admission from the Commander-in-Chief of the second largest battlefleet in the world, and a tacit admission that control of the North Sea could not be wrested from the Grand Fleet by his dreadnought squadrons under the existing circumstances.

If the overall strategic situation on both sides pointed towards a future stalemate in the North Sea, it did not promise the same for the Channel region, however. The German destroyer forces there were to assist the submarines based in Belgium in getting through the Straits, and to dislocate the British hold on the Dover-Calais region generally. In doing so they would convince the German people that their surface forces were still active while assisting the greater struggle of the U-Boat against British commerce. 'Clear in the North Sea, squally in the Channel' might well have been the forecast for the future development of the Anglo-German naval conflict as the year 1916 drew to a close.

Further Reading
Corbett, Sir Julian, *Naval Operations,* Volumes 3 and 4 (Longmans, Green)
Der Krieg zur See 1914-1918 (Berlin: E. S. Mittler & Sohn, 1925)
Marder, A. J., *From the Dreadnought to Scapa Flow,* Volumes II and III (OUP 1965)

Illuſtrirte Zeitung

Unſere U-Boote

Felix Schwormstädt 1917

Verlag J. J. Weber · Leipzig

Our U-Boats — the front page of the Leipzig *Illustrated News*, July 1917. In February the Germans had estimated that under unrestricted U-Boat warfare they could destroy sufficient shipping to drive Britain out of the war within five months. By July the five months were up, and Britain's naval supremo, Jellicoe, was uttering pessimistic warnings of imminent starvation. Germany was the first country to rely heavily on the submarine's strategic possibilities, and the gamble appeared to be paying off. . . .

The Submarine War
FIRST ROUND TO GERMANY

On February 1, 1917 Germany's leaders decided on a bold strategic gamble: to attempt to destroy Britain economically by sinking on sight any shipping, Allied or neutral. Such an act would bring America into the war, but would Britain be forced out before American involvement tipped the scales in favour of the Allies?
Vizeadmiral (Retd) Friedrich Ruge.
Left: U-Boat lookouts on watch for hostile aircraft

When in the autumn of 1916 the U-Boats received orders to resume their war against merchant shipping no steps were taken to adapt the organisation of the submarine force to that vastly increased task or to create a staff competent to clarify the technical and political problems, and to co-ordinate the military effort. Command remained divided, and several authorities continued to deal with submarine questions. The most important staff dated back to the times when submarines were considered exclusively as weapons to attack larger warships. Before the war the U-Boats were organised as a flotilla consisting of two half-flotillas, just like the torpedo boats, and, like these, under Fleet Command. In August 1914 the Senior Officer of the Flotilla, Fregattenkapitän Hermann Bauer, received the title of *Führer der U-Booten* (FdU). He was given a lieutenant-commander as his one and only staff officer, who among other duties kept the war diary of the FdU in longhand (which may explain why it is not exhaustive).

Hermann Bauer was a good choice for he was energetic, clever and experienced. Born in 1875, he joined the navy in 1892. As early as 1905 he and a classmate of his were the first officers to volunteer for submarine duty. They were nominated commanding officers of *U 1* and *U 2*, but Bauer's *U 2* never got beyond the trial stage and he was put in charge of submarine affairs in the *Reichsmarineamt* (Navy Office). Later on he served in several ships until he was made Senior Officer of the U-Boat Flotilla in March 1914.

As new submarines came along two more half-flotillas were founded under the FdU. In October 1916 they were all named 'flotillas'. However, they were not the only U-Boat forces. After German troops reached the coast of Flanders in autumn 1914 a Marine Corps under the tough Admiral von Schröder took over the defences there. For the most part it was formed from the surplus of naval reservists, but small torpedo boats and patrol vessels were attached. In February 1915 the 'U-Boat Flotilla Flanders' was created of *B I* and *C I* class submarines. The senior officer was Korvettenkapitän Bartenbach, who also had submarine experience. He was not under the orders of the FdU. Three more units were in a similar position: U-Boat Flotilla Kurland for the eastern Baltic, with only a few submarines; U-Boats of the Mediterranean Division for operations in the Black Sea, with again only a few UB and UC-boats; German U-Boat Flotilla Pola, operating in the Mediterranean with the Austrian Adriatic port of Pola as their base. At Pola there were 20 and more submarines, at least half of them large boats.

The *Inspektion des Ubootswesens* (Inspection of U-Boat Matters) under the Navy Office was responsible for the technical and some of the tactical developments. The Admiral Staff was directly in charge of the Mediterranean operations and had a say in the others. The very active Commander-in-Chief of the High Seas Fleet, Admiral Scheer, quite naturally was much interested in having strong submarine support available for the fleet operations he planned, whereas Marine Corps Flanders counted on its U-Boats as a defence against attacks on the coast which might also endanger the northern flank of the army in Belgium.

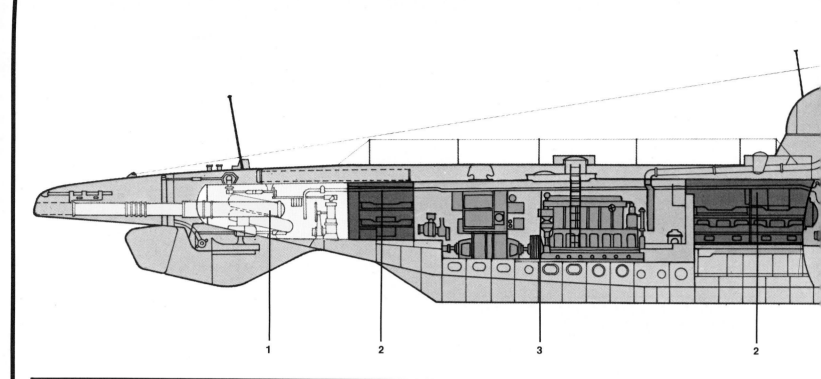

1   2   3   2

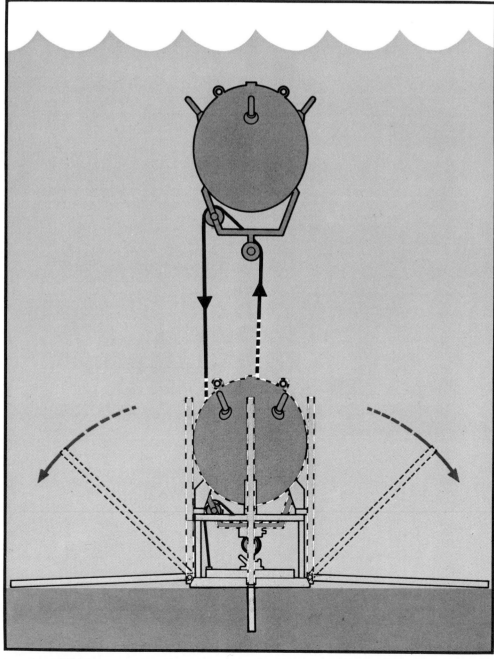

Above: The **UC 26**, representative of the *UC II* class, Germany's most numerous coastal mine-laying type. *Length:* 173 feet. *Beam:* 17 feet. *Displacement:* 434/511 tons. *Power/speed:* 600 (diesel) and 620 hp/12 and 7.4 knots. *Armament:* 18 mines in six obliquely mounted bow tubes, three 19.7-inch torpedo tubes (one stern and two bow, above water) and one 3.4-inch gun. *Crew:* 28. *Key to diagram:* **1.** Aft torpedo tube. **2.** Living quarters. **3.** Engine room. **4.** Control room. **5.** Mines and mine tubes. **6.** Forward torpedo tubes. *Left:* The deployment of a German submarine-laid mine. In Allied mines, the mine and the sinker (the part which rested on the bottom and anchored the mine) separated almost immediately after they had been dropped, the sinker towing the mine down to a predetermined depth above the sea floor after the correct length of cable connecting the two had been unreeled. In the German mine, however, the complete mine/sinker combination went to the bottom together. There the dissolution of a solvable plug permitted the partially air-filled mine to float towards the surface until a hydrostatic device was activated at the desired depth below the surface, which gave better results in service. Here the line was snubbed automatically. This system had much to commend it, principally in that the mines could be laid much more accurately, but it also had two inherent drawbacks: the mine

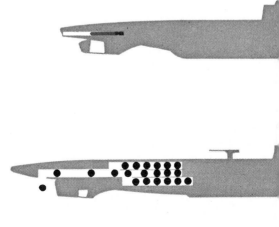

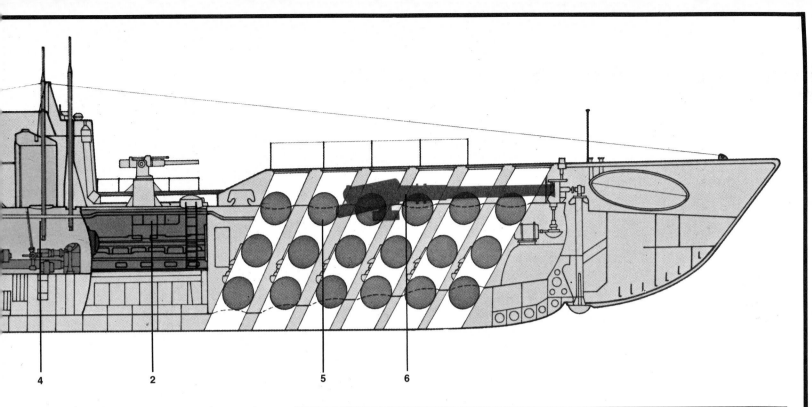

4 2   5   6

was connected to the sinker by two lines, and this meant that it was more prone to swaying, and therefore altering its depth, in strong currents, and the soluble release device tended to dissolve as soon as the mine was released, which meant that the mine might come up under the laying submarine and explode. The sinker was stabilised on the bottom by four arms, held flush with the sides of the whole package until it reached the bottom, where the arms swung out. *Below:* The two types of minelaying submarine used by Germany: *U 117* (bottom), a stern-laying type (42 mines and 18 torpedoes), and *UC 16* (top), a bow-laying type (18 mines and fewer torpedoes). The former was safer, as the submarine had time to get away before the mine and sinker separated. *Right:* The German 'Egg' mine. **1.** Hertz horn (lead tube containing sulphuric acid in a glass container. Impact with a ship breaks the glass, allowing acid to flow onto carbon and zinc elements, thus producing an electric current to fire the detonator). **2.** Mine casing. **3.** Detonating charge (allowed to fall to detonating mechanism by deactivating of safety device). **4.** Safety device (deactivated as mine is laid) and electric firing mechanism. **5.** Blocks of explosive. **6.** Wooden chocks. **7.** Electrically controlled firing-pin mechanism. **8.** Hydrostatic depth setter. **9.** Mooring line in horizontal drum. **10.** Mine sinker (acts as anchor when mine is operational)

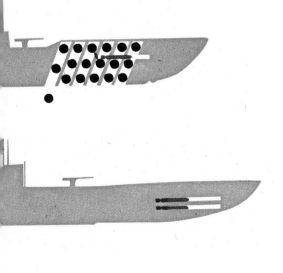

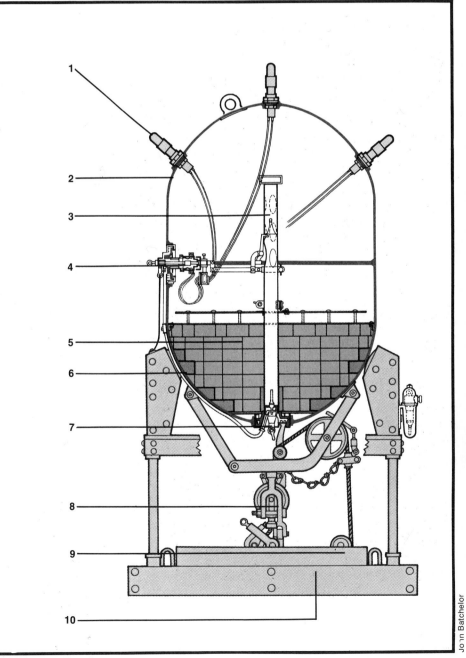

John Batchelor

Minelaying was not enough: unrestricted U-Boat warfare was Germany's only hope of destroying Britain's trade

Right: A party from a German minesweeper defuses a Russian mine in the Baltic by unscrewing its horns with a spanner

Opposite: Raiding into the Atlantic, the forward gun of a U-Boat is photographed from the conning tower as it submerges. Owing to the limited number of torpedoes that the U-Boats could carry, the gun armament was of great importance, and shipping was sunk by gunfire rather than torpedo whenever possible

Below: A German minesweeping team marks a mine with a buoy. Although extensive, minefields claimed far fewer victims than submarines, and the work of laying them was as hazardous as the task of identifying and marking those laid by the enemy

The Navy Office, Admiral Staff, Fleet and Marine Corps were all independent of each other and directly under the orders of the Kaiser who was supposed to give a ruling when their plans and opinions differed. That was no mean task under the best of conditions. Nothing like the present situation had been taken in account in the Kaiser's education and training. He had no adequate assistance in the shape of a combined staff or a well-selected 'brains trust' to help him in his decisions on the difficult political and military problems of the U-Boat war, which, in itself, was something quite new in international relations.

The scope of the task

In the autumn of 1916 the overall military situation pointed to unrestricted U-Boat war as the only means left that could bring a decision in a comparatively short time. Neither the German attack on Verdun nor the Franco-British offensives in Flanders and on the Somme had succeeded in a breakthrough, and both sides were exhausted. On the Eastern Front a dangerous situation was overcome by the quick victory over Rumania, but if Russia was exhausted Austria was distinctly weakening, and a very long front had to be held.

Great Britain was the key to the situation. If she could be cut off from her supplies she could not survive. The German naval staff calculated as follows: of a total British tonnage of 20,000,000, 8,600,000 at least were requisitioned for military purposes, 500,000 were needed for coastal traffic, 1,000,000 under repair or damaged, 2,000,000 had to serve the Allies. In this way about 8,000,000 tons of British origin were available. Actually, in the summer of 1916 no more than 6,750,000 tons of British shipping carried supplies to the British Isles and France, but about 4,000,000 tons of neutral and Allied ships transported cargoes to Great Britain. Unrestricted warfare would destroy about 600,000 tons per month and in addition dissuade two-fifths of the neutral ships.

In this way maritime traffic to England would be reduced by 39% in five months whereas submarine war under prize regulations would destroy only 400,000 tons per month and reduce maritime traffic by no more than 18% in five months. This would not be sufficient to force England to give up, whereas unrestricted warfare would achieve this end.

But much depended on the political consequences of the un-restricted war, particularly how President Wilson would react to it. From the point of view of international law and agreements there was not much difference between war zones declared and mined by the British, and zones barred to merchant ships under threat of unannounced submarine attack. Nobody was compelled to enter them whereas hundreds of thousands of German civilians were starving without having any choice in that matter, with the food situation in the winter of 1916/17 worse than ever. However, Wilson did not seem to mind that but had very forcibly declared that he was against submarine war.

A point he completely neglected was the fact that British merchant ships were armed, that they often sailed under false colours or no colours at all, and that a number of apparently harmless ships operated which were armed to the teeth with concealed guns. These Q-ships had already destroyed some German submarines which observed prize regulations.

To get a personal picture of the situation, Commander Bauer took part in a cruise of *U 67* around Scotland in April 1916. South of Ireland they encountered a steamship under the Swedish flag. When *U 67* fired a shot across her bows to stop her she answered with gun fire, all the time under the Swedish flag, hit *U 67* and forced her to dive. Another steamer opened fire under the Red Ensign. These experiences obviously contributed to Commander Bauer's stand in the question of the tactics to be followed. In any case, he felt responsible for his U-Boats and their crews. Therefore he advocated either unrestricted warfare or purely naval operations together with the surface ships of the Fleet. Admiral Scheer vigorously expressed the same view.

In contrast to them the Admiral Staff, closer to political currents and less in contact with the fighting men, favoured submarine war under prize regulations. On October 6, 1916 Admiral von Holtzendorff, the Chief of the Admiral Staff, carried his point with the Kaiser, and a number of orders were issued governing prize regulations. These regulations remained in force until February 1, 1917.

Raiding the shipping routes

In the autumn of 1916 heavy gales in the northern waters were costly in time to the submarines taking the route around Scotland. In some cases members of the watch on the conning tower were flung against the casing and seriously injured or even killed, others were hurled overboard and drowned. After consulting the commander of Marine Corps U-Boats on conditions in the Channel, the FdU gave orders to his U-Boats to take the short cut through Dover Straits unless they were newly commissioned and their crews therefore not yet experienced enough.

Not all large boats were employed for merchant warfare. Between beginning of November and middle of December three were directed to the Skagerrak and the Norwegian coast to scout for the raiders *Möwe* and *Wolf* on their way to the Atlantic and to assist them if they were attacked. To keep this protection at hand *Wolf* towed *U 66* submerged at ten knots for eight hours off the Norwegian coast opposite the Shetlands. After dark she cast the towing line off and proceeded at full speed northward. Both raiders succeeded in passing the British patrols without being sighted. The three submarines scuttled six small ships (none larger than 1,000 tons) and examined 43 more.

Three other U-Boats cruised along the Norwegian coast up to the Vestfjiorden (port of Narvik) where the Admiral Staff expected iron ore traffic to England. They found only one larger ship which turned out to be a British Q-ship. In the heavy sea neither side obtained hits. The weather was mostly very bad, and the guns were covered by ice, the men on the bridge exhausted, and there were no more than three hours of uncertain daylight. Altogether the operation was a waste of men and material.

Once the U-Boats reached the waters south of Ireland and the Bay of Biscay conditions were generally better. They met heavy traffic, and the British patrols were frequent only in the approaches to the Channel and near the coast. Some U-Boats even put a man or two as prize crews on board suitable ships which were used to receive the crews of the ships they scuttled, and to put them ashore in Spain. In this way, *U 46* 'worked' first with a small steamer and then with a trawler. Altogether she sank nine ships totalling 15,000 tons. Some more escaped after gun duels.

On December 17 *U 70* stopped and scuttled a British steamer of 5,600 tons in the middle of the Channel. Then she continued to the Bay of Biscay. Her total haul consisted of 16 ships with 26,000 tons. There were about ten more cruises of this type, and not all were finished on February 1, 1917. As a rule they lasted about four weeks, with a stay of one to two weeks in the waters to the southwest of the British Isles. They were all successful with the exception of two boats which had technical trouble. One lost oil through leaky tanks, in the other the propeller shaft of the port engine broke.

On January 5 *U 48* tried to stop a French steamer north of Cape Finisterre but the Frenchman returned the fire, altered course and escaped in a westerly direction. The German captain calculated that she would haul round again to reach the French coast. He was right and intercepted his quarry the following morning. His torpedo missed, he steamed ahead and sank her with another torpedo after a chase of 15 hours. Five hours earlier the Frenchman had already reported 'I am safe'. Altogether *U 48* destroyed 11 ships totalling 27,000 tons.

At that time there were six *UB II* boats under Fleet Command, mainly used for hunting British submarines which were supposed to watch the swept channels near Horns Reef and Doggerbank, and to report any movements there. The UB craft did not meet any of their opposite numbers, and very little traffic. They searched a number of ships, sank one small steamer and made two prizes. They, too, were much hampered by rough weather and might have destroyed more tonnage if they had been stationed nearer to the English coast.

What really could be done was shown by the UB-Boats based on the ports of Flanders. Even the few one-engined *B Is* stopped 17 neutral steamers, with machine gun or carbine, and made one prize. The *UB II* boats were much more successful. In two cruises between November 22 and January 9 *UB 18* stopped and scuttled 15 steamers totalling 17,400 tons, and also 11 trawlers and small coastal sailing ships. Twice she encountered Q-ships but escaped unharmed thanks to the watchfulness of her experienced captain.

U-Boat casualties

UB 19 met with a different fate. On November 22 she left Zeebrugge under a new captain. In the central part of the Channel she stopped and scuttled five ships totalling 5,200 tons. On the way back she sighted a tanker without a flag and took her under fire. The ship first tried to get away, then stopped and lowered two whalers which pulled away. *UB 19* thought her adversary harmless and approached to 500 to 600 yards. Now the captain felt misgivings and gave the order to dive but it was too late. It was the Q-ship *Penshurst* which opened fire with several guns and at once damaged *UB 19* so seriously that she had to be abandoned. Eight of her crew were killed, 15 saved by the whalers, and some injured, among them the captain.

In a similar way a few days later the same Q-ship sank *UB37* which had approached to 700 yards. There were no survivors. *UB 29* was also lost, probably hit by the British destroyer *Landrail* which early in the morning of December 13 dropped depthcharges on a diving submarine southeast of the Goodwin Sands. Much oil came to the surface after that attack, *UB 29* did not return to her base. Almost all the other boats had encounters with armed steamers or Q-ships.

In this period four *UC I* and eight *UC II* boats operated from Flanders. Only the larger type passed Dover Straits or went north of Great Yarmouth to drop the mines. *UC 19* was lost, probably hit by an explosive kite towed by the destroyer *Ariel* in the western Channel on December 6, 1916. *UC 18* had a weird experience in the night of January 24/25 when she returned through the Dover Straits after laying mines off Brest and St Nazaire and scuttling 13 ships totalling 14,600 tons. In the very dark night she sighted a destroyer and dived. To give it time to depart the captain stayed on the bottom for half an hour. When the boat rose again to the surface the crew felt a shock, and the stern would not come up. Opening the hatch of the conning tower they saw the stern of a destroyer on the after part of the submarine. The destroyer tried to get free by going astern, *UC 18* assisted these endeavours by diving quickly. Then she went on as deeply as possible and remained unmolested.

Other U-Boats had difficulties with nets but succeeded in getting rid of them, mostly by going down as deeply as possible, sometimes by going astern. This was dangerous, however, because the wires might foul the propellers. On January 18, 1917, *UC 21* torpedoed the destroyer *Ferret* which did not sink but could be towed in. A number of steamers of 5,000 and more tons were also brought in after hitting mines.

Seven *UC II* boats attached to the flotillas under Fleet Command undertook 11 operations, each time laying 18 mines. By these fields 11 ships of 14,300 tons were sunk. These UC-Boats also stopped and examined 31 neutral steamers. Four of them were scuttled because they carried contraband, and also some trawlers. *UC 31* took one as a prize and put a coxswain on board. Soon afterwards the submarine had a fight with an armed steamer and was compelled to dive. In this way she lost contact with the trawler which later was retaken by a British patrol vessel.

In November and December 1916 six large minelayers of the class *U 71* to *U 80* were used for merchant warfare under prize regulations, mainly in the North Sea because their engines were unreliable. However, *U 79* was sent to the Bay of Biscay as an experiment. She passed Dover Straits on Christmas Eve and went south to the coast of Portugal scuttling nine ships totalling 14,200 tons. On account of engine trouble she went around the Shetlands but used so much fuel that she could not hope to reach a German North Sea port. East of the Shetlands her captain there-

Above and opposite: Two stages in an unusual fight in the North Sea. A German seaplane, commanded by *Kapitän* Christiansen, engages the British submarine *C 25* with gunfire, damaging the conning tower and injuring the crew on it. After half an hour the seaplane exhausts its ammunition and is forced to break off the fight, leaving the *C 25* wallowing out of control until eventually she is towed into harbour by another British submarine, the *E 51*

fore stopped a small Norwegian steamer with a cargo of salt from England to Norway, declared her a prize and used her for towing the submarine. After three days they reached the German Bight and destroyers took over. The prize was later released.

In January 1917 two of the large minelayers were sent on minelaying operations to distant waters again. *U 76* went to the Polar Sea in order to mine Kola Bay. There she was rammed at night by a darkened ship when she tried to avoid it by diving. She got away but her pressure hull was so much damaged that she had to stay on the surface. She tried to return to Germany but after some days the engines broke down. With the last of the electric power the boat reached sheltered water near Hammerfest. There the crew was taken off by a Norwegian fisherman, and *U 76* sank with opened seacocks. *U 80* laid several small minefields off the Orkneys, the Hebrides and the north coast of Ireland. Here an auxiliary cruiser, the *Laurentic* (14,900 tons) struck a mine and sank. She was on her way to the USA with a large cargo of gold which, according to newspaper reports, was valued at $35 million.

The losses were lower than could reasonably be expected under the dangers inherent in fully observing prize regulations. From October 1916 to end of January 1917, 11 U-Boats were lost in all theatres of war, but only four were destroyed by enemy action in the waters around the British Isles and off the coast of France.

February 1 – the great decision

In all areas taken together the total results of the submarine operations were:
- October 1916 – 337,000 tons
- November 1916 – 325,000 tons
- December 1916 – 308,000 tons
- January 1917 – 328,000 tons

These figures were carefully calculated after the war with the help of all available sources. In 1916/17 the estimates of the Admiral Staff were about one-third higher. Yet it was evident that even these results would not be enough to force Great Britain to give up the struggle. Therefore the advocates of unrestricted submarine warfare continued to plead their cause.

After discussions with the Austrian government the German Chancellor Bethmann-Hollweg declared the willingness of the Central Powers to enter negotiations for peace in a speech before the German Parliament on December 12, 1916. President Wilson, re-elected 'for peace' on November 7, 1917 took these proposals up but in only a very general fashion. In their answers (Lloyd

Südd Verlag

George in the Commons on December 19, and in the Allied note of December 30) the Allies declared the German offer an attempt to deceive the world, put the whole blame for the war on Germany and practically demanded the disintegration of the Austro-Hungarian Empire and the removal of the Ottoman Empire from European soil. These facts, as well as the discourteous tone used on both occasions, were taken by the German military leaders as a complete rejection of the peace proposals. The Chancellor still had hopes and tried to induce President Wilson to act. However, in a conference at the Emperor's HQ on January 9, 1917, Bethmann-Hollweg was persuaded to consent to a declaration of unrestricted submarine warfare as from February 1, 1917, as the only means of ending the war in a reasonably short time.

On February 1, 1917 the German government declared a large area around the British Isles and off the French coast as well as the central and eastern Mediterranean as barred zones where all ships would be attacked and sunk without warning. In April the Polar Sea east of the North Cape outside Norwegian territorial waters was added. Neutral shipping was given time to leave these zones, and shipping channels were arranged for neutral countries like the Netherlands and Greece. All armed merchant ships were to be treated like warships even outside the zones.

On February 1 the submarine force comprised 105 submarines in all – a rather modest number after two and a half years of war, and the organisation was substantially unchanged.

There was agreement between the staffs that the best prospects for playing havoc with the flow of supplies going to Britain and France were to be found in the approaches to the Channel and the Irish Sea, in the Bay of Biscay and off the larger ports. Therefore the large U-Boats were sent mainly to the waters west and southwest of the British Isles. The smaller boats of the FdU operated off the east coast of England and Scotland, those of the Marine Corps in the Channel and in the approaches to the Thames. A few large boats were sent north to intercept traffic between Norway and the Shetlands or going to northern Russia.

To save time the large U-Boats had orders to take the route through the Dover Straits. In view of the concentration of defences there and the tricky navigation with rapid currents and large changes of depth, many captains were against this short-cut, all the more so as there were repeated delays. After a month the order was rescinded, the captains were given free choice. In May they were urged again to use the shorter route but no direct order was given, and few did so. The few large minelayers were sent to the waters around Scotland and Ireland, only one to northern Russia.

These arrangements worked comparatively well but there was not enough co-ordination, and the U-Boats generally acted as independent units. The map of the operational area was subdivided by a grid, and according to their importance the resulting squares were allotted to individual U-Boats which could no longer freely choose where they wanted to go. No concentrations

or reconnaissance lines were attempted as had been done during fleet operations. Only in a few cases, more or less by accident, did two submarines co-operate against the same target.

Commander Bauer received the title of 'Commodore' but an interesting and promising plan of his was not accepted by the Admiral Staff. Fully realising the necessity of utilising the U-Boats to the utmost he suggested the conversion of the merchant submarine *Deutschland* into a command ship. Equipped with additional wireless she was to take up a position in the western part of the barred zone, with FdU or a deputy on board. Specially trained personnel were to watch Allied wireless traffic. This would give the officer in charge valuable information and enable him to inform and possibly concentrate the U-Boats on rewarding targets or in promising areas. Moreover, *Deutschland* was to carry oil for other boats.

The Admiral Staff was not over enthusiastic about this plan. It wanted the *Deutschland* to conduct cruiser warfare in distant waters, and thought that a normal large U-Boat could be fitted for the duties envisaged by Commodore Bauer. But this project which might have led to 'wolf pack' tactics was not pursued with any energy, and it was shelved when Bauer was relieved of command early in June, 1917.

A new stage in the war
The declaration of unrestricted submarine warfare had considerable influence on the situation in the North Sea and the tasks of the High Seas Fleet. In an Order of the Day of January 31, 1917 Admiral Scheer said that every effort of every component of the entire navy was to be put into the service of the U-Boat war. On the following day he wrote in his war diary: *We now enter a new stage of the war in which the submarine arm is to bring the decision by strangling British economic life and sea communications. Every means of naval warfare must be put into the service of our U-Boat operations. Of course, this will principally apply to the light forces and auxiliary units charged with escort and minesweeping duties. However, the situation created by opening unrestricted submarine warfare will have to be taken into consideration for the employment of the Battle Fleet itself, too.*

The main task of the Fleet now was to get the U-Boats safely through the mines and submarines in the southeastern part of the North Sea. Any actions of the Fleet or of its light forces were to be directed against the British anti-submarine units or against Allied shipping. At first there were doubts if surface ships were permitted to attack merchant ships without warning. On February 28 the Admiral Staff ruled that in the 'barred zones' no difference was to be made between attack by submarine or by destroyers or other surface warships.

Scheer now planned an operation against the traffic between the Dutch ports and the Thames. There comparatively fast and well-protected steamers carried mainly food to Britain. However, nothing came of Scheer's plan for various reasons, among them restrictions on fleet movements without airship reconnaissance, ordered by the Kaiser.

In February and March 1917 an uncommonly hard winter hampered the passage of the U-Boats from and to their bases on North Sea and Baltic, and repairs were delayed by difficult working conditions. In the open North Sea the British mining campaign which had started in early 1915 became more effective by the use of fast minelayers, submarine minelayers and improved mines (with Hertz horns). Whereas from November 1916 to end of January 1917 only one German minesweeping vessel struck a mine and sank, the figures were four in February, seven in March, two in April and 13 in May 1917.

However, the German navy was prepared. The main results of the early British attempts to block the exits of the German Bight was to show how necessary large and well-equipped minesweeping forces were to ensure relative freedom of movement to the German units, whether surface ships or submarines. Before the war there were three minesweeping divisions of about 15 very old torpedo boats. These little ships had not been built for minesweeping for their draught was too great. During mobilisation local divisions of tugs and fishing vessels were added, one at least for every naval port.

In the first years of the war more auxiliary units were commissioned, among them a flotilla of *Sperrbrecher*, medium-sized steamers, made almost unsinkable by a cargo of wood and empty barrels, equipped with a primitive mine-detonating gear at their bows. Simultaneously, special minesweepers were built (called M-Boats), of 450 tons, with two propellers and a draught of only 6½ feet. These replaced the torpedo boats for actual sweeping. In addition, a great number of small torpedo boats were built, in three classes, displacing 110, 220 and 350 tons respectively. They were equipped for minesweeping, too, but used mainly for escort duties, laying marker buoys, etc. Then there were large minesweeping motor launches carried on the deck of special steamers, called 'motherships', to fields of particularly shallow mines. Eventually, all the older destroyers of the Fleet were equipped with light minesweeping gear and used for exploring the channels.

There were two kinds of minesweeping gear, a heavy one which did good service as long as the British mines were laid in long rows, and a light one which was very accurate but tricky to handle. To protect the minesweepers themselves, a kind of very simple paravane was introduced. These forces and means were sufficient for getting the Fleet and the submarines into open water between the barred zones, with small losses to the combat vessels. Those of the minesweepers were heavy.

A staggering kill ratio

During every month of unrestricted war in 1917 on an average almost 100 cruises were undertaken, about 250 torpedoes launched (hits slightly over 50%) and 700 mines laid. Conditions were now easier for the U-Boats, at least as long as the British anti-submarine weapons and methods were not substantially improved. The apparent results were much higher than the Admiral Staff had calculated, but even the actual sinkings surpassed the German expectations:

- February 1917 — 520,000 tons
- March 1917 — 564,000 tons
- April 1917 — 860,000 tons
- May 1917 — 616,000 tons

These results were gained with the loss of 16 U-Boats, with one interned, including eight off the Flanders coast and only one in the Mediterranean.

These losses were higher than before but acceptable in view of the increased number of cruises. Yet only 18 U-Boats were commissioned in the first four months of unrestricted war whereas in the preceding four there had been 43. No such augmentation was to be expected for the rest of the year. Therefore the causes of the losses were of particular interest in order that corrective measures might be taken. At the time they could be ascertained in only a few cases, but the experiences of those submarines that escaped attack gave valuable hints.

Four were destroyed by the weapons of surface ships. UB 36 was rammed by an armed steamer during the attack on a small convoy, UC 26 was rammed by night and under a full moon in the Dover Straits by the destroyer Milne. UC 46 surfaced under similar conditions a few hundred yards in front of the destroyer Liberty and was also rammed. UC 39 was surprised by destroyers when she stopped a steamer near Flamborough Head with gun fire. She dived but a depth charge damaged her and she had to return to the surface where she was received with heavy fire. Her captain and several men were killed, the rest jumped overboard and were saved. UC 39 did not go down at once. She was taken in tow but sank after some hours. U 83, U 85 and UC 18 fell victims to British Q-ships. Quite a number of other boats were luckier and got away from Q-ships, some by the skin of their teeth.

Some damage and losses could have been avoided if the captains and lookouts had been more distrustful. Yet in the times when prize regulations were in force the U-Boats had stopped so many ships that it took them some time to become cautious enough and go only for rewarding tonnage.

In some cases the Q-ship had the worst of the encounter. U 62 (Kapitänleutnant Hashagen) sighted a small steamer, apparently unarmed and harmless, about 150 miles west of Fastnet. But Hashagen did not trust appearances and manoeuvred submerged until he could fire a torpedo which hit amidships and caused the boilers to blow up. Even now U 62 remained under water and closely scrutinised her quarry through the periscope. In this way she discovered several guns which were still partly camouflaged. When one began to fire on the periscope U 62 went about 2,200 yards ahead, came to the surface outside of the arc of fire of her opponent's guns and sank the steamer with her two guns (105-mm and 88-mm). Then U 62 approached and searched the wreckage drifting about. In a small wooden box they found a postcard addressed to a sailor in HMS Tulip (Q12). They asked for the captain and took him on board. It was Commander Lewis, and his first question was: 'Will you kill me now?' Hashagen was greatly taken aback but managed to answer in a noncommittal tone: 'No, not yet.' Actually, Commander Lewis was treated like a member of the crew during the 19 days he stayed on board U 62. After the war the two captains got in touch and met in England.

Submarines were another danger. The British E 54 torpedoed

U 81 which was about to sink a ship with guns after damaging it with a torpedo. In spite of a considerable sea E 54 saved the commanding officer and six men. U 81 was at the end of a cruise which brought the total of her three operations to 86,000 tons sunk and 3,000 damaged. North of the Shetlands UC 43 was hit by a torpedo from the British submarine G 13 and sank with all hands. (The only loss in the Mediterranean, UC 24, was also due to a submarine, the French Circe.) Others were luckier. Shortly after leaving Zeebrugge UB 10 sighted the British C 7 on a dark night. C 7 fired a torpedo, the German turned quickly away, the torpedo detonated on the bottom of the sea about 200 yards off. Some weeks later UB 10 sighted the periscope of a submarine and the tracks of two torpedoes at the same moment. One passed ahead, the other hit but did not detonate. A third torpedo fired immediately afterwards passed under UB 10 which understandably avoided further enemy action by diving.

The human element

Of the other losses two (probably three) blew up owing to failures of their own mines (UC 68, UC 32 and probably UC 36). U 59 got into a German minefield through a mistake in the navigation of the escorting vessels, UC 30 and possibly UB 39 perished in the combination of nets and mines in the Dover Straits. Quite a number of U-Boats had disagreeable experiences when they passed this area. Trusting in their low silhouette and in the difficulties of the patrols in keeping alert all through the long nights of uneventful waiting, they generally started on the surface, always with the tide. The strong current exerted considerable force on the nets which helped the net-saw of the U-Boat to make a breach when it ran on the upper guy of the net. Some boats preferred to try their luck by going as deep down as possible, and most of the others had to follow their example for part of the trip at least. Some succeeded without any incident, others went clean through a net they met, not a few stuck and got free again, and some heard noises from steel wires scraping along the hull without knowing whether they were mine ropes or part of a net. In any case, passing the narrow part of the Channel was a nerve-racking experience which nobody liked. In contrast, the dangers of the open sea and the enemy there were borne with equanimity.

The human element played a prominent part in submarine warfare. The U-Boat arm received the pick of the young officers and men of the whole navy, but the natural gifts for this special type of action, and also luck, were not at all evenly distributed. Promising captains made unproductive cruises, others seemed to have all the breaks. Of course, chance could not be ruled out, but quiet determination and tenacity, a flair for the ever-changing situation, the ability to calculate the risks, and good shooting were decisive.

The most successful captain of small submarines was Otto Steinbrinck, who was based in Flanders. From February to May

Opposite page: The crew of the *U 35* take a cold shower. *Left:* A U-Boat rescues survivors of a merchant ship it has just sunk—a painting by Felix Schwormstädt. *Below:* The theory and practice of unrestricted U-Boat warfare. When she launched the campaign on February 1 Germany gambled that she would be able to sink a sufficient percentage of the shipping available to Britain from all sources to drive her before the war before America was propelled into joining the Allies. The gamble was based on estimates of the total tonnage available to Britain (10,700,000 tons) and the amount the Germans could sink each month if they were not obliged to warn the victims (600,000 tons): the estimate was that within five months Germany could sink 39% (compared with only 18% under prize regulations) and Britain would be forced to sue for peace. Indeed, the first *three* months of the campaign showed a great increase in sinkings, alarmingly high to Britain's leaders but equally alarming to Germany's because Britain was by no means anxious to sue for peace

GERMAN U-BOATS
2 ▬▬ LOST
(5) UNDER REPAIR
(5) IN DOCK
(5) AT SEA
BRITISH SHIPS
(5) LOST

1916				1917			
September	**October**	**November**	**December**	**January**	**February**	**March**	**April**
84 596 tons	14 689 tons		109 945 tons	109 954 tons			
		145 195 tons			256 394 tons	283 647 tons	516 394 tons

BRITISH SHIPPING LOSSES IN THE WESTERN APPROACHES, CHANNEL & EAST COAST.

September 1916– January 1917

February – April 1917

CAPTURED 9		NEUTRAL 3			BRITISH 6·75	Shipping available to Britain (In millions of tons)
		1·2 (frightened away)			3	German estimate of British losses in 5 months of U-Boat warfare (In millions of tons)

129

Another link in Britain's vital chain of supply is shattered

1917 he undertook four operations in the Channel and the Irish Sea with *UC 65*, laid 18 mines on each, torpedoed seven steamers, stopped 54 vessels ranging from a fishing smack to a steamer (one with a rifle, another one with a megaphone) and scuttled them all with gun fire or explosives, beat off a French flying boat with machine gun fire, crossed a net and searched for another one but did not find any trace of it. In these four months Steinbrinck sank 72,311 tons and damaged 51,452 tons by mine or torpedo. In his whole career he destroyed about 210,000 tons. Among the ships damaged by his exertions was the US steamer *New York* which struck a mine off Liverpool but did not sink (10,000 tons). The US Admiral Sims was a passenger, and was on his way to London where he was to discuss the naval situation and the participation of the US navy.

From a military point of view the first phase of unrestricted U-boat warfare fulfilled what the Admiral Staff had promised. Yet it contributed to bringing the USA into the war and this extra weight on the Allied side was not compensated by the withdrawal of Russia after the Revoultion.

Further Reading
Bauer, H., *Als Führer der U-Boote im Weltkrieg* (Germany 1941)
Bauer, H., *Reichsleitung und U-Boots-Einsatz* (Germany 1956)
Doenitz, Admiral Karl, *Memoirs: Ten Years and Twenty Days* (Weidenfeld & Nicolson 1959)
Gibson, R. H., and Prendergast, M., *The German Submarine War, 1914-1918* (Constable 1931)
Grant, R. M., *U-boats Destroyed* (Putnam 1964)
Grant, R. M., *U-Boat Intelligence, 1914-1918* (Putnam 1969)
Hashagen, Commander E., *The Log of a U-Boat Commander* (Putnam 1931)
Michelson, A., *Der U-Bootskrieg 1914-1918* (Germany 1925)

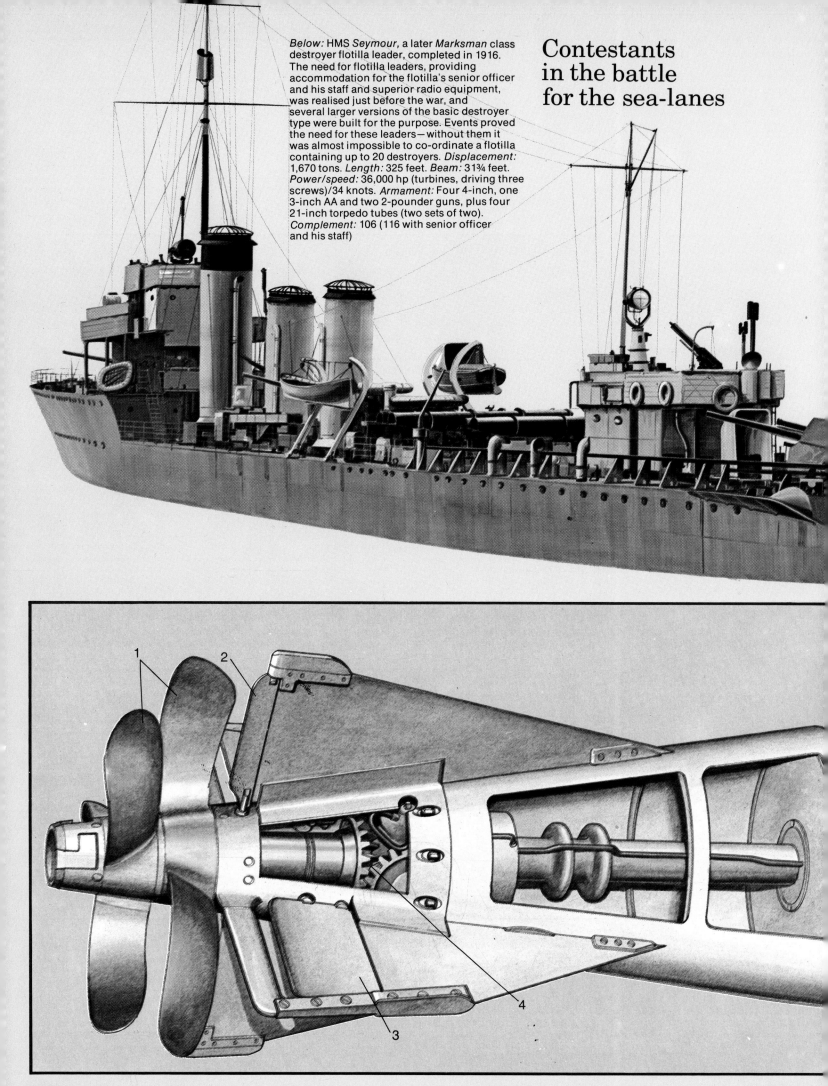

Below: HMS *Seymour*, a later *Marksman* class destroyer flotilla leader, completed in 1916. The need for flotilla leaders, providing accommodation for the flotilla's senior officer and his staff and superior radio equipment, was realised just before the war, and several larger versions of the basic destroyer type were built for the purpose. Events proved the need for these leaders—without them it was almost impossible to co-ordinate a flotilla containing up to 20 destroyers. *Displacement:* 1,670 tons. *Length:* 325 feet. *Beam:* 31¾ feet. *Power/speed:* 36,000 hp (turbines, driving three screws)/34 knots. *Armament:* Four 4-inch, one 3-inch AA and two 2-pounder guns, plus four 21-inch torpedo tubes (two sets of two). *Complement:* 106 (116 with senior officer and his staff)

Contestants in the battle for the sea-lanes

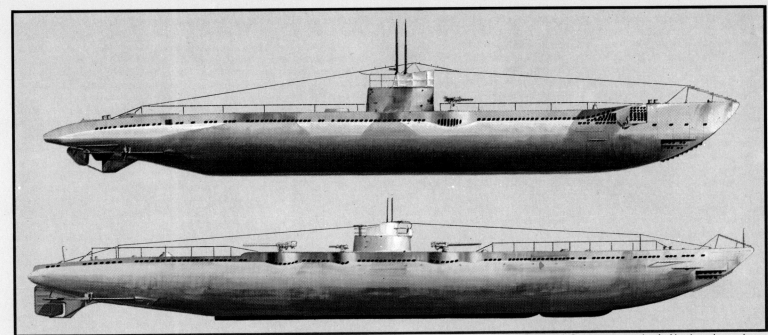

Above: The German submarine *U 139.* This boat, launched on December 12, 1917, was one of the last classes of big boats to be built by Germany. It was also one of the few boats to be named: *Kapitänleutnant Schweiger,* after one of the war's great U-Boat captains. *Displacement:* 1,930/2,483 tons. *Length:* 311 feet. *Beam:* 29¾ feet. *Draught:* 17¼ feet. *Power/speed:* 3,300 hp and 1,780 hp/15.8 and 7.6 knots. *Armament:* Six 19.7-inch torpedo tubes (four bow, two stern) and two 5.9-inch and two 4.1-inch guns (one of the latter is not visible). *Crew:* 62-80. *Top:* The coastal U-Boat *UB 80,* launched on August 8, 1917. *Displacement:* 516/646 tons. *Length:* 182 feet. *Beam:* 19 feet. *Draught:* 12 feet. *Power/speed:* 1,060 hp and 788 hp/13.4 and 7.8 knots. *Armament:* Five 19.7-inch torpedo tubes (four bow, one stern) and one 3.4-inch gun. *Crew:* 34. This boat was of the final (UB III) type of coastal U-Boats, incorporating the lessons of the earlier classes

Below: A German torpedo. **1.** Air charging valve. **2.** Fuel charging valve. **3.** Fuel tank. **4.** Air cylinder. **5.** Warhead. **6.** Exploder charge. **7.** Primer. **8.** Detonator horn. *Bottom:* The motive parts of a German torpedo. **1.** Contra-rotating propellers (one propeller was impractical as its torque would have deflected the weapon from its course). **2.** Rudder (another below). **3.** Hydroplane. **4.** Differential gears for propeller drives. **5** and **6.** Fuel tanks. **7.** Mechanism for regulating the depth at which the torpedo was to run. **8.** Starter latch (engaged as the torpedo was fired). **9.** One of four cylinder heads on the engine. **10.** Air cylinder. Up to 1908, all torpedoes had been driven by compressed air alone, but the later type illustrated used two fuels and an engine, this giving the torpedo a much higher speed and greater range. Range and speed had to be balanced out, increased speed severely curtailing the maximum range

1. AIR CHARGING VALVE
2. FUEL (WATER) CHARGING VALVE
3. FUEL AND WATER TANKS
4. AIR FLASK, AIR VESSEL
5. WARHEAD
6. EXPLOSIVE CHARGE
7. PRIMER
8. HORN

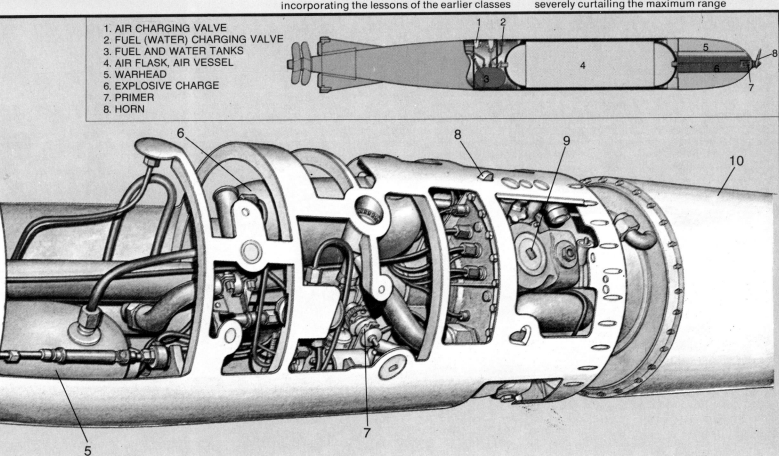

John Batchelor

Q-SHIPS
KILLERS IN DISGUISE

Searching for an answer to the U-Boat, the British hit upon the so-called Q-ship, a merchant vessel fitted with a concealed armament to lure the submarine to close range and then destroy it before it had a chance to escape. Below we reprint an account of one such meeting in the Irish Sea. *Rear-Admiral Gordon Campbell*

Above: Part of a Q-ship's main armament. On the gun's right and in front of it can be seen the walls of the false compartment concealing the gun from prying eyes on the decoyed submarine. This gun could be exposed and brought into action in six seconds. *Below:* A typical Q-ship, armed with three main guns—in the bows, the stern and amidships, the last being concealed under a small boat designed to be pulled apart in the middle to expose the gun. Note also the droppable railings

We did everything we could to try to get contact with a submarine. Each day we plotted carefully all the reports received to try and see whether the Germans worked on any 'system', but apparently, except that they sometimes seemed to be working in pairs, I could only imagine that each captain of a submarine had his own system.

There were one or two places that they all seemed to make for, such as the principal lighthouses. This was possibly to check their positions for navigational purposes. It appeared to be something to go on, and we frequently made for such lighthouses, so as to be off them at daybreak.

We also tried our previous scheme of stopping and being 'not under control', or 'disabled'. On another occasion we heard two submarines talking to each other one night and they appeared to be fairly close. We thought to encourage them by making en clair wireless signals to our 'owners' at Liverpool, such as, 'Have been delayed by weather; am now in latitude — longitude —; expect to arrive Liverpool 6 am Friday.' I would then change my tune and answer myself, saying, 'Your message received.' By this means we hoped to convey to the submarine where we were and what course we would be steering. It never came off; possibly he was not listening on our wavelength.

We frequently sailed neutral, which needed a lot of preparation during the hours of darkness, as in addition to the funnel wanting some special painting, alterations in the ship had to be made —the colour boards put in place, the name and port of registry painted on, and we generally removed the Plimsoll marks, as I noticed so many neutral ships had not got them. It was no use pretending to be something you were not unless you attended to every detail. There was one disadvantage of sailing neutral, and that was that it was expected that submarines would sometimes follow neutral ships, perhaps to find out what routes were being used or to allay the suspicions of other ships.

After a few weeks of trying to secure a meeting with the Germans, we got news of a submarine coming down the West Irish coast, and, guessing that he would probably try to sight one of the lights at the south-west corner before starting on his career of destruction in the Channel or Bay of Biscay, we set our course accordingly for the next two days. I always had in mind that it would be an additional help to our side to get a submarine before he started his career of sinkings, as thereby many valuable lives

would be saved. Daylight on March 12, 1916, found us steering up the west coast at eight knots, representing a collier flying no colours bound for the north, and keeping just at the extreme submarine visibility range from the coast.

At 0640 hours the port look-out—Kaye—reported a suspicious object on the horizon on the port bow, about five miles distant. A quick look with glasses disclosed the fact that it was a submarine awash. It was barely daylight, and a small object so far away is very deceptive and might easily be a small fishing craft, especially as submarines frequently disguised themselves as sailing craft; but after watching carefully for a few minutes the submarine submerged, leaving no doubt as to what the object was. Our position at the time was latitude 57° 56′N, longitude 10° 53′W.

There was nothing to be done except steam quietly on, the men having already gone to their action stations at the first report of a 'suspicious object'. The submarine, on his part, would naturally expect that he had sighted us (a fairly big object with smoke) before we had seen him; so, if we wished to be attacked, no attempt must be made to escape—in fact, we had to pretend we had not seen him.

This was a fairly easy matter for the next 20 minutes, though it was rather a novel sensation to us all when we realised that practically for certain in a short time we should be attacked by an invisible enemy and perhaps blown sky high without the chance of a shot in reply. I think the most apt expression I have seen applied to this sort of game is 'live human bait'. It seemed strange also to think that, although we made no alteration of course or speed, yet we were really the attackers, simulated ignorance, and eventually defence in order to make our offence.

So with the guns loaded, their crews concealed beside them, the man on the bridge watching for the next move of the Germans, and all the time the disinterested crew of this tramp lounging about chatting and smoking, we waited, wondering whether we would be attacked by gun or torpedo. The wait may not have been very long by the clock, but it was terribly long to those on board.

The answer came at seven o'clock, when the track of a torpedo was seen approaching, which we made no attempt to avoid. It was fired from our starboard quarter—a bad position from the submarine point of view. The bubbles of the track passed under the fo'c'sle, which meant that the torpedo had just missed us ahead. We therefore maintained our course and took no outward

1 The Q-ship, bringing up the rear of an ordinary convoy, deceives the U-Boat into believing that she is merely a straggler. Taken in by this ruse, the U-Boat surfaces and opens fire with her gun, to conserve torpedoes for more valuable targets.

2 The Q-ship's 'panic party' abandons ship to further the deception, while the U-Boat closes the range cautiously, shelling all the time.

3 If the U-Boat fires a torpedo, fearing a trap or making sure of the kill, the Q-ship ensures that it hits her, relying on her 'cargo' of timber or the like to keep her afloat.

4 After the U-Boat has closed to point blank range, the Q-ship breaks out her White Ensign, drops her gun shields and opens up a hail of fire on the U-Boat.

5 If the U-Boat is not sunk by this hail of fire, but pulls back and resumes shelling at long range, the Q-ship goes into her 'Abandon Q-ship' routine, to persuade the U-Boat that the Q-ship has finally been completely abandoned.

6 Tricked again, the U-Boat closes to point blank range once more, and is blown out of the water by the Q-ship's gunners, who have remained by their guns as the U-Boat makes her final approach, convinced that all opposition from the Q-ship has ceased

Q-ship   U-Boat
Gunfire from Q-ship   Gunfire from U-Boat
Merchantmen in convoy   Torpedo from U-Boat

notice, as a tramp steamer (at that time) could not be expected to know what a torpedo track looked like, and in any case the 'lookouts' would neither be numerous nor very bright at that hour of the morning.

We could have escaped with ease if we had been an ordinary steamer by putting our stern towards him and steaming off at full speed. He might have opened fire with his gun, but under the weather conditions prevailing the steamer would have got away.

To the men concealed at the guns and elsewhere, this was the first great test of the discipline and drill we had been training for, as it was obvious that the submarine might fire another torpedo and perhaps successfully. All remained quiet, and the men, lounging about, continued to smoke their pipes.

A prearranged pantomime

One young seaman was whistling at his gun, because, as he explained when asked what he was doing, 'if he didn't whistle he would get scared'. A few minutes after the torpedo had missed us, the submarine came to the surface astern of the ship and steamed up on our port side. As he came up, his gun was manned and he fired a shot across our bows as a signal to stop. After firing his shot he closed down and partially submerged again, obviously ready to dive in a few seconds if we attempted to ram. But in the meantime we had proceeded with our pantomime as prearranged, and, as soon as the shot fell, the engines were stopped, steam was blown off and the panic party got busy.

They entered into the spirit of it with more zeal than ever – a great scrambling for boats took place, which apparently satisfied the submarine as to our bonafides, for he came right on the surface again and closed towards the ship – this before we had even got to the stage of lowering the boats. I was still rushing about the bridge and had not yet been relieved of my cap by the navigator. The submarine was evidently in a hurry to get on with the business and go after another prey, as he fired a shot at us which fell just short of the magazine, a matter of a few feet.

He was now about 800 yards off, showing full length, and although the range was a little bit greater than I wished, the time had come to open fire before he might touch off our magazines. I therefore blew my whistle. At this signal the White Ensign flew at the masthead, the wheel-house and sideports came down with a clatter, the hen-coop collapsed; and in a matter of seconds three

12-pounder guns, the Maxim and rifles were firing as hard as they could.

The submarine had been successfully decoyed to a suitable position with his lid open and gun manned. Everything now depended on the accuracy of the fire; but the target was a comparatively small one, and we had no rangefinders to help us, so that the distance of the target was reckoned by eye. The fire was accurate, and before the submarine could get closed down again we had hit him several times as he slowly submerged. In all, 21 rounds were fired from the three 12-pounders, one gun getting off 13 rounds. The Maxim and rifles wasted no time in getting off some 200 rounds at the personnel on the deck of the submarine, who were manning the gun, but now rapidly sought shelter inside.

As soon as he had submerged and there was nothing more to fire at, we steamed at full speed to the spot where he had gone down, for at the moment there was nothing actually to show whether he had been destroyed or not, although we knew we had hit him, as he had closed his conning tower before diving. Two depth charges were therefore dropped, and almost simultaneously the submarine, that had obviously been trying to rise, came up nearly perpendicular, touching our bottom as it did so. We were still steaming ahead when the submarine passed down our side a few yards off, and it could now be seen that in addition to a periscope having been shot off there was a big rent in the bows.

Our after-gun was leaving nothing to chance and put a few more rounds in at point-blank range. A couple more depth-charges were released, and the surface of the sea became covered with oil and small pieces of wood – but there was no living soul.

This boat, it was ascertained afterwards, was *U 68,* and by destroying her before she got to her hunting ground, we had done exactly what we set out for. The great feeling of rejoicing and relief to all on board showed itself in the whole crew rushing to the bridge and cheering. . . . When all were present, I read the 'Prayer of Thanksgiving for Victory' from the Book of Common Prayer, followed by three cheers for the King, and then all went back to 'cruising stations', but not before one of the wags had produced the gramophone and put on the record of 'Down among the dead men let him lie'.

[*Reprinted from* My Mystery Ships *by Rear-Admiral Gordon Campbell VC.*]

Opposite: The tactics of Q-ship warfare. *Below:* A Q-ship shows its teeth – in harbour. *Right:* A hydrophone in operation, too late in the war to detract from the important rôle of the Q-ship. *Below right:* The *U 93,* participant in one of the most exciting contests between U-Boat and Q-ship. She was seriously damaged by the Q-ship *Prize,* but was able to limp home to Germany after a magnificent feat of seamanship by one of her junior officers. The *Prize,* also seriously damaged, got home too, and her captain was awarded the VC. Four months later she was torpedoed by the *U 48* with the loss of all her crew

1 Depth charge hatches. 2 12-pounder QF gun in collapsible deck house. 3 Shell locker. 4 4-inch magazine. 5 Ward room. 6 Officers' quarters. 7 4-inch gun (sides of deckhouse drop sideways to reveal gun). 8 PO mess and quarters. 9 Electrical and gunnery stores. 10 Bomb thrower magazine. 11 Royal Navy 200-pounder bomb thrower. 12 12-pounder QF gun on a revolving mounting with counterbalance weight, allowing the space to change from a clear deck to a gun ready for action in 20 seconds

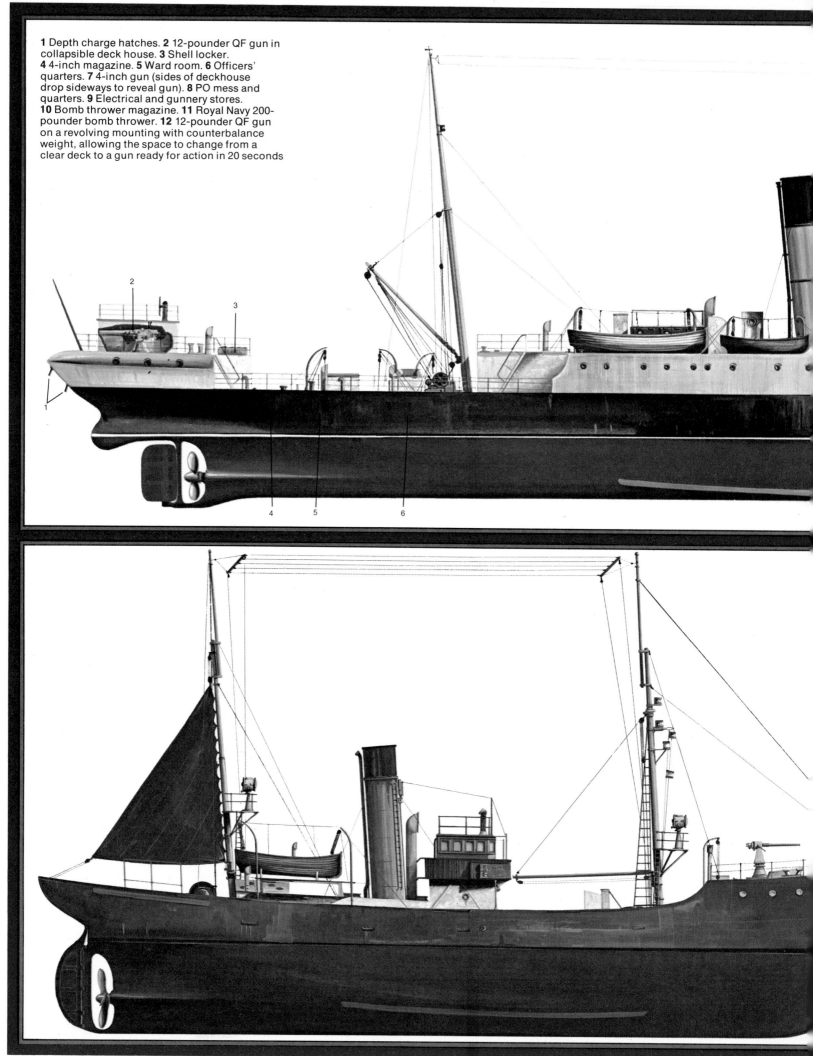

7   8   9   10

11

12

John Batchelor

In the unsafe seas—weapons of defence

Above: A British Q-ship. Disguised as an innocent merchantman, she carried a hidden armament of two 4-inch and two 12-pounder guns as well as depth charges and bomb throwers. *Left:* A British armed trawler. These were used to protect fishing trawlers and were also employed in mine-sweeping operations.
Below: A paravane is lowered as a British cruiser enters a minefield. Paravanes were the only effective weapons against mines known at this time; they were lowered to a depth of several feet on heavy cables which would pass under the mine cable and bring the mine to the explosive head of the paravane.
Right: One of the many that were lost: a minesweeper keels over after striking a mine

John Batchelor

Imperial War Museum

The Submarine War
a U-Boat commander's view

Bapty

Typical of many of the daring U-Boat commanders who raided commerce in the Atlantic was Freiherr von Spiegel, commander of the new *U 93*. On its first raid the *U 93* sunk 27,000 tons of shipping before it was damaged by a Q-ship. Spiegel was captured and the U-boat, badly damaged, began to limp back to base. *Vizeadmiral Ruge. Opposite, left to right:* Spiegel, commander of the *U 93;* the *U 93* showing damage by shell-fire from the *Prize,* a British Q-ship; and Sanders, the *Prize's* commander

The *U 93,* commanded by *Kapitänleutnant* Freiherr von Spiegel, left the submarine base at Emden on April 13, 1917, and after a short dive to test all components, human and mechanical, she proceeded in the wake of a group of minesweepers. After passing the mined area the sweepers turned back and *U 93* moved north in the neutral channel between the British and German war areas via the Dogger Bank Light Vessel. The southwest wind increased to Force 10, and heavy seas forced the submarine under water for some time. On April 15, on the latitude of Dundee, she sighted a small Danish sailing ship with a cargo of British coal and sank her with gun fire after the crew had taken to a boat. In the afternoon Fair Isle came in sight but the weather became too rough to pass Fair Isle Straits on the surface. Therefore Freiherr von Spiegel decided to go around the Shetlands. On April 18, 100 miles west of them, a large British ship was stopped. She carried 2,100 tons of maize and 500 tons of oil cake. Her captain handed his papers over, and the crew were given time to get away in the boats before the ship was sunk by a torpedo.

A few hours later, a Norwegian steamer was sunk in a similar way. After passing a line of patrols between the Orkneys and the Faroes undetected *U 93* had gyro trouble but succeeded in repairing it. The weather improved but there was still a heavy swell. She tried to cut off a steamer which was too fast, however. In order to regulate the gyro and overhaul the torpedoes *U 93* dived and proceeded at 100 feet for several hours. On April 21, she sighted two boats under sail evidently from a ship sunk by another U-Boat, then exchanged recognition signals with *U 67,* and wireless messages with *U 60.* On the following day a large Norwegian full-rigged ship with a cargo of pitch-pine for Liverpool was stopped and scuttled by explosive charges. At that time gunfire was heard to the north.

After that no shipping was met off the North Channel, and *U 93* moved to an area 100 to 200 miles west and southwest of Fastnet where she sighted a British patrol vessel. On April 23, she attacked the steamer *Stanmore* with a bronze torpedo which did not reach its target, and then with a newer make which also missed because

it had a gyro failure. Then *U 43* surfaced nearby and attacked the steamer with artillery fire. *U 93* surfaced too and also began to shell her, but the steamer zigzagged cleverly and replied so vigorously that both submarines broke off the engagement. A few hours later, however, the *Stanmore* was sunk by a torpedo from *U 50.* The destroyers she had called by SOS had arrived too late.

In the following days several patrols were sighted and a small Danish sailing ship was rendered useless and left, deep in the water, floating on its cargo of 300 tons of pitch-pine. *U 93* towed its crew of six a considerable distance to the east.

On April 29, *U 93* unsuccessfully attacked two steamers and then sank two others (each about 5,000 tons with cargoes of grain and ammunition) by torpedo. The first started to burn and blew up with considerable loss of life; the second had to be sunk by a bronze torpedo and some shells. The captain and two gunners were made prisoners. On the following day two more steamers were sunk. The first, with a cargo of ore from Africa to England, went down at once. *U 93* rescued 14 men, some seriously injured, and took them on board where they were fed, clad, and their wounds dressed. The second steamer, Italian (3,200 tons, with a cargo of ammunition), blew up in two detonations, and nobody was saved.

On the following day *U 93* put the Danish crew on a Finnish ship keeping only the gunner. Recognition signals were exchanged with *U 21.* Then a steamer came in sight. On diving *U 93* got too much forward angle and went too deep, rose with the help of compressed air, got too deep again and surfaced to attack with the guns because the opportunity for torpedo attack was past. However, the tables were quickly turned because the opponent was armed with six guns which forced *U 93* to dive. Some hours later, another steamer with food and ammunition was sunk by torpedo.

Only two torpedoes were left and the captain decided to go north again before returning home. Towards evening a three-masted schooner came in sight and was stopped by gunfire. She turned into the wind and her crew left in a boat while *U 93* approached from the port quarter and began to shell the apparently deserted vessel at a distance of no more than 300 yards. At the first hit the

schooner hoisted the White Ensign and returned fire with four guns and some machine guns. It was the Q-ship *Prize*, commanded by W. E. Sanders, who had caught his adversary napping, with all the officers in the conning tower and a number of men sight-seeing on deck, including the gun crews. *U 93* at once received several hits on the starboard side as Spiegel shouted 'Hard aport, emergency full speed ahead.' Fire from the machine guns and a shell through the base of the periscope made it necessary to clear the bridge. Captain, quartermaster and pilot jumped aft, the Chief Engineer down into the control station, the executive officer took shelter in the lee of the conning tower. The forward gun continued to hit the schooner, doing much damage, and there were loud screams. Hits in the fuel and diving tanks now caused *U 93* to take up a list of 14 degrees to starboard. The gunlayer of the after gun was wounded, the quartermaster tried to get it going again, the blast of another hit threw the captain, quartermaster and machinist's mate overboard unobserved by the others. Now the forward gun was put out of action by a hit and Lieutenant Ziegner, the executive officer, took over and tried to get away from the schooner, zigzagging at high speed. After one or two more hits *U 93* succeeded in getting out of range.

Detection seemed unavoidable

When the captain could not be found Ziegner decided to steer westwards until noon on the next day to throw off pursuit. Several men had been seriously injured and one died during the night. The pressure hull was pierced in one place, elsewhere rivets were leaking and the boat could not dive. When the damage was examined on the next morning it was found that *U 93* had been hit at least nine times. Both guns and the periscope were out of action, several fuel and regulating tanks damaged, a number of valves, compressed air flasks and the wireless masts wrecked and more than half the fuel lost. What remained would just be sufficient to reach the German Bight of the North Sea, without reserves for high speed or other emergencies. Attempts were made to stop the leak in the pressure hull but were not successful.

As long as the boat remained on the surface the hole was above water, but diving was impossible. Nevertheless, Lieutenant Ziegner decided to try to return to Germany, giving the Shetlands a wide berth.

It took them six days at economic speed until they were well to the north of the Shetlands. Once they sighted a German submarine at a great distance but were not able to contact her. The weather was fairly good, with moderate winds and the sea from astern or from the quarter. On May 6, gyro and magnetic compass failed but after an anxious half hour the gyro worked again. When it was time to change course the wind increased to Force 9 from the west with snow squalls. It was difficult to steer a straight course, the seas rolled over the conning tower where the officer and the petty officer of the watch were secured with safety belts. On the following morning, about 100 miles east of the Shetlands, several destroyers and trawlers came in sight at distances down to 4,500 yards. Detection seemed unavoidable. *U 93* turned away to where there was a gap in the line of patrols. A heavy snow squall set in, but the submarine went on at high speed. After an hour when the weather cleared there was nothing in sight. The course was now set for the west coast of Jutland which was reached at Bovbjerg in the night of May 8/9. Attempts at wireless communication failed. The boat followed the coast southwards, avoided a number of small ships, passed inside Horns Reef and contacted a German trawler which accompanied her to Sylt Island. Here they did not take oil because they thought they had still enough to reach Wilhelmshaven. After two and a half hours the engines stopped. Not a drop of fuel was left, and they were towed in. All ships they passed cheered them, and Admiral Scheer, C-in-C Fleet, came on board to congratulate them. They had sunk 27,000 tons.

Some weeks later they were informed through the Red Cross that *Kapitänleutnant* Spiegel and the other two men had been rescued. In August, 1917, *UB 48* sank the *Prize* with a torpedo. She blew up. There were no survivors.

U-BOATS
the tide turns

Close though the German U-Boat campaign came to success, it was in fact a case of too little and too late. This was well recognised by the German naval authorities, and Tirpitz described the campaign as 'a measure of despair'. The difficulties lay in keeping enough U-Boats at sea to inflict the required losses, at the same time making good their own losses, which were heavy. *Bryan McLean Ranft.*
Below: A diminishing threat to Allied shipping. German crewmen range in a U-Boat gun on a target

The German naval chiefs conviction that the U-Boat was going to do what Germany's armies had failed to do, drive Britain out of the war, was turned into a dogma by the successes of the first three months of the unrestricted campaign launched on February 1, 1917. Like their British counterparts they exaggerated the difficulty of organising a complete convoy system covering British home waters, the North and South Atlantic and the Mediterranean. They were unchanging in their belief that if only they could get the necessary industrial manpower and resources to increase substantially the number of submarines operating against the convoys, they would carry out their promise to the Emperor. Britain, the centre of enemy power and will to resist, would be defeated by the new form of the *guerre de course,* waged ruthlessly by the submarine and the mine.

Two distinguished German admirals, Tirpitz and Scheer, did not share this confidence. Although Tirpitz admitted that the opening of the unrestricted campaign in 1917 was inevitable because it was the only possible way to defeat Britain, he thought that it was too late. He bitterly condemned the weakness of Germany's political leaders who had called off the earlier campaign in April 1916 under American pressure. This had raised doubts about Germany's tenacity of purpose and above all, had given the British time to improve their countermeasures. If the 1916 campaign had been continued, British morale would have crumbled while the German people would have been more steadfast under the blockade, knowing that their enemies were suffering too. Now in 1917 Germany had got the worst of all worlds. America was in the war against her, domestic morale was low, and, at least from April, Allied countermeasures were beginning to take a heavy toll of the U-Boat force. Moreover, Tirpitz considered that the civil authorities were so lukewarm in their support of the campaign, that they would never provide the industrial resources necessary for its success. 'As a measure of despair, half-heartedly, and with already broken prestige, we undertook the unrestricted campaign, which, a year earlier, would

Leaving a tell-tale wake a U-Boat periscope scans the sea for victims. A scarcity of targets was to be the lot of U-Boat Commanders after June 1917

have appeared as the act of a strong people confident of victory.' Scheer, in command of the High Seas Fleet until his appointment to be Chief of the Naval Staff in August 1918, shared Tirpitz's views that if Germany had persisted in 1916 she would have won a decisive victory before America entered the war.

A great deal was to depend on Germany's ability to build new submarines relative to the enemy's capability to destroy those

already in commission. German official sources show that in 1917 she had 138 U-Boats in commission at the beginning of the year. She built 103 as compared with losing 72, a net gain of 31. She thus began 1918 with a force of 169 of which 81 were lost. These losses exactly equalled the new construction during the year and she thus ended the war with 169 boats. The additions in 1917 marked the climax of the building programme and the 1918 figures show quite conclusively that she was not capable of achieving the strength needed to overcome the convoy escorts.

More mines, and better mines

The German Naval Staff realised that if they were to gain the rapid success they had promised, they must attack Allied merchant shipping where it was most concentrated—in the English Channel and its Western Approaches. To get to these hunting grounds without excessive expenditure of time and fuel, the U-Boats must penetrate the Dover Straits. Commanders were given detailed instructions for this dangerous passage. It should always be made at night, with the current, and, if possible, on the surface. If forced to dive by British patrols, the submarine was to submerge deep enough to go beneath the net barrier known to be there. They were also to dive when minefields were suspected. Up to the autumn of 1917 the U-Boats had little trouble with British mines which were usually found near the surface and were notoriously inefficient. Submarine commanders in 1917 were also warned of the growing number of patrol vessels equipped with hydrophones. These could be evaded by diving deep, running quietly on one electric motor and turning off all auxiliary machinery. Once through these dangers and nearing the shipping routes, submarine captains in 1917 were not given the free hand they had had in previous years. In an effort to use their resources more efficiently, the command gave each boat a priority area so that all likely killing grounds were covered. After the introduction of the convoy system in April 1917, a few farsighted U-Boat captains saw that a possible countermeasure was to concentrate a number of boats in a simultaneous attack. Some boats were equipped with special radio apparatus to direct others into the attack and experiments were made in the last year of the war.

After September 1917 the U-Boats found that they could no longer afford to despise British mines. A new type, based on a German model, was now being laid in great quantities. Offensive

minelaying operations in the Heligoland Bight were frequently mounted and in the second half of 1917 accounted for at least six submarines. Similar fields were laid off the Flanders submarine bases and these in the same period claimed another five victims. An equal number were sunk in the defensive minefields in British home waters. In the year as a whole 20 U-Boats were sunk by enemy mines, as well as another six which accidentally hit their own. The mine was by far the most effective anti-submarine weapon of the time. In 1918 it was to destroy another 18 victims. New techniques in the Dover Straits were to present the U-Boats with their chief mining threat in that year, but they also found increased danger nearer home. New fields in the Heligoland Bight claimed their first victim in January, and further laying in the Kattegat threatened those who tried to emerge via the Kiel Canal and the Baltic. That the total losses for the year were not proportionate to the vastly increased British minelaying effort was due entirely to the great resources and determination which Germany put into minesweeping.

But against the increased dangers in the Dover Straits she could do little, except launch an occasional destroyer raid at night. Up to the end of 1917 the mined net-barrage had been easy to evade. By the beginning of June no less than 190 safe passages had been made, mostly on the surface at night. Only eight U-Boats had actually touched the mines and another eight forced to dive by patrols. None were sunk. By October the defences were strengthened by a deep mine barrage, which was continually increased for the rest of the war. Simultaneously plans were being discussed to have the barrage much more heavily patrolled and the Straits so brilliantly illuminated that no submarine could hope to slip through on the surface at night. That something more was needed was established by the fact that despite the new mines, at least 35 submarines got through in November and December. On December 14 the Admiralty ordered additional patrols and illumination to be inaugurated. With the new leadership of Admiral Roger Keyes, the new methods soon brought results. Under the glare of searchlights and flares and constantly threatened by a patrolling force of about 100 ships supplemented by aircraft, the U-Boats found surface passages equally impossible by day or night. If they dived there was the danger of the new deep mine barrage. In January 1918 five submarines were sunk in the Straits as compared with only two in all the previous years of

Top: Mines. Second only to the depth charge as an anti-submarine weapon, mines accounted for 14 of the 63 U-Boat losses in 1917.
Editor's note: The figures for U-Boat losses are difficult to arrive at, as primary sources often conflict.

the war. In February the German-based boats were ordered to use the safer but much longer northern route round Scotland. The smaller Flanders boats, however, were still getting through the Straits and this led to a raid on their base at Zeebrugge in April 1918. Despite what was believed at the time, the raid did little to delay the submarine sailings and it was the strengthening of the Straits barrage and air-bombing raids on the bases which were ultimately effective. In June and July only nine U-Boats attempted the passage. The last one to do so was blown up on September 16. Henceforward the Flanders boats too had to use the longer northern route before they could attack their prey.

German sources give a vivid picture of the succession of perils which faced the Flanders boats before September 1918. With their brief rest periods disturbed by air raids, they sailed from their bases only to be immediately confronted by the 35 miles of minefield between Dunkirk and the Scheldt. They had either to make a long detour through Dutch waters or else to try to slip over the danger at night; the sea was not deep enough to dive beneath the mines. This peril surmounted there was then the Dover net barrage to be evaded and then the Straits themselves with their mines, searchlights and ubiquitous patrols now abundantly equipped with the deadly depth charges. Even if they got through it was with nerves already strained that captains and crews arrived on the hunting grounds to face the ever-increasing strength of the convoy escorts. At the back of their minds was the haunting thought that all their earlier dangers had to be faced again before they returned to base. It was with great relief that they received the order to use the northern route in future.

Even this was soon to have its own dangers. Encouraged by the success of the Dover defences, the Allies decided to mine the 240-mile channel between Orkney and Norway. Laying began in March 1918 and over 70,000 mines were used. It was a magnificent technical feat, but the material results were small, chiefly due to faults in the new American mines and the depths at which they were laid. A further weakness came in August when the craft patrolling the barrier were withdrawn for other duties. No more than six U-Boats were actually destroyed by the Northern Barrage. It is now known that the passages through it increased from a monthly average of 30 in the first half of 1918 to 42 in July/September. Although it must have had an additional depressing effect on the U-Boats' morale, its laying was probably an unnecessary burden for the Allies to assume. By the time it was operational, the convoy system had already defeated the submarine, but the British and American naval leaders were still doubtful that it was the decisive weapon.

This can be accounted for partly by the fact that more submarines were still being sunk by other methods. As already mentioned, mines in 1917 accounted for 20 U-Boats, while another 22 were sunk by ships and aircraft on patrol and hunting operations. Against these figures, only six were destroyed by convoy escorts. In 1918, the patrols and hunters came out on top with 24 successes, as against 18 by mines and ten by convoy escorts.

Convoy – the answer to total war

Germany's aim was to sink so much Allied shipping that not enough tonnage would remain to feed the British people, maintain war industries and bring American troops and munitions across the Atlantic to confront the already weakened German armies in France and Flanders. It was this aim which the convoy system frustrated. As it was more widely applied the tonnage destroyed decreased significantly. Simultaneously, the Allies, by more efficient use of the ships available and by stepping up their building and repairing effort, gradually made good some of the devastating losses suffered in the early months of 1917. By resorting to unrestricted submarine warfare Germany had turned her struggle with the Allies into a total war. This was her undoing. In such a contest economic strength and staying power were equally as important as military strength. Germany's mode of total warfare had brought the richest nation in the world into the ranks of her enemies and the sea power of the Allies was to prove just sufficient in the summer of 1917 to hold the ring in the waters of the Channel and its approaches until that power could be brought to bear.

The six months from February to July 1917 had certainly been a period of staggering losses. Britain herself had lost 2,350,000 tons of shipping in addition to the loss of 1,500,000 tons by Allied and neutral nations. There had already been an appreciable shipping shortage at the end of 1916, so the position was indeed serious. Yet even before the full effects of convoy could be assessed, the underlying position in the food and materials essential to Britain was not so precarious as the loss of merchant ships might suggest. This was due to the development of a more effective rationing system which cut down non-essential imports to make shipping space for those which were vital, and of organisation to ensure a more rapid turn round of ships in port. Financial arrangements made by the government had prevented the withdrawal of Scandinavian shipping which Germany had hoped would be caused by the submarine campaign. In addition, steps to increase shipbuilding and speed up repairs were instituted in both Britain and America which began to bear fruit by the end of 1917. As a result of all this, in the first six months flour imports were actually 450,000 tons up on the corresponding period of 1916. This increase was to be maintained for the rest of the war, largely by concentrating on bringing in American supplies in fast liners to replace grain from the more distant South America and Australia. There were, however, substantial reductions in other essential foodstuffs, particularly meat and sugar, and supplies for the civil population had to be more stringently limited. In essential industrial materials there were few serious shortages, largely because of the shipping space made available by import limitations of non-essentials. Supplies of the two most important raw materials, wool and iron ore, were well maintained, but the priority given to grain and munitions on the Atlantic run did result in a serious shortage of cotton. There was enough for war purposes, but again the civilian population suffered. The government's most serious worry was over oil supplies. The U-Boats had made heavy attacks on tankers and new building fell far behind. Moreover, as the majority of wartime construction for the navy was oil-burning, and increasingly motorised armies were swallowing up fuel, shortages could directly limit operational efficiency. By the beginning of June, stocks in Britain amounted to only 750,000 tons, under three months' supply. Drastic action was required and took the form of fitting liners and tramps in the Atlantic trade with double bottoms to their ballast tanks in which oil could be carried. This meant reduction of their food and munition carrying capacity, but oil was the priority and the first

Below: In happier days. After the adoption of convoying, U-Boat commanders could rarely run the risk of picking up their victims

shipment in July was the beginning of a regular traffic. Fortunately the work required was easy and took only three days to complete. At the same time an accelerated tanker building programme was begun.

Germany's failure

Thus at the end of July, although the British government was anxious about the general shipping situation and particularly concerned about oil, they realised that if shipping losses could be gradually decreased, victory was in sight. In Germany, although the picture was superficially similar, the long term prospects were very different. The winter of 1916/17 had been endured by the German people, but it had been a bitter struggle. In May some relief came with the arrival of grain supplies from the newly conquered Rumania. Meats and fats, however, were critically short and there was evidence of the effects of undernourishment in the armed forces as well as among civilians. Added to this

was a growing weakness in future military capacity because of the virtually complete success of the Allied blockade in stopping imports of war materials by sea. The U-Boat campaign offered the only hope, not now of victory, but perhaps of exhausting the Allies so that they would accept a peace favourable to Germany.

Such was the hope of the German naval command in the second half of 1917, even although their original plan to defeat Britain within six months had already failed. Political and military leaders were full of doubts, and if they had known exactly how the war against shipping was developing, their doubts would have been confirmed.

Yet there was no complacency in Britain. Convoy, introduced in April and gradually extended, had produced no miracle. It was true that the staggering losses of April, when 373 ships were sunk, were not repeated. In May the losses had reassuringly dropped to 287 ships of 593,206 tons, but this was a false dawn. In June there was a significant rise to 683,000 tons; of the 290 ships sunk

U-Boats in dock at Kiel. Over the period May 1917 to December 1918 Germany's serviceable U-Boats numbered between 120 and 140. At any one moment only one third of these would be at sea; the remainder would be in dock for servicing and repairs

all but 18 were victims of U-Boats. The May results had been all the more encouraging because the decrease had been most marked in the really critical area of the South-Western Approaches, and had been accompanied by the sinking of seven submarines in home waters compared with only three in April. The June increases were most serious in these same waters, a rise of almost 50%, and the total losses would have been even more depressing but for a drop of 27% in the Mediterranean sinkings. The initial decline in losses in the Mediterranean was not due to the introduction of convoy, there were neither the escorts available nor any confidence in its efficacy on the part of the British, French and Italian naval chiefs on the spot. The method of protection adopted was a mixture of patrolled and unpatrolled routes, although occasional convoys were formed for groups of not more than three especially important ships sailing between Malta and Alexandria. Great hopes were put into the provision of a net barrage across the Straits of Otranto, to bar the entry of U-Boats into the Medi-

terranean from their Austrian Adriatic bases. Italian refusal to provide destroyers to patrol it prevented its being constructed for some time. One good omen for the future was the creation of a better working relationship between the French and British commanders-in-chief.

Even more promising for the future was the beginning in May of a small scale convoy organisation for ships sailing in both directions between Malta and Alexandria. Although the convoys were never of more than four ships and the escorts only armed trawlers, only two of the 275 ships which sailed in them up to mid-July were sunk. Overall success in the Mediterranean became a reality; except for a temporary setback in August there was a constant decline from the 32 British ships sunk in April to 17 in June, eight in July and seven in September.

Although in the Mediterranean itself convoy was slow to be generally adopted, as early as May 10 there was an experimental ocean convoy from Gibraltar to Britain. It was a complete

success—all of its 17 merchant ships arrived safely. Station keeping was well maintained, and at the end of the trip the merchant ship Masters were completely convinced of its practicability. Equally significant, in the light of the strong economic arguments previously advanced against convoy, the voyage took two days less than it would have done on the diversionary routes hitherto used. Ships and time were saved, two essential commodities in this kind of war, and yet it was not until July that another Gibraltar convoy was organised. On the Admiralty's credit side, however, was their insistence on starting Atlantic convoys despite the lack of enthusiasm shown by the US Navy. On May 24 the first eastbound convoy left Hampton Roads, Virginia. Despite fog and heavy weather, formation was maintained and only one of the 12 merchantmen was torpedoed. This success continued in June. None of the 61 ships which sailed in convoy was lost and it was found possible to handle convoys of up to 20 ships, with a consequent increase in the economical use of escorts. Despite these successes, and the report of the Admiralty's Trade Convoy Committee in early June that a regular system should be inaugurated, this was not done until the end of the year. As yet, Jellicoe and the admiral directly responsible for the security of merchant shipping, Duff, were still not completely convinced of convoy's efficacy. Jellicoe refused to set up a regular ocean system until a far greater number of escorts was available, and refused to take destroyers from the Grand Fleet to meet the need. These doubts were shared by the US Navy, where many officers shared their British counterparts' preference for hunting and patrolling. A view was held at the time that the increased losses in June 1917 were directly attributable to the taking away of ships from these duties to supply convoy escorts. Jellicoe was still pessimistic about the ultimate outcome and in June warned the Cabinet that shortage of shipping might make it impossible to continue the war throughout 1918. More ominous were slight signs that the shipping community was beginning to lose faith in the Admiralty and might soon refuse to send their ships to sea unless more effective security was provided. These facts must have been in Lloyd George's mind when he removed Jellicoe from the Admiralty at the end of 1917.

In fact the situation had improved substantially by then. In July, thanks to the arguments of Admiral Sims, the US Navy dropped its opposition to the extension of convoy and a regular North Atlantic schedule was instituted, operating at three/four day intervals. Outward bound ships to the United States were still sailing independently and in August the U-Boats began to concentrate on them with a consequent increase in losses. Equally heavy damage was being sustained on the unescorted South Atlantic and Mediterranean routes and even Jellicoe was convinced by the contrast. In mid-August regular westward-bound Atlantic convoys followed the institution of regular convoys from Gibraltar at the end of July. In August, too, a beginning was made on the South Atlantic route to Sierra Leone and Dakar. Of all the 600 ships which sailed in convoy during July and August only three were torpedoed and it became increasingly clear to both the British and German Admiralties that the great proportion of ships still being sunk were either sailing independently or else, for various reasons, had parted from their convoy.

Sinkings fall dramatically

Thus, by November 1917, a complete ocean convoy system was in full swing. On an average day 16 homeward-bound and seven outward-bound convoys would be at sea; neutral as well as Allied ships were included. Experience had shown that not only were large convoys perfectly manageable but also that they gave greater security. The average size on the Atlantic run was 20/25 ships; the largest in the whole war was of 47 ships, in June 1918. Behind the ships at sea was a worldwide organisation for the control of shipping, the assembling and sorting out of the ships into convoy according to their destinations and speed; for the provision of appropriate escorts at the right place at the right time; and, most fascinating of all, for the gathering and interpretation of Intelligence about the movements of the U-Boats. This last was largely the work of the mysterious Room 40 in the Admiralty in London. An extract from an official Admiralty publication describing the scene on the operations room gives some indication of how it all worked: *Midnight at the Admiralty. The Atlantic Homeward Convoy, passing through Rendezvous H, is due and has been picked up 200 miles from Cape Clear. Down the pneumatic tube from Room 40 comes a cylinder rattling noisily into the wire basket—a directional perhaps from U65 and an intercepted signal from U69. They are quickly plotted and their positions lie only a few miles off the track of the incoming convoy. There is a rapid consultation. A message goes out within a quarter of an hour to the Commodore of the Convoy. He has received it by 1 am and the whole convoy has been swung off its course. At dawn when the two submarines rise to the surface the convoy is many miles away.*

The percentage of losses of ships in convoy of the total number sailing shows the true significance of what was happening. In all the convoys sailed in 1917 the total loss rate was no more than 1.23% of sailings. The U-Boats themselves began to incur heavy losses, particularly from the British minelaying effort which increased every month. Especially significant was the fact that in the last four months of 1917, the 32 U-Boats sunk almost equalled those newly commissioned. Here were two vital factors in the war against merchant shipping which were turning against Germany. The Naval Staff's confidence in the submarine war had been proved unjustified, but only just in time for the Allies. From now onwards further weaknesses in the German position began to emerge. U-Boat attacks were made with less skill and determination owing to the loss of experienced captains and crews and the decreasing morale of those who replaced them. In Germany itself, the High Command accepted the failure of the campaign before the end of the year and decided that a last desperate effort in France must be made.

1918 saw a continuation of the fall in merchant ship losses. In June, for the first time since the unrestricted campaign began, new shipbuilding exceeded the total lost at sea. These successes were achieved despite desperate German attempts to throw more U-Boats than ever into the war against the convoys. But they failed even to equal the strength achieved in 1917. The total operational strength available, 123, was six less than in the previous year and the average monthly number of boats at sea was 60 as compared with the 70 of 1917. Despite great efforts, the monthly average commissioning rate of submarines was only eight, with the result that, between January and November the loss of 83 exceeded by three the total number built. This element too had turned against Germany; but it was not the decisive one. Claims made after the war by Tirpitz and Scheer, that it was only lack of new construction which caused the U-Boat campaign to fail, are invalid. As 1918 continued, convoy protection was extended to coastal traffic and intensified on the ocean routes. The figures show conclusively that, unless Germany had found some means to defeat the defensive strength of the convoy, no practicable increase in her U-Boat strength would have swung the struggle in her favour.

When the war ended and it was possible to examine the workings of the convoy system in detail, its claim to have been the decisive factor in saving Allied shipping from the submarine was established beyond any doubt. Of the 16,070 ships sailing on ocean convoys throughout the war, only 96, or 0.60%, were sunk; in home waters convoys, 161 of the 67,888 sailing were sunk, 0.24%. The victory was not absolute; in the last six months of the war British losses still averaged more than 140,000 tons a month. But it was sufficient to ensure the survival of the Allies until their armies went into the final offensive in summer 1918.

There is no need to look any further into the reasons for the success of convoy than the words of Karl Dönitz, whose own U-Boat fell victim to a convoy escort in the Mediterranean. After the war he thought deeply about the reasons for his country's defeat at sea, and wrote: *The oceans at once became bare and empty; for long periods at a time the U-Boats, operating individually, would see nothing at all; and then, suddenly, up would loom a huge concourse of ships, thirty or fifty or more of them, surrounded by an escort of warships of all types. The solitary U-Boat, which most probably had sighted the convoy purely by chance, would then attack, thrusting again and again and persisting, if the commander had strong nerves, for perhaps several days and nights, until the physical exhaustion of both commander and crew called a halt. The lone U-Boat might well sink one or two of the ships, or even several, but that was but a poor percentage of the whole. The convoy would steam on. In most cases no other German U-Boat would catch sight of it and it would reach Britain, bringing a rich cargo of foodstuffs and raw materials safely to port.*

Further Reading

Doenitz, Karl, *Ten Years and Twenty Days* (Weidenfeld & Nicolson 1959)
Fayle, C. E., *Seaborne Trade,* Vol III (Longmans Green 1924)
Gibson, R. H. & Prendergast, M., *The German Submarine War 1914-1918* (Constable 1931)
Grant, R. M., *U-Boats Destroyed* (Putnam 1964)
Hezlet, Vice-Admiral Sir A., *The Submarine and Sea Power* (Peter Davies 1967)
Marder, A. J., *From the Dreadnought to Scapa Flow,* Vols IV & V (OUP 1969)
Scheer Admiral R., *Germany's High Seas Fleet in the World War* (Cassell 1920)

THE OTRANTO BARRAGE

Until the end of the war the Allies maintained their faith in a barrage across the Adriatic. It was a fruitless and wasteful exercise. *Peter Kemp. Below:* Squadron of Italian destroyers on patrol in the Adriatic

Map labels:

AUSTRIA-HUNGARY

■ AUSTRIAN BASES
● ALLIED BASES
▨ BLOCKADE ACROSS STRAITS OF OTRANTO

Venice
Trieste
Fiume (Rijeka)
Pola (Pula)
Rimini
Zara (Zadar)
Ancona
Sibenik
Split (Spalato)
ITALY
Ragusa (Dubrovnik)
Cattaro (Kotor)
Bari
Durazzo
Brindisi
ALBANIA
Taranto
Valona
Otranto
Smyrna (Izmir)
Malta

Throughout 1917 the Adriatic remained the key to the U-Boat war on shipping in the Mediterranean. Cattaro (Kotor), some 140 miles above the narrow Straits of Otranto, was the main U-Boat base, while farther north, at Pola (Pula), lay the as yet virtually undamaged Austrian fleet. A few U-Boats still operated from Constantinople, emerging through the Dardanelles into the eastern Mediterranean, but extensive minelaying from the tip of Gallipoli to the Anatolian coast was making their passages increasingly hazardous. Almost the entire threat to Mediterranean shipping came from Cattaro.

The presence of three Allied navies in the Mediterranean made any measures of co-ordination and common doctrine extraordinarily difficult. The great inland sea was divided into 11 zones, of which the British naval authorities were responsible for four, the French for four, and the Italians for three. Differing command structures, national pride and the language barrier all contributed to a lack of cohesion in the application of Allied sea power, producing a situation in which the U-Boat attack on shipping flourished. In the rest of the oceans, the violent American

John Batchelor

reaction to the torpedoing of the cross-Channel steamer *Sussex* had forced Germany to modify her first 'unrestricted' U-Boat warfare, but in the Mediterranean, where few American ships sailed, Germany felt it safe to continue her sink-at-sight policy. Shipping losses in that sea continued to mount alarmingly.

As around the British Isles, the system of protection of merchant shipping was based on the ineffective method of patrol of routes. Important ships, such as troop transports and ammunition carriers, sailed singly escorted by a destroyer, but too often this arrangement broke down when such a ship passed out of one national zone into another. As an example of this lack of co-ordination, the Italian troop transport *Minas,* bound from Italy to Salonika, was torpedoed in one of the British zones in February with the loss of 870 lives. An Italian destroyer had brought her to the western limit of the British zone, but no British destroyer was there to continue the escort because of a misunderstanding in the British headquarters in Malta.

Great faith, contrary to all the evidence, was placed in the net barrage across the Straits of Otranto which was designed to stop

Opposite page. Top left: The Otranto net barrage, supported by 120 net drifters and 30 motor launches, across the Straits of Otranto—'a large sieve through which U-Boats could pass with relative impunity'.
Top right: A British motor launch, part of the Otranto Flotilla. Built in 1915, it had a speed of 19 knots, and like the Italian motor launches it was painted in diagonal stripes so that it should not be mistaken for a U-Boat—however, it was so conspicuous that U-Boats could easily avoid it.
Bottom: British drifters at anchor, Taranto harbour. Armed with a six-pounder gun and fitted with hydrophones and depth charges, they formed part of the flotilla engaged in net sweeping against the Austrian and German submarines.
This page. Above: An Italian motor torpedo boat, the **MAS 57**. *Displacement:* 11 tons. *Length:* 52 feet. *Beam:* 8½ feet. *Armament:* One 47-mm, one 6.5-mm machine gun, plus six depth charges. *Power/speed:* 400 hp/ 24 knots. *Crew:* Eight. Launched in 1917.
Below: The *Novara* (of the improved *Spaun* class), one of the three Austrian cruisers which attacked the Otranto Barrage on May 14/15, 1917. *Displacement:* 3,500 tons. *Length:* 424 feet. *Beam:* 42 feet. *Armament:* Nine 3.9-inch, two 12-pounders, plus four 17.7-inch torpedo tubes. *Power/speed:* 25,000 hp/27 knots. *Armour:* Belt 2½ inches, deck ¾ inch

John Batchelor

the passage of the U-Boats from their base at Cattaro into the Mediterranean. This faith echoed that held in Britain in the similar Dover Straits barrage, again in spite of all the evidence to the contrary. Both, in fact, were really no more than large scale sieves through which the U-Boats were able to pass with relative impunity. Since its inception at the start of 1916, the Otranto Barrage had caught but two U-Boats, the Austrian *U 6* and the German *UB 44*, out of the hundreds of passages made.

The Otranto Barrage consisted of 120 net drifters and 30 motor launches, all equipped with depth charges to be dropped on any U-Boat which ran into the nets. All these small ships carried a gun, but in no single case was the gun as large or efficient as the gun mounted in the U-Boats. In the Dover Barrage, the drifters were reinforced by destroyers, whose function it was to force the U-Boats to dive deep so that they should become tangled in the nets, but this refinement was lacking in the Adriatic. The barrage lay in the Italian zone and was under the overall orders of the Italian Commander-in-Chief, though with a British officer in operational control. The Italian destroyers allocated to the bar-

rage normally lay at anchor at Taranto, proceeding to sea only if the drifters signalled for assistance. At first the Italian authorities had not permitted the motor launches to be out at night in case they were mistaken for U-Boats, but this difficulty had been overcome by painting them in diagonal stripes. An unforeseen result of this was that they were now so conspicuous that U-Boats had no difficulty in avoiding them.

The Austrians strike first

A three-power conference to discuss measures for a more successful approach to the U-Boat and shipping problem was convened at Corfu on April 28, and among the subjects discussed was a more offensive strategy in the Adriatic. The Italians were not prepared to consider any big ship operations while the Austrian fleet was still at Pola, and seemed to have little stomach for any other form of offensive operations. It seemed that none of the Allies was prepared to move alone against the Austrians, and none was prepared to act in co-operation with another in trying to tempt the Austrians out for full scale battle. The mere fact of

The combat of May 14/15.
Opposite page. Top left: A ranging shot goes wide. *Top right:* The three Austrian cruisers which raided the Otranto Barrage, the *Novara, Saida* and *Helgoland.* *Below:* The *Novara,* making a lot of smoke, fires her forward guns. *This page. Top left:* Destroyers rush to shield the *Novara,* her steam supply damaged by a shell from the *Dartmouth* (which in turn was hit by a torpedo from the *UC 25*). *Top right:* The *Novara* (centre) limps home

Austrian ships at Pola, even though inactive, was enough to paralyse all Allied naval initiative in the Adriatic.

Yet the Austrians were not entirely inactive, and even as the Allied conference was in session in Corfu, they were planning an offensive operation against the Otranto Barrage. There had already been four small scale attacks, on March 11, April 21 and 25, and May 5, but none of them had amounted to anything. Now a more ambitious operation was being planned. The net drifters were to be attacked by three cruisers, and a simultaneous operation was to be carried out by two destroyers on the Italian transport traffic approaching Valona (Vlonë), near the eastern end of the barrage. Two U-Boats were despatched to lay mines off Brindisi, with a third patrolling the exits, in case Anglo-Italian forces could be drawn out by the attack on the drifters. The whole operation was timed for the night of May 14/15.

The first to strike were the two destroyers, the *Czepel* and *Balaton.* An Italian convoy of three ships, escorted by the destroyer *Borea,* was approaching Valona when, out of the darkness, the *Czepel* and *Balaton* fell upon them. The *Borea's* main steam-pipe was severed by the first shell fired at her, and she was disabled and left sinking. Of the three merchant ships, one loaded with ammunition was hit and blown up, a second set on fire, and the third one hit. The two destroyers then steamed off northward.

Meanwhile the three cruisers had passed through the barrage before turning back to attack the trawlers. Although Admiral Acton, the Italians' Commander-in-Chief, had some Intelligence of a movement by the enemy and had in fact sent out four French destroyers under the command of Captain Vicuna in the flotilla leader *Mirabella,* to patrol north of the barrage, he had failed to warn the drifters that enemy operations were suspected. As a consequence, the three Austrian cruisers, *Novara, Saida* and *Helgoland,* were thought to be friendly ships, and allowed to pass unchallenged. It was not until the easternmost group of drifters heard the gunfire of the attack on the Italian convoy that they had any indication that enemy ships were out.

Each Austrian cruiser took one-third of the line of drifters and began slowly and systematically, to destroy the barrage. The drifters were hailed as they were approached and ordered to

abandon ship. In those cases where the crews obeyed, they were taken prisoner before their ships were sunk; where they did not do so, they were engaged at point-blank range by the 4-inch guns of the Austrian cruisers.

There were some scenes of great gallantry, of which that of Skipper Joseph Watt of the drifter *Gowan Lea* was perhaps the most outstanding. The *Novara* was sighted at a range of 100 yards and Skipper Watt, ignoring her orders to abandon ship, turned the *Gowan Lea* towards her at full speed, firing her one 57-mm gun. When the gun was put out of action by a 4-inch shell, the crew set to work to try to repair it. Again the drifter was hit, a box of ammunition on deck exploded and took off the leg of one of the crew, but still the men worked on, trying to repair their tiny gun. Finally the *Novara* passed on, confident that no drifter could have survived the hammering that the *Gowan Lea* had received. Even when the cruiser was out of sight, the men of the *Gowan Lea* were still working on their gun. For his gallantry in this action, Skipper Watt was awarded the Victoria Cross.

Forty-seven drifters were out on the barrage that night, and when the Austrian cruisers had finished their work, 14 of them had been sunk and three seriously damaged. Of those that escaped to the north, several made signals reporting the attack, but no one at Brindisi read them. The first that Admiral Acton knew of the action was when the shore station at Valona reported hearing the firing of the destroyer attack on the Italian transports.

His first action was to order the *Mirabella*, with the four French destroyers (now reduced to three through mechanical trouble in one of them), to steer to intercept. His next was to go on board the British cruiser *Dartmouth* and order such ships as were ready to proceed to sea. First away were the British cruiser *Bristol* and two Italian destroyers. The *Dartmouth*, with two more Italian destroyers, followed about half an hour later. A third light cruiser, the Italian *Marsala*, with two more destroyers, sailed from Brindisi three hours after the *Dartmouth*.

Although the Austrian cruisers had completed their action against the barrage before Admiral Acton's ships had left Brindisi, they still had further to go to reach Cattaro than the Anglo-Italian ships. By steering to the northeast, the *Dartmouth* and her consorts could well cut them off and bring them to action. So far, of course, Admiral Acton did not know of their presence in the area; he had sailed his ships only on the information received from Valona. It was only two hours after sailing, when he received a signal from the *Mirabello* that she was in combat with three cruisers, that he was able to learn the strength of the enemy force. But even with the benefit of the signal from the *Mirabella* he was not yet in possession of the full facts, for he had no knowledge of the presence or the position of the two destroyers which had attacked the convoy. In fact, these were now about half-way between him and the Austrian cruisers, some 40 miles SE.

Captain Horthy, commanding the three Austrian cruisers, was similarly placed. He knew the position of the *Mirabella* and her three destroyers because they were in sight, but he had received no reports of Admiral Acton's force. Horthy turned to engage the destroyers, but the action was broken off when one of the two Austrian destroyers, the *Czepel*, sighted the cruisers and destroyers from Brindisi and reported them.

First blood went to the Austrians. Admiral Acton sent in his destroyers to deal with the *Czepel* and *Balaton*. In a long range gun duel a shell from the *Czepel* hit a boiler in the Italian *Aquila* and brought her to a stop. The two Austrian ships then made off at high speed and finally reached Durazzo (Durrës) in safety.

The crippled *Aquila* brought the two main forces into contact. Admiral Acton, thinking that the Austrian cruisers were to the north of him was actually steaming away from the *Aquila*, but fortunately smoke was just then sighted from the south. It came from the Austrian ships, which were closing in on the *Aquila* to finish her off. At once, the British and Italian ships reversed their course and arrived just in time to cover the crippled Italian ship and bring Horthy's ships to action.

Horthy was now in a difficult position. Ahead of him was the Brindisi force of two cruisers and four destroyers, with, as yet unknown to him, another cruiser and two destroyers (*Marsala* and her escort) still to the west. Astern of him was the *Mirabella* and her three French destroyers. There was nothing he could do but settle down to fight his way out of the trap.

Almost at once his ship, the *Helgoland,* was hit on the bridge by the *Dartmouth*. It was not a decisive hit though it killed Horthy's second-in-command and damaged the *Helgoland's* communications system. To open the range, and also because he was becoming worried by the *Mirabella* and her three destroyers astern of him, he turned away towards the north-west. In fact, he need not have worried, for the *Mirabella* was now a spent force. She had

been forced to stop by water getting into her fuel tanks. At the same time one of the French destroyers was also experiencing trouble with her steam condensers, and was also brought to a standstill. The two remaining destroyers decided to stay with their consorts to guard against possible attack by U-Boats. So far as the main action was concerned, they played no further part.

The two main forces, now more evenly matched, continued to fire on each other, but the *Bristol* which had not been in dock for a long time and thus had a foul bottom, began to fall astern, leaving the *Dartmouth* to bear the main brunt of the action. A splinter from one of her shells wounded Horthy, and the command of the *Helgoland* passed to one of her lieutenants. Another shell from the *Dartmouth* hit the *Novara* and damaged the steam supply to her main engines. The situation was beginning to look promising for the Allied squadron, but Admiral Acton now decided to slow down to allow the *Bristol* to catch up. By the time she had done so, the Austrian cruisers had drawn ahead and there now seemed little chance of catching them.

The situation, however, was in fact a good deal more promising than it looked, though the true position was not fully apparent to the Italian admiral. The *Novara* was slowing down as a result of the *Dartmouth's* hit and was soon to come to a complete stop. The third Austrian cruiser, the *Saida,* had fallen some distance astern of the other two, and Admiral Acton saw a chance of cutting her off and driving her down onto the *Marsala* and her two destroyers which, having left Brindisi some three hours later than the other ships, were now approaching the scene of battle from the south. The *Saida* was heavily engaged by both the *Dartmouth* and the *Bristol*, but was not so badly hit that she could not continue her course. It was at this moment that the *Novara* came to a stop, and Lieutenant Witkorocski, who was commanding the *Helgoland* after the wounding of Horthy and the killing of her commander, ordered the *Saida* to take her in tow.

This was seen in both the *Dartmouth* and the *Bristol,* and it seemed that the fate of these two ships was sealed. But even as Admiral Acton turned to a closing course for the kill, smoke was sighted to the north, which soon revealed itself as coming from a large cruiser and five torpedo-boats which had sailed from Cattaro on receipt of a signal from Captain Horthy that he was being engaged. Feeling that the odds were now too heavily weighted against him, Admiral Acton broke off the action and set his course for a return to Brindisi.

Two of the Allied destroyers were now in tow; the *Aquila,* which had been hit by the *Czepel,* and one of the French destroyers which had broken down. Both reached Brindisi in safety. But the day was yet to end badly for the Allies. While she was still some 40 miles from Brindisi, the *Dartmouth* was hit by a torpedo from the mine-laying submarine *UC 25,* one of the three sent by the Austrians to patrol off Brindisi before the start of the operation. At one time the *Dartmouth* was in danger of sinking, and her crew was taken off by the attending destroyers, but in the end she was saved and finally reached Brindisi the following day in tow of a tug. This, however, was not the end of the Allied discomfiture. One of the French destroyers which had been ordered out to assist the *Dartmouth* struck one of the mines which had been laid by the *UC 25* and was sunk.

This small engagement, conducted with singular lack of skill, was to have considerable repercussions on the conduct of U-Boat warfare in the Mediterranean. One immediate result of the whole operation was that the Italian Commander-in-Chief came to the conclusion that it was impossible to defend the net drifters on the Otranto barrage during the hours of darkness; they were therefore withdrawn each night, leaving the Straits unguarded against the passage of U-Boats into the Mediterranean. This, of course, was a counsel of despair, and the figures of tonnage losses rose to new heights. The average of monthly loss was more than doubled during the second quarter of 1917 compared with the first. It was not until July that the Italians felt themselves able once again to provide naval support for the drifters on which the maintenance of the barrage rested. And even that, of course, was not the real answer to the problem. The whole conception of trying to deny the passage of U-Boats by a barrage was wrong, whether in the Straits of Dover or in those of Otranto. The real wonder of all these vast and costly operations in trying to close such stretches of water was the continuing faith in their efficiency in spite of vast and conclusive evidence to the contrary.

Further Reading
Naval Staff Monographs, *The Mediterranean 1917* (Copy in the Naval Library, Ministry of Defence)
Chatterton, E. K., *Seas of Adventures* (Hurst & Blackett 1942)

THE LAST SORTIE OF THE HIGH SEAS FLEET

Beatty had long been waiting for an opportunity to engage the HSF in favourable circumstances. But when Scheer made what was to be the German navy's 'last throw of all', inadequate information on both sides and the breakdown of the *Moltke* caused the operation to founder. *Paul Kennedy. Below:* Battleships *Royal Sovereign, Resolution* and *Revenge*

Ever since the battle of Jutland in May 1916, a strategic stalemate had existed between the British and German surface forces, broken only by destroyer battles in the English Channel area and by a few tentative sweeps by the respective battlefleets in the North Sea. The latter had not led to any decisive results, even when contact between the opposing forces had been made, partly because of tactical mistakes and confusion during the actual engagements, but chiefly because of the reluctance of the respective commanders-in-chief to fight unless the circumstances were favourable to their own vessels. But, of course, what was suitable for one side could not be so for the other, and therefore the prospects for a decisive 'Trafalgar' in these waters were not at all promising at this stage in the war.

To the German Commander, Scheer, there could be no question of an all-out battle with the Grand Fleet. His vessels had had a narrow escape at Jutland, and he was now well aware that he could employ only 19 dreadnoughts and 5 battle cruisers against Beatty's 34 and 9 respectively. In any case, the submarines necessary for reconnaissance work for the High Seas Fleet could not be diverted from their crucial campaign against Britain's sea lanes. Finally, the Kaiser still opposed any risky sorties involving his precious battleships. As ever, therefore, Scheer's basic policy was to plan for the isolation and destruction of *part* of the British battlefleet, which would change the entire strategic situation immediately. Only if the Grand Fleet ventured close to the German coast, where it could be reduced first of all by submarines, torpedo-boats and mines, would it be engaged in close combat by the High Seas Fleet.

However, there was absolutely no chance of the British undertaking so risky an operation, eager though they were to get to grips with the German fleet. Ever since the alarming action of August 19, 1916 the Grand Fleet had been instructed to avoid going further south than the Farne Islands and further east than 4°E unless the need were 'very pressing', such was the fear of

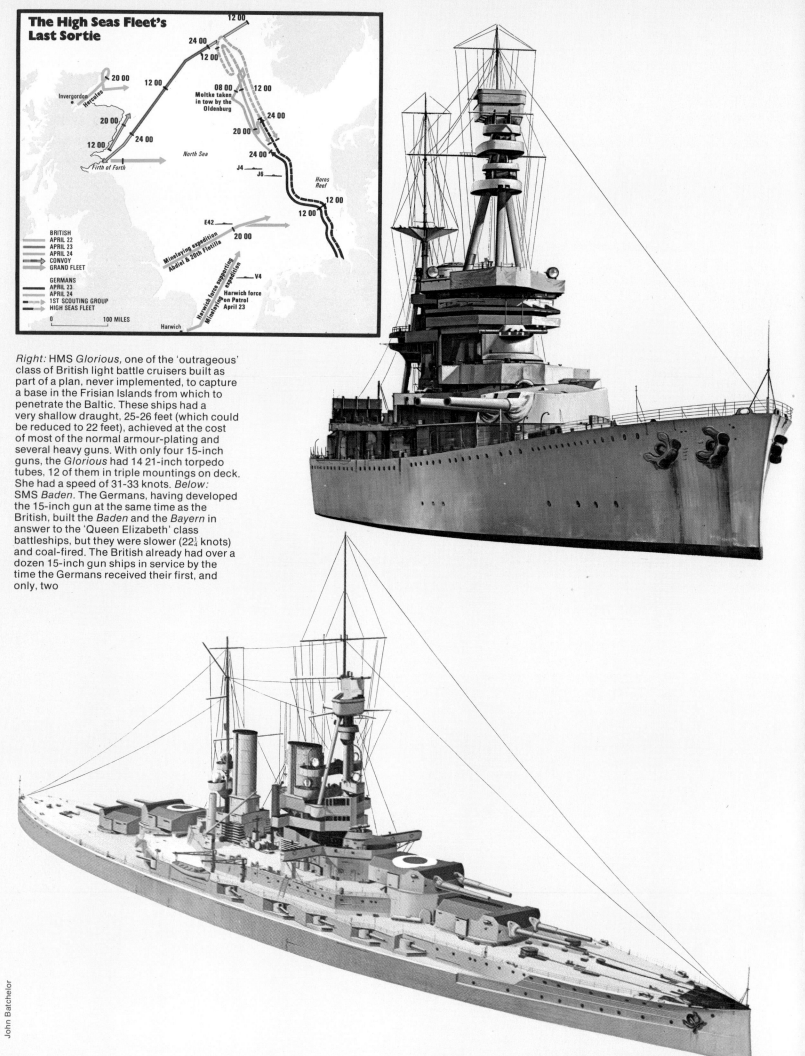

BRITISH
APRIL 22
APRIL 23
APRIL 24
CONVOY
GRAND FLEET

GERMANS
APRIL 23
APRIL 24
1ST SCOUTING GROUP
HIGH SEAS FLEET

0   100 MILES

Invergordon
Hercules
Firth of Forth
North Sea
Harwich

08 00
Moltke taken
in tow by the
Oldenburg

Horns Reef

J4
J6

E42
V4

Minelaying expedition
Abdiel & 20th Flotilla

Harwich force supporting
Minelaying expedition

Harwich force
on Patrol
April 23

Right: HMS *Glorious,* one of the 'outrageous' class of British light battle cruisers built as part of a plan, never implemented, to capture a base in the Frisian Islands from which to penetrate the Baltic. These ships had a very shallow draught, 25-26 feet (which could be reduced to 22 feet), achieved at the cost of most of the normal armour-plating and several heavy guns. With only four 15-inch guns, the *Glorious* had 14 21-inch torpedo tubes, 12 of them in triple mountings on deck. She had a speed of 31-33 knots. *Below:* SMS *Baden*. The Germans, having developed the 15-inch gun at the same time as the British, built the *Baden* and the *Bayern* in answer to the 'Queen Elizabeth' class battleships, but they were slower ($22\frac{1}{4}$ knots) and coal-fired. The British already had over a dozen 15-inch gun ships in service by the time the Germans received their first, and only, two

John Batchelor

German submarine attacks. Moreover, Beatty was extremely worried about the structural weaknesses of the British battleships, the inefficiency of the shells, and, most important of all, his chronic shortage of destroyers. The latter were being continually detached for anti-submarine duties, leaving the Commander-in-Chief with insufficient numbers with which to protect his capital ships from submarines and mines. In view of all this, Beatty had argued in an important memorandum of January 9, 1918 that 'the correct strategy of the Grand Fleet is no longer to endeavour to bring the enemy to action at any cost, but rather to contain him in his bases until the situation becomes more favourable to us'. Although this did not exclude minelaying ventures and operations by British forces in the Channel, and although it was stated to be a purely temporary measure until the destroyer shortage was surmounted, the conclusion about the employment of the battlefleet was one towards which Beatty had been moving ever since he had assumed his post. Moreover, his arguments were accepted in full by the Admiralty and the War Cabinet. Scheer's fond hopes of a British sortie into the Heligoland Bight were, therefore, not likely to be realised.

However, by the spring of 1918 there was considerable pressure upon the German navy to take the initiative in breaking this deadlock. On March 21 Ludendorff's big offensive in the west began, throwing the navy's inactivity into even greater contrast than before: surely something could be done to boost the name of the High Seas Fleet at home and to assist this great land struggle by diverting the enemy's attention? It was also possible that aggressive sorties into the North Sea would, as the German official history puts it, 'effectively ease the strain on the U-Boats operating in the Channel and around England'. The most obvious way of achieving these aims, Scheer realised, was a successful attack upon a Scandinavian convoy and its escorting force. This traffic had been twice interrupted by small German forces in the previous year, for it was not very difficult to steam swiftly under cover of darkness from Wilhelmshaven to the waters between Scotland and Norway, strike at the merchantmen, and retreat before more powerful British vessels arrived on the scene. Following the attack of December 12, during which an entire convoy and an escorting destroyer had been sunk by the German raiders, the British had decided that in future an entire battle squadron should accompany the merchantmen. But this counter-action, far from deterring Scheer, prompted him to consider taking his whole fleet into the northern North Sea to interrupt this traffic. It was a risky venture, but a successful mission would kill many birds with one stone: not only would the destruction of a convoy stop the Scandinavian trade, divert British attention from the Channel and be warmly applauded at home, but there was a distinct chance that the High Seas Fleet might be able to trap and sink the escorting British battle squadron, thereby altering the whole strategic balance. It was, Scheer reckoned, a risk worth running, provided that the Grand Fleet itself was not at sea. All would depend upon keeping secret the movement of the High Seas Fleet.

This self-same thought had been worrying Beatty also. It would not be difficult for the enemy to discover that the Scandinavian convoys sailed at regular 4-day intervals, and that they were nearly always escorted by a force of battleships. Unknown to Scheer, the Grand Fleet was now based upon Rosyth instead of Scapa Flow, but unless it was kept at sea or at least in a state of continual readiness to sail, it would be unable to prevent a surprise attack on the escort by superior forces unless the Admiralty was forewarned by its own intelligence services in Room 40. By this stage of the war, however, the Germans had become suspicious that their wireless messages were being deciphered by their foes, and had severely restricted this method of communication. In this case, the risks were so great that Scheer virtually banned the use of the wireless. He also did without airship reconnaissance and advance minesweeping, which were normally two other indications to the British that a sortie was under way.

Bold and well contrived

Having assembled the High Seas Fleet in the Schillig Roads on the evening of April 22 on the pretext of large-scale exercises, therefore, Scheer led out his vessels at 0500 hours on the following morning. His plan was to let Hipper's battle cruisers and escorts attack a Scandinavian convoy on the 24th while the High Seas Fleet (three battle squadrons and escorts) cruised some 60 miles to the south-south-west, ready if need be to support the raiders if they met up with the British battle squadron. The only thing wrong with this bold and well-contrived scheme was that the German Naval Staff were mistaken in believing that a British convoy would be midway between Scotland and Norway on that day. Had they bothered to obtain information on this from their

consuls in Norway instead of relying solely upon U-Boat reports, this error might have been avoided; and had the sortie been advanced or postponed by one day, the Germans would most probably have sighted one of the convoys.

All this Scheer was not to know until later and throughout April 23 his ships steamed northwards in pursuit of their imaginary prey. Secrecy had been complete, and the operation was assisted by a thick haze. His luck held even when the High Seas Fleet was sighted by the British submarine *J6* at 2000 hours; for that vessel's commanding officer for some unaccountable reason believed that this was a British force and did not send any report to Beatty. Had he done so, the entire story might have been different. As it was, the German forces made uninterrupted progress northwards until 0510 on the 24th, when the battle cruiser *Moltke* suddenly broke down. By that time, Hipper's advance force was only 40 miles west-south-west of Stavanger and was searching in vain for the Bergen-Methil convoy, which was then steaming into the Firth of Forth. The *Moltke's* breakdown was a serious one, for a propeller had dropped off and a gear wheel had disintegrated, sending pieces into the condenser. Unwilling to abandon the operation because of this mishap, Hipper merely ordered the slowly-moving vessel to retire towards the battlefleet. But the trouble got worse and at 0643 hours *Moltke* reported by wireless that her speed was only 4 knots; at 0845 hours she was forced to inform Scheer and Hipper that she was out of control.

About two hours later, the High Seas Fleet came upon the stricken battle cruiser, which was taken in tow by the battleship *Oldenburg*. Since his vessels were now at a latitude slightly north of John o' Groats and would be hampered in any action by the presence of this cripple, Scheer ordered that the battlefleet should return to base, escorting the *Moltke*. Nevertheless, he coolly decided that the expected British convoy should still be attacked and he instructed Hipper's forces, which had steered south to within sight of the main force, to press ahead again with the search. Carrying out this order, the German battle cruisers reconnoitred to almost 60°N, Hipper's eagerness being increased by wireless reports from the German Naval Staff that a convoy of 30 ships should be in the area. In fact, the accompanying German light cruiser force went within sight of the Norwegian coast but all to no avail. The incoming British convoy was now docked at Methil, while an outward-bound one was still hugging the Scottish coast as it proceeded northwards. Therefore, at 1410 on the 24th Hipper's ships turned south and worked up speed to regain contact with the main force, which was making a steady 10 knots back to Wilhelmshaven (the *Moltke's* port engines were still working). By midnight on the 24th/25th they had rejoined the High Seas Fleet by then in the middle of the North Sea and 150 miles to the east of the Grand Fleet, which had eventually realised that something was up.

It was the *Moltke's* wireless calls of distress, picked up by the British directional stations, which had alerted the Admiralty in London about this operation, although it was already generally on its toes because of the Zeebrugge raid (April 22/23) and because of certain wireless messages to the German minesweepers in the Heligoland Bight. Realising that large enemy forces were right up to the northern entrance to the North Sea, further from base than they had ever been before, Beatty was galvanised into action. Clearly, this daring raid by the High Seas Fleet was an example of the 'favourable opportunities' for which the Commander-in-Chief had been waiting so long, and the reservations upon a fleet action which he had expressed in his memorandum of January 9 no longer applied. After strengthening the Methil-Bergen convoy and warning Scapa Flow against a surprise attack, he led out the Grand Fleet in the early afternoon in the hope of blocking the German vessels from their return to Wilhelmshaven. A pea-soup fog obscured what must have been a splendid sight—31 battleships, 4 battle cruisers, 2 heavy cruisers, 24 light cruisers and 85 destroyers setting out at full speed from the Firth of Forth into the North Sea. Four of the battleships were American, under Rear-Admiral Rodman and now tactically integrated with the Royal Navy. It was to be the last time in the duration of the war that the entire Grand Fleet was to go to sea.

Only a miracle

It was also, incidentally, the first time that this force had been despatched in such strength since the disappointing operation of August 19, 1916; and although Beatty was not to have such a harrowing time of it as Jellicoe did then, his mission was to prove equally fruitless. By midnight the Grand Fleet was 90 miles out from May Island and steering east, but both Scheer and Hipper's vessels were past this line of advance and moving steadily southwards. In order to have interrupted the High Seas Fleet that day,

Main picture: SMS *Baden* and *Karlsruhe II* passing the nets at the mouth of the Jade River. It was possible for small forces to steam quickly out of Wilhelmshaven and attack the convoys with impunity. *Inset right:* German destroyers at Heligoland, *S 65* (right) and (left) one of the G 37 class. Both types carried 6 19.7 inch torpedo tubes and 24 mines, but the S 53s had larger guns. *Far right:* SMS *Moltke,* the battle cruiser whose mechanical failure disrupted the German attack on the Bergen-Methil convoy and who, by reporting her accident, broke the radio silence which had shrouded the operation.
Below left: The *Revenge* leading the *Resolution* and the *Royal Sovereign* (nearest the camera). The five 'Rs', the second class of British battleships to be built with 15-inch guns, were massive and powerful, but slower than the 'Queen Elizabeths'

HMS *Iron Duke* in a heavy swell. The 'Iron Duke' class were the first large British ships to be built with anti-aircraft guns.

Imperial War Museum

the British force would have needed to have left Rosyth some 12 hours earlier. As it was, only a miracle could now prevent the Germans from escaping, especially since Beatty did not realise until the following morning that the enemy had evaded him.

Only a few British submarines on patrol duty in the North Sea had the chance to delay Scheer's retreat. At 0400 hours on the 25th, the hapless *J6* once again sighted various squadrons of the High Seas Fleet but it did not attack and only sent out a message $2\frac{1}{2}$ hours later, when these ships had disappeared from view. That evening, however, the submarine *E42*, which had been steaming at full speed to reach the entrance to one of the main minefield channels into the Bight, spotted the *Moltke* slowly steering southwards about 40 miles north of Heligoland. By this time the battle cruiser had been repaired enough to cast off the *Oldenburg's* towline and was under its own steam, though still presenting an ideal target. The commander of *E42*, Lieutenant C. H. Allen, let off four 18-inch torpedoes as the *Moltke* turned into the channel down which the rest of Scheer's battleships had already gone, and he then had the satisfaction of hearing a distant explosion. More he could not do, for his submarine was subjected to depth-charge attacks by German destroyers for another hour before he got clear. In fact, the *Moltke* had been hit near the port engine-room, took in 1,800 tons of water and was out of control for a while; but she later managed to put herself right and to rejoin the High Seas Fleet in the Jade Estuary during the night.

The lost opportunity

Even before the *E42* had attacked, the Grand Fleet was on its way back to Rosyth, it being clear from *J6's* signal that morning that the enemy had eluded them once again. As ever, Beatty was most disappointed and annoyed, and he insisted to the First Sea Lord that 'we must reconsider the outlook which permits apparently considerable forces, indeed the High Seas Fleet, to get out without our knowledge — otherwise we might meet with a disaster of some magnitude over this cursed convoy supporting force.' Nevertheless, there was little that could be done to improve Room 40's powers of detecting when the German fleet was on the move. Scheer was now restricting his ships' wireless transmissions very severely, and indications of an impending sortie had to be gleaned instead either from cryptic messages to U-Boats returning from patrol into the North Sea or from activities such as minesweeping and Zeppelin patrols; but the former were most erratic, and the absence of the latter could never be a sure guide that all was well, since Scheer was in the last resort prepared to do without them to maintain secrecy. As it was, therefore, the Scandinavian traffic continued, as did the deployment of a battle squadron to cover each sailing of the outward and homeward convoys. To withdraw this protecting force, even though it ran the risk of being overwhelmed by the High Seas Fleet, was impossible: yet to keep the Grand Fleet constantly at sea was both physically exhausting and dangerous, in view of enemy sub-

marines and mines. Luckily, Scheer never again attempted to interrupt the shipping route between Scotland and Norway.

Despite Beatty's disappointment, the overall strategy in the North Sea had not been altered by this incident. Britain still controlled the southern and northern exits to the Atlantic, and the Royal Navy maintained in battleships a comfortable lead over its enemy; and while this situation remained, Beatty had no incentive to put his supremacy at risk by rash ventures into the eastern and southern zones of the mine and submarine-ridden North Sea. Scheer could still not afford to face the Grand Fleet in a toe-to-toe battle, and yet he was aware that, while Britain could not lose by this strategic stalemate, Germany could not win by it. Though he was constantly to seek ways of destroying a portion of the British battlefleet, numbers, geography, and Beatty's caution were to prevent him from ever achieving this aim.

On the German side generally, the sortie of April 22-25 was not seen in the grave light in which Beatty viewed it, chiefly because it was not realised that the Grand Fleet was now based upon Rosyth instead of Scapa Flow, and that the British had had a good chance, given earlier notification of the German moves, of cutting off the High Seas Fleet from its base. Scheer's bold sortie, which was the farthest yet undertaken by the German battlefleet, had been skilfully planned and executed. The only blunder, apart from the completely unforeseen breakdown of the *Moltke,* was the failure of the German naval staff to calculate the correct sailing dates of the Scandinavian convoys. If, as mentioned earlier, the operation had been carried out one day earlier or later, Scheer would have most likely succeeded in finding and destroying a convoy and its escorts. As it was, the raid turned out to be somewhat of an anticlimax.

In retrospect, it was more than that. The April sortie of the High Seas Fleet and the Grand Fleet was the last time in which those two great forces were engaged, even if they did not meet each other. Thereafter, much as Scheer might plot and Beatty impatiently fret, there was to be no further opportunity of a naval Armageddon in the North Sea. Instead, while the Royal Navy retained its command of the sea and beat off the U-Boat challenge, the German battlefleet was to remain in harbour, with serious consequences for the morale of the crews. The next time the High Seas Fleet was to emerge from Wilhelmshaven in any strength would be on November 21, 1918.

Further Reading
Gladisch, Admiral Walther, *Der Krieg in der Nordsee,* Vol 7 (German Official Naval History; E. S. Mittler & Sohn, Berlin 1965)
Marder, A. J., *From the Dreadnought to Scapa Flow,* Vol 5, *Victory and Aftermath* (OUP; London 1970)
Newbolt, Sir Henry, *Naval Operations,* Vol 5 (Official Naval History; Longmans, Green & Co, London 1931)
Scheer, Admiral Reinhard, *Germany's High Seas Fleet in the World War* (Cassell & Co; London 1920)

PRINTED IN BELGIUM

proost Turnhout (Belgium)